An Activist Handbook for the Education Revolution

United Opt Out's Test of Courage

An Activist Handbook for the Education Revolution

United Opt Out's Test of Courage

Edited by

Morna McDermott

Peggy Robertson

Rosemarie Jensen

and

Ceresta Smith
United Opt Out

INFORMATION AGE PUBLISHING, INC.
Charlotte, NC • www.infoagepub.com

Library of Congress Cataloging-in-Publication Data

A CIP record for this book is available from the Library of Congress
http://www.loc.gov

ISBN: 978-1-62396-932-5 (Paperback)
       978-1-62396-933-2 (Hardcover)
       978-1-62396-934-9 (ebook)

CONTENTS

ACKNOWLEDGMENTS

If we were to name every individual or group who has inspired us, helped us, supported us, and worked (as hard if not harder, and as long if not longer) in our shared journey to reclaim public education, the list would go on ad infinitum. But suffice it to say we have never done this alone. That would be impossible and counterproductive. Many of you who are reading this now (perhaps even those of you we have never met) have been "with us" since the beginning—in body, mind, and spirit.

There are only seven of us. And there is a mighty ocean of passionate people fighting this battle everyday ... and we fight with and for them. Our journey, our struggles, and our vision for the future are not ours alone. They belong to all of us.

But 2014, when we crafted the first draft for this book, was a year of sadness as we mourned the loss of two of the world's greatest intellectual inspirations: Maya Angelou and Maxine Green.

We are heartened throughout our journey by Maya's words: "One isn't necessarily born with courage, but one is born with potential. Without courage, we cannot practice any other virtue with consistency. We can't be kind, true, merciful, generous, or honest."[1]

And we remain inspired by Maxine's vision: "To break with the 'cotton wool' of habit, of mere routine, of automatism, is (as we shall see) to seek alternative ways of being, to look for openings. To find such openings is to discover new possibilities—often new ways of achieving freedom in the world" (1998, p. 2).

An Activist Handbook for The Education Revolution:
United Opt Out's Test of Courage, pp. vii–xi
Copyright © 2015 by Information Age Publishing

Our book is dedicated to their memory.

But if we are to acknowledge individuals, we would have to start with our own families. It is because of the loving and patient support of our partners, our parents, our children, our siblings, and our friends that we are able to do the work that we do.

For every Occupy event we held, there were children, husbands, wives, and friends we left at home. For every night we stayed up late crafting an action, we were negligent of our lives "at home" and sometimes (ironically) our jobs. For every phone call we took for an interview or to quell a crisis, we put aside the ones we love and our daily lives to accomplish our goals. The work of activism exacts a price: a physical, emotional, financial, and psychological price. Not only a price paid by us, but on some days by our families. We risked hurting close personal relationships and our careers.

We must acknowledge that without their support, we would not be able to have sustained as a group. So our book is dedicated to them.

Ceresta Smith: I want to first and foremost acknowledge and thank my family—Scott for withstanding the blows of market-based reform via the school sanctioning process, which labeled his beloved Northwestern High as a "failing school" long before I understood what was going on; Aisha for being courageous enough to opt out of and speak out against high-stakes testing with the threat of a denied high school diploma looming over her head; and my mother for showing me what it means to take a political stance and exercise a social justice voice. I also want to acknowledge and thank all the other colored girls that have gone before me to model how to stand up and courageously fight for truth and justice in a patriarchal world that systemically demeans us and in various different ways attempts to silence our collective and individual voice. And last, but not least, I want to acknowledge and thank the generation of students whom I playfully call "the standards"—the heart-warming folk who enter and exit my classroom year after year who have and will suffer under the intellectually stymied and oppressive rein of market-based reform and its money-grubbing misuse of standardized testing.

Laurie Murphy: Organizing for change is never quick or easy, and it does not occur in a vacuum. Many people are responsible for exposing me to the world of advocacy and for educating me on the art and science of strategic organizational development. First and foremost, I would like to thank my husband, Tim, for his wisdom, patience, and guidance as he assisted me in understanding the complex realities of today's educational system and the forces that undermine its success. I am also deeply grateful for the support received from my children who spent many family dinners staring at my empty chair while I was busy with yet another conference call. I would like to also acknowledge the incredible gratitude I have for my parents for instilling within me a love of learning, curiosity about life, and appreciation for the arts; and for my grandchildren for allowing me to witness each of these coming to life within them. I wish to thank my fellow education advocates for sharing large chunks of their lives with me, allowing me to learn from their successes and gently guiding me to learn from my own failures. I owe a special debt to Chris Janotta for sharing with me his expertise in social media, community organizing, public relations, and new technologies and for inspiring within me the desire and confidence to fight for change. Finally, words cannot express the gratitude that I have for the administrative team of *United Opt Out National* for accepting me into their lives as part of their family, sharing with me their experiences, wisdom, pain, and humor, and teaching me the true meaning of respect. Because of them, my life—personally and professionally—is forever changed.

Peg Robertson: First, I must acknowledge my husband, Darrin. I am not sure how he tolerates me and my work that takes me from my family on a daily basis. He is patient when I rant and rave and when I type furiously at the computer as though the sky may come crashing down at any minute. He listens when I come to him with a story or a problem, while looking me in the eye (rather than multitasking), and he respects our work at *United Opt Out*, even though he'd be thrilled if he never heard the words "corporate education reform" ever again—as would I. When I head out the door to an event, away from my family, he always reminds me to enjoy myself—he knows these folks give me sanity. Next, I must acknowledge my two boys, Sam and Luke, who are wise to the world and have accompanied me to many events, locally as well as nationally. Sam and Luke, thank you for tolerating my absences, my immense number of quarters in the cussing jar, and the many meals we have eaten in which the conversation veered in the direction of education—you each shine a light on this world and I know you will move mountains someday. Finally, I must acknowledge my parents, Jake and Patsy Wolf. My father was a political reporter and my mother was a public school music teacher—I never understood until just recently how that combination was destined to send me down this path—thank you for all that you did, and all that you still do. Much love to all of you.

Tim Slekar: My thanks, gratitude, and love go to my wife Michelle, my son Luke, and my daughter Lacey. I never asked them if they were willing to become education activists. I never asked them if they were willing to share me and our precious time together. However, after 5 years of opt out activism, blogging, radio shows, television interviews, phone conferencing, and speaking to groups all over the country, they are still standing with me. That is what you call real love.

This book is for you Michelle!
This book is for you Luke!
This book is for you Lacey!

Rosemarie Jensen: I need to acknowledge my husband, Rick, who has supported my need to always stand up for what is right in the classroom and has encouraged me to become more involved and more vocal at both the local and national level. He gave me the courage to get on that plane to the SOS March, which led me to *United Opt Out*. Also, my deepest gratitude to my two kids, Danielle and Connor, who made me realize even more who I was fighting for—them and for all children present and future who deserve more than a test-prep education. I know that many of the children I taught would not have had a chance in this underfunded punitive educational environment. They are the ones who continue to shoulder the ill effects of the testing culture. Also, for my cousin Darlene and my former colleagues who continue to teach with as much integrity and fidelity despite the antichild edicts handed down by the corporate reformers. And lastly to Peggy Robertson, who was my lifeline when Rick and I were considering opting out and had no idea that there was support for our decision; and to the entire Opt Out group, who pushed my thinking, solidified my resolve, and encouraged my participation at the first event in DC. My gratitude to you is without measure.

Morna McDermott: I need to acknowledge first and foremost my husband, Len, who knows more about corporate reform than any self-respecting master plumber ought to know—he is my sounding board and my reality check. I am grateful for all the times he listened and reminded me when I "needed to talk in a way that normal people might understand." I practiced many a presentation or speech with him as my sounding board. He has lugged cemetery gravestones to Washington DC, attended rallies, and watched the kids while I left either for a day or a week. And to my children, who have the courage and wisdom of the best budding activists around. So many days I wondered why I was putting the collective idea of saving "childhood" and schools above being present for their own childhood and attending to their own school needs. The future I am fighting to create is for them. And they continue to be my greatest teachers and inspiration. My deepest thanks and gratitude also go to my dear friend Bess Altwerger, founding organizer of Save Our Schools. Little did she know on that fateful day in 2011 on the elevator at Towson U., when I offered to help her with the SOS March, that it would lead here. Bess is a model to me of what integrity, courage, and respect in activism looks like. And finally, the entire UOO team: You have changed my life ... for the better.

Shaun Johnson: For the kids.

Ruth Rodriguez: Giving thanks to all the people who have accompanied me in this journey, riding on the train whose destination is justice, will probably take more space than I am allowed. So I'll limit myself to the time when first I became involved with this noble struggle. I give thanks to Maryanne Hardenbergh, who introduced me to Citizens for Public Schools.

I was later elected President and since have collaborated with some of the most amazing people; Barbara Fields, Marilyn Segal, Lisa Guisbond, Ann O'Halloran, and Monty Neill. I thank Liza Womack, Nancy Carlsson Page, Rosalie Friend, and Judy Rabin, for their courage and commitment which helped me to see the value of fighting for the preservation of our public schools. To my sister Lourdes, who reads my Facebook postings, then researches what I write to keep me honest, gracias. Of course my most sincere gratitude go out to my seven pissed-off-real-radicals comrades, Tim, Sean, Rosemarie, Morna, Ceresta, and Peggy—thank you all for sharing your passion for justice. And finally, I thank my higher power for the precious gift—my adoring daughters—they are my true inspiration, the reason why I do anything for the cause of justice; they show me every day what a real fighter looks like. It's why when I wake up some morning wanting to throw in the towel, their image pops up right before my eyes, and suddenly the strength within me blasts out. Thank you all for sharing your passion for justice. Thank you Joselina and Kelly!

NOTES

1. http://www.goodreads.com/quotes/71312-one-isn-t-necessarily-born-with-courage-but-one-is-born

REFERENCE

Greene, M. (1998). *Dialectic of freedom*. New York, NY: Teachers College Press.

FOREWORD

Ricardo Rosa

Plentiful and persuasive books have been written about the utter despair racialized capitalism has inflicted on communities and people. The brilliance of this book, aside from the sobering fact that it is written by deeply courageous people refusing to be servants to power and willing to put their careers and bodies on the line, is that it begins with contestation. Far too many "critical" texts truncate, tuck away, or evade struggling with alternative visions. Disabling neoliberal capital requires that we not reify neoliberalism by subjecting it to the exclusive entry point of our critique. Rather, we need to take the words of the late Howard Zinn (2004) seriously, "If we see only the worst, it destroys our capacity to do something ... to live now as we think human beings should live, in defiance of all that is bad around us" (p. 1). The authors are also clear that unless we perpetually examine the form that resistance takes, the exclusions that it forges, and actively shape its direction so as to be both constitutive of the voices of and responsive to those who bear the most social cost, we risk disabling its critical edge and worse, we allow it to be co-opted.

We also risk undermining the movement, as the authors so accurately point out, by not animating it within a larger history of "leftist" educational resistance. Zinn (2004) is, again, instructive here:

An Activist Handbook for The Education Revolution:
United Opt Out's Test of Courage, pp. xiii–xvi
Copyright © 2015 by Information Age Publishing

If we remember those times and places—and there are so many—where people have behaved magnificently, this gives us the energy to act, and at least the possibility of sending this spinning top of a world in a different direction. (p. 1)

And, like those that came before it (and they're certainly not totally subject to the dustbins of history), the struggle is not restrictive to the sphere of education. In 1895, some 19 Hopi men were incarcerated on Alcatraz Island for refusal to allow their children to attend school (Tuck & Yang, 2014), given that schooling was an instrument of manifest destiny and cultural erasure. From 1900 to 1940, politically clear Native American youths routinely rebelled against placement in boarding schools by running away. In both cases, whether or not explicitly articulated, the struggle was not against schooling only but against imperial authority. Resistance to schooling was a form of counter-colonial resistance. Likewise (although the stakes and anxieties are different), the current opt out movement is both an effort at creating more responsive schools and a struggle against the reign of neoliberal capital (or what has also been called market fundamentalism). The authors are brilliant, given their realization that schools are not totally independent institutions. They are informed by the wider social, political, and economic context and are also active in shaping that context.

The authors also realize that the analytical focus should not be on the United States only (since policies travel) and ground the revolt into a more politically vibrant and long-term movement to end human exploitation and American global imperialism. It is only here that the opt out movement will be significant, since it may very well become a nerve center where numerous struggles against authoritarianism coalesce and where radical democratic ideals may be redesigned. Conversely, it has the potential of bridging the rage that high-stakes tests breed and assist people in crossing into other spaces of resistance.

Last academic year, during the day the Massachusetts Comprehensive Assessment System (MCAS-Massachusetts' high-stakes test) was to be administered, my son was visibly sick. He insisted that he wanted to attend school to take the test. He opened the test booklet and proceeded to answer test items when his teacher noticed that something was wrong. She sent him to the nurse. I received a call. The nurse stated, "He is clearly not well, but he opened the test booklet and risks having his test invalidated if he is sent home. We'll have him sit for a little then send him back to the classroom to take the test. After the test we'll send him home." I was appalled. Ultimately, my son returned to take the MCAS, despite the early onset of the flu, and my resistance. Although he did not support the test, he felt compelled, given the pressures. I don't mean to impress upon readers that nurses in our school system are incompetent. I think they perform quite well and would perform stellar if our educational system was adequately funded. What I do mean to say is that the regime of high-stakes testing in our schools is not only deeply disturbing, but inhumane! My son's experience is certainly not as severe as the brilliant young adults routinely abandoned by accountability structures that not only do not work, but are designed to move wealth upward.

High scores on high-stakes tests do not prove that true learning is occurring. Countless educational research studies have concluded that the use of high-stakes tests narrows the curriculum and encourages test preparation as a substitute for engaged learning. Furthermore, our continuous focus on scoring well evades more important public dialogue about funding inequities and the root cause of educational disengagement—poverty. Allowing corporations to continue reaping billions of dollars in profit off public education only exacerbates the problem. Any administrator, school committee member, or school functionary still standing before students, teachers, and families touting the virtues of high-stakes tests should be ashamed. And, if they know it's wrong but remain silent, they're complicit in educational malpractice.

Subjecting English-language learners to the high-stakes tests after only having been in the country for one year is immoral. Emergent bilingual students are 9 times more likely to drop out of high school than their peers. These tests are part of the problem. Not only are they culturally biased, given their history in IQ testing, eugenics, and the social efficiency movement (Au, 2009) the assumption of unidimensional cognitive processes (Swope & Miner, 2000), they also contribute to the expansion of school cultures marked by the hegemony of English. I recall a conversation with a colleague, a middle school language arts teacher who was frantically preparing her students for the Florida Comprehensive Assessment Test (FCAT). After overhearing my conversation with a student, she pointedly asked, "Why do you speak to her in Spanish! She's very smart and speaks perfectly good English." My response was, "Because she also speaks perfectly good Spanish." In her estimation (as related to other colleagues), my interaction with youths in the hallway was detrimental to their success on the FCAT. Worse, it was an impediment to their literacy and intellectual development. The ability to manipulate multiple linguistic repertoires and registers could not possibly count as deep literacy and intelligence at work.

A high percentage of students with disabilities are not meeting graduation requirements as a result of these tests. Countless educational researchers have concluded that measuring teacher effectiveness and school quality through high-stakes test scores is unreliable and unethical. Evaluating teachers in this manner does very little to improve the profession. Rather, it encourages great teachers to resign.

All of the authors writing in this book believe in the high expectations of all students, teachers, and administrators. Yet they correctly claim that imposing high-stakes tests are about securing low expectations. Portfolios, performance based, and other forms of authentic assessments are more educationally sound. Standardized tests also have their place, but they should not be in the form of high stakes.

The opt out movement documented and theorized in this book is not simply about resisting high-stakes tests. If testing regimes were to be dismantled in the morning, I would hardly think that any of the activist-authors of this book would cease their work. The movement is essentially about opting for democracy as an unfinished and ongoing process that must be struggled for. It realizes that radical democracy is not just born out of our option to participate in the ordinary political infrastructure. It is a process involving the ongoing democratization of civil society. A democratic political system cannot come to fruition if the institutions of that society are undemocratic, antidemocratic, or fail to (re)create the structures and conditions that lead to further democratization. Democracy flourishes when democratic cultures are the norm. The authors herein therefore "claim no easy victories" (Cabral, 1974, p. 1), since the work before us requires long-distance runners.

This book exemplifies the very best of what critical scholarship should be and do. The contributors do not engage in intellectual accommodation by raising disquieting questions from a balcony. All of the authors included in this text are fiercely courageous in their activism and organizing. The text should be read widely! Anyone wishing to examine the intricacies of educational resistance, to "engage education as the practice of freedom" (hooks, 1994, p. 207) and to channel political and moral outrage into positive and productive political projects would be served well by this text.

REFERENCES

Au, W. (2009). *Unequal by design. High-stakes testing and the standardization of inequality.* New York, NY; London, UK: Routledge.

Cabral, A. (1974). *Revolution in Guinea.* London, UK: Stage 1.

hooks, b. (1994). *Teaching to transgress: Education as the practice of freedom.* New York, NY: Routledge.

Swope, K., & Miner, B. (2000). *Failing our kids: Why the testing craze won't fix our schools.* Milwaukee, WI: Rethinking Schools.

Tuck, E., & Yang, W. K. (Eds.). (2014). *Youth resistance research and theories of change.* New York, NY; London, UK: Routledge.

Zinn, H. (2004, September 2). *The optimism of uncertainty.* Retrieved from http://www.thenation.com/doc/20040920/zinn

INTRODUCTION

Peggy Robertson

On behalf of the *United Opt Out* (UOO) team, I wanted to share our purpose in writing this book. First and foremost, we had a story to share. A story about a group of individuals who waded into the complex world of activism and found one another, and realized that each of us held one piece of a puzzle. We came together as a result of chance, timing, and necessity. We were by no means the first group on the block to share opt out strategies or any other strategy for that matter. We were simply a group of six who clicked, who enjoyed one another's quirkiness, and who felt incredibly passionate about doing what is right for all children. Each of us refused to accept soft actions as a way to move forward. Each of us wanted to play hardball. And so play we did, and still do. I myself did not even meet the team until a year later at our first occupation in Washington, D.C. in 2012. Our work and our relationships were built via free Skype phone calls every Monday night from our individual homes, where each of us would hear the noises of one another's life in the background—families were eating, TVs were blaring, children chattering, dogs barking—all while we bantered on about our daily lives and hammered away at strategy—planning to save public education. We quickly found out one another's strengths and found that together our collective strength generated ideas and actions beyond our individual imaginations.

An Activist Handbook for The Education Revolution:
United Opt Out's Test of Courage, pp. xvii–xix
Copyright © 2015 by Information Age Publishing
All rights of reproduction in any form reserved.

Our team also created a space for us to feel sane, away from our day jobs and for some of us, away from our communities, where folks were still asleep to the crumbling democracy staring us in the face wherever we turned. As we worked together and saw that we could have an impact, it made us work even harder, and faster, and with greater intensity, at times pushing ahead too fast and crashing. And at other times sailing ahead at a steady pace with patience, deliberation, and careful planning. Our story is one story of many in this time period in which activists everywhere are pushing forward to reclaim public schools.

We share our story for a reason. Stories create action. The UOO story may be a catalyst for other small pockets of resistance out there who are right now asking, *Is it possible? Can our small group do this? Can we make a difference?* Yes. You can. Read our story and see how six individuals (now seven) with no money, in different locations, from different backgrounds, each working a day job, managed to make something happen. But we didn't do it alone. We were simply seven individuals who reached out in the hopes of finding others, and did. We built relationships with activists all over the country—individuals who were talented and brought their own strengths to the fight. Some individuals worked in tandem with UOO, and still do. Others created their own activist groups and attacked reform from a different angle—all angles being equally as important. We take no credit for any of this; I simply share it here because it's important to recognize the ability we each have to share our story, build relationships, collaborate, and create an even greater impact, as we each chip away at the corporate takeover of public schools.

We also share this book in the hopes of showing the human side of this work. Corporate reform has no human side—they have only greed, ego and power. Our side—*the ethical* side—is one of humanity—we have heart, we make mistakes, we play, we work hard, we care for others—we care very much about our country, our public schools, and America's children. We care so deeply, that at times we are driven to do things that place us in harm's way. But our relationships with one another carry us through these difficult times, and that is what activists must always do for one another. Hold hands tightly—together we can lift one another up.

Finally, we hope to share knowledge that will help our readers fill their activist tool boxes with research, ideas, and a checklist of what to do and not to do, as you move forward in your fight to make this world a better place. The landscape is always changing, but heart and truth always remain the constant—and this is what keeps us going.

Thank you to everyone who has been a part of our journey or has helped us along the way. We are always here and available to talk should you need us. You can find us online at www.unitedoptout.com. Or simply,—give one of us a call. Our contact information is on the website as well. The UOO team sends out a solid fist in the air in solidarity to each of you. We are on the right side of history. With this truth, we continue to push forward. We look forward to seeing each of you along the way as we work together to create a world that is a better place for all children.

CHAPTER 1

PREDATORS, COLONIZERS, AND CORPORATE-MODEL REFORM

Morna McDermott

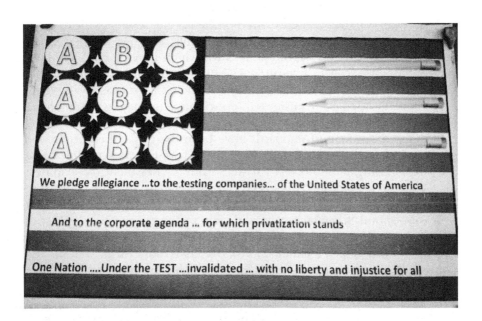

We pledge allegiance ...to the testing companies... of the United States of America

And to the corporate agenda ... for which privatization stands

One Nation ....Under the TEST ...invalidated ... with no liberty and injustice for all

United Opt Out's **Pearson flag**

An Activist Handbook for the Education Revolution:
United Opt Out's Test of Courage, pp. 1–15

WHAT IS CORPORATE REFORM?

There's a lot of growing resistance to the Common Core State Standards (CCSS) and to high-stakes standardized testing. And there are a lot of reasons for this opposition: invasion of privacy of information; shoddy, confusing content; federal and corporate intrusion; questionable standards in terms of content or developmental appropriateness; costs/expenditures being funneled to private corporations; and its indelible and damaging attachment to high-stakes testing. What's also concerning is the way in which CCSS is directly intertwined with other education reforms as a multipronged effort toward one goal: *privatizing public education*.[1] Federal overreach, through the nationalized imposition of these reforms, allows corporations to manage and control (and own) every facet of public education, including what children learn, how they will learn it, and who serves as the beneficiaries of their efforts (spoiler alert here: it's not children).

Pearson publishing spent large sums lobbying for the legislation to create new tests, new curricula, and new teacher evaluations (McDermott, 2013a) and then waits on the other end with their hands out, receiving the millions of dollars to deliver the new tests, new curricula, and new teacher "training" needed to implement the polices for which they lobbied. Achieve, Foundation for Excellent Education, the Business Roundtable, and testing companies like ACT pushed for and wrote the CCSS standards to reflect their own educational and business interests, micromanaging the outcomes of education for children toward their own agendas (McDermott, 2013b). Nationalized testing and standards have been the goals of corporate-led interests ever since No Child Left Behind (NCLB). Efforts to push for *more and newer* testing methods (via Partnership for Assessment of Readiness for College and Careers/PARCC and Smarter Balanced Assessment Consortium/SBAC) are led by Bill Gates, along with inBloom[2] and no longer in business, and other tech-savvy data-interested corporations. Most of these corporations are members of the conservative-led American Legislative Exchange Council (Schneider, 2013) such as State Farm, Walton, and Lumina, who have their own vested interests in having access to "big data." The governing boards[3] for PARCC and SBAC are political and economic footballs for the politicians who serve on their boards.

The federal government uses abusive, intrusive, and invasive techniques (ironically, in the name of "equity") to serve the interests of the corporations with whom they partner. Additionally, some of these same corporations are being paid handsomely to collect the 400 points of data[4] embedded in both CCSS and the new PARCC and SBAC tests that go along with it. And when our schools, our children, and our teachers "fail" to meet the expectation set forth by the aforementioned corporate interests, hedge fund corporations and billionaires line up to fund the charter schools and other forms of "reform" designed to privatize our public schools, because there's profit to be gained (Bernstein, 2013). These same private interests promise to "fix" the problem, which of course they created in the first place. This, despite research that has shown again and again how and why such "reform" efforts have failed our children (Thomas, 2012). *It's not rocket science. It's simple. It's greed.*

How to Privatize Public Education in 12 Easy Steps

1. Manufacture a crisis and instill public fear. See *Waiting for "Superman"* (Guggenheim, 2011).
2. Create a rallying cry for the need for *(re)action* to save citizens from some danger, which involves eliminating those ideas or people posing a threat. In this case, public educators. Bring in your own "private" troops (Blackwater? No. Teach for America) and people trained at new "innovative leadership centers."
3. Create a system which becomes a self-fulfilling prophecy. High-stakes testing policies will doom schools and children to failure, which is a convenient way to "prove" the grounds for numbers 1 and 2 (see Ohanian, 2009).
4. Use of "savior" language. Create sound-bite messages which co-opt terms that most people identify as favorable such as "innovation," "reform," and "choice."
5. Deflect *the facts* with spectacular dog-and-pony-show media blasts and hide the truth under glossy presentations of the agenda. Disguise this ideology of greed under the umbrella of "freedom" and "saving children."
6. Create legislation that politically and financially benefits the stakeholders of those same policies by forging under-the-table alliances between big business and state legislators.[5]
7. Launder these policies through seemingly beneficial nonprofit agencies and corporate philanthropy where the origins cannot be traced easily.
8. These same corporations now open for-profit charter schools and online schools and other "options" in lieu of "failing public education." When children attend these "schools," the per-pupil funding that would have gone to support the local public schools is now funneled into the new for-profit alternative.[6]
9. Make inside deals with the textbook and testing companies that these schools will use, generating billions of dollars of profits for these companies while public schools languish from lack of resources. Mandated testing forces schools to redirect monies to

testing that could have otherwise been spent hiring teachers to
reduce class size or provide needed learning materials.[7]

10.   Hide and twist the data that shows that charter alternatives perform
no better than their public counterparts (Schemo, 2006).

11.   Manipulate legislation in ways that benefit "choice" alternatives so
that certain populations of students who would make their schools
"look bad" can be denied access to those schools and can be provided with ample resources that could have also improved public
schools if only THEY had they funds.[8]

12.   Public schools, as result of steps 10 to 11, would now, in fact, be
failing and as a result, the free-market ideology prevails and can
appear justified in their actions. The cycle back to step number
1 is now complete. Public education now becomes Education
Incorporated.

Colonizing for Land and Profit: A Brief History ... Repeating Itself

How We Got Here

A glance at the history of modern public schooling reveals how power has
been a front and central agenda for determining who, what, and how schools
shall educate "the masses" (the elite have always had private education as
the option of choice). Public education has largely been manipulated by
those in power, assigning to schools their purpose and meaning according
to their own image. And these policies have mostly been intended for
urban centers populated by people of color and immigrants. These policies
were constructed for people with little financial or professional means to
fight back, while suburban schools remained safe havens protected from
the ravages of these policies intended for the "Other."

In the early 1900s, even though newly emancipated Black people could
now receive a public education, institutional powers ensured that their
education was still "separate and unequal." Following *Brown v. Board*, state
and federally sanctioned laws (and unchecked racism in general), including block busting and redlining, ensured that even if schools could no
longer segregate, housing and employment practices would make sure they
remained separate—and unequal. And the legacy of separate and unequal
continues today because of corporate-style reforms (Brown & Dianis, 2014).

In the height of the industrial era, we introduced factory models of
schooling to prepare children for a factory model way of thinking and
producing. We've used testing to sort and track children like widgets on
a conveyer belt. Throughout the 1900s into today, dominant cultural
influences often determine that public education would (will) be the place

to "Americanize" immigrants, whitewashing their history and their cultural identity (Kliebard, 2004; Mirel, 2010).

In the 1950s, politics demanded we push for more math and science to keep up the "Space Race" with the Russians. And we introduced physical education (PE) during World War II so we could physically condition young men going to war. And now we live in the age of multinational corporate domination and efforts to privatize every public good or human right from education to clean drinking water. The agenda for what and who and how to teach within a public education system has been crafted by the interests of everyone it seems, except the most important and fragile of all stakeholders—children.

Of course within each of these eras there has remained great schools, great teachers, and great learning experiences. Again, in spite of all of this, we believe it's not the idea of public education that is failing. It's not our children or our teachers who are failing. What is failing is our promise to our children and our commitment to this grand democratic experiment which requires an informed, compassionate, critically minded, and healthy citizenry to survive.

Manifest Destiny?

Remember how White Europeans used "Manifest Destiny" to justify taking over lands occupied by the Native Americans? First, the government, in tandem with corporate interests, launched a campaign that identified the "Indians" as a "dangerous threat," calling them "savages" who needed to either be civilized or eliminated (privatizing step #1). This threat justified the use of "state force" to curtail this supposed threat (step #2). Then, when attacked, the Native Americans fought back. These skirmishes were twisted around to "prove" how "savage" Native Americans were (step #3). Then they used the term "Manifest Destiny" (that they were chosen by God) to take these lands in the name of "progress." Further, they would "civilize the savages" in the name of Christianity and European superiority (step #4). The Native Americans, they said, would be better off for it—they were "helping" them.

Facts about the savagery of the White Europeans themselves (small pox on blankets for example) were hushed up and kept from public knowledge (step #5). Even today in many history books, this continues to be the case. Steps number 6–10 can be found in an accurate history book such as *People's History of the United States* (Zinn, 2003). The current policy "reforms" in American public education are a 21st century land grab. This time around, the land grab is in urban neighborhoods, being gentrified by land developers and corporations, as well as a land grab for our nation's public schools in general.

Manifest Destiny 2.0: Meet the New Colonizers

Drawing from the work of Jay Griffiths' book *A Sideways Look at Time* (2004), we can understand how colonizing bodies, emerging out of the Enlightenment era, needed to control how other people understood and experienced time as a means to solidify their hegemonic ideology. And it took decades, if not centuries, to really erase the sense of time and space of non-Western (and non-Christian) predecessors; to create a "new normal," which to date, most of us take for granted as "natural." Griffiths states, "With its dominant ideology, the West declares its time is *the time*" (p. 27, emphasis in original).

What standardized concepts of time and space (i.e., clocks, calendars, and maps) were to the Western colonizers of previous eras, data collection/ownership is to corporate ownership of the 21st century. This is not just happening—poof!—now out of nowhere. Dominance and hegemony don't happen overnight, in one year, or even one decade. They operate under the slow creep of time, creating a subtle yet pervasive effect on the social mindset and the worldview of a people. Griffiths points out that, "Society begins to think in the forms it has structured for itself, linear and artificial, over-fragmented, modeling itself in the imagery of its machinery" (2004, p. 75).

Today's obsession with the streamlining, collection, and surveillance of data—from collecting phone records, wire-tapping, Internet cookies, Facebook advertising, and now children's test scores and other private records—makes evident that the streamlined and synchronous effect of the Common Core and standardized testing mandates demand that we regulate our bodies and minds to this new generation of corporate shape-shifters until we think it a natural and normal act to do so. Even years before now, the global consulting firm McKinsey & Company was on the trail of this idea:

> Data have swept into every industry and business function and are now an important factor of production, alongside labor and capital. We estimate that, by 2009, nearly all sectors in the US economy had at least an average of 200 terabytes of stored data (twice the size of US retailer Wal-Mart's data warehouse in 1999) per company with more than 1,000 employees. (Manyika et al., 2011, para. 4)

The corporate takeover of public education, as a form of profit as much as it is a form of control and social engineering, has been in the works for a while. Every generation believes it is the "it" generation. It's the end of the world, it's the Age of Aquarius, it's the … fill in the blank. And they're all equally right. Each generation defines itself in response to the broader sweep of history in relationship to the sociopolitical, economic, and ecological events of the moment. This is why having a historical perspective in understanding what corporate-controlled education is, how it got here, and how to fight it is so important. Know your enemy.

Much of what we're seeing today started back in the 1980s—the age of Reagan. Reagan was a huge fan of eliminating federal programs, specifically the U.S. Department of Education:

> As recently as 1996, the Republican Party platform declared, "The Federal government has no constitutional authority to be involved in school curricula or to control jobs in the market place. This is why we will abolish the Department of Education." (Charen, 2010, para. 7)

Going a little farther back in time, we must remember that federal oversight, or decision making, has (in its shining moments) brought us both the end of slavery in the 1800s and the desegregation (at least on paper) of schools and other public institutions in the 1950s. This has everything to do with everything. The free-market approach toward education today is quite possibly a long-planned scheme to essentially erase (or override) the rulings of *Brown v. Board*. Current (circa 2012) reform policies have decimated Black and Brown communities, their schools, and have done nothing but bring in major monies to charter school investors. The school-to-prison pipeline is doing quite well these days. Gentrification is the new red-lining and real estate investors are "all in" on new charter polices. Low-income schools or community services in impoverished areas have *never* been adequately funded or staffed; so how can we claim that *they've* failed? We ignore the fact that as a society we have consistently failed them.

It was in the 1980s that the notion of "standards" and high-stakes testing were born (Bower & Thomas, 2012). Sure, we've had standardized testing ever since the eugenics movement of early 20th century, but Reagan's folks really nailed it. They laid the groundwork, *the slow creep of public acceptance*, for the supposed need for standardized testing and national standards to aid "failing" public education. Remember, this was the decade of "A Nation at Risk" report (Gardner, 1983). Among other things, the report called for "Standards and Expectations … and standardized tests of achievement at major transition points from one level of schooling to another and particularly from high school to college or work" (p. 35).

The 1980s also brought us the birth of the American Legislative Exchange Council (ALEC).[9] Corporate dominance met at the crossroads of technology, and things have been going their way ever since. Without technology to create enormous vehicles for data collection (both known and unknown to us) and clouds in which to store this information, corporations would not have nearly the stranglehold today that they are gaining. Again McKinsey and Co. celebrates this fact: "Computer and electronic products and information sectors, as well as finance and insurance, and government are poised to gain substantially from the use of big data" (Minyaka et al., 2011, para. 9).

Even Rupert Murdoch, owner of *FOX News* and huge ALEC proponent, created his million dollar database gathering and storage company called *inBloom*. Without the Common Core, there is no universal data to be mined. It's a data-palooza![10] But this brings me back to author Jay Griffiths. The standardization of time was central to the global colonization of other (non-White) cultures, countries, and peoples. According to Griffiths

> Synchronization is highly political; totalitarian states adore it, from the vast synchronized gymnastics of fascist countries to the synchronized *Heil Hitler* salute. Synchronization illustrates the totalitarian desire to subsume the individual into the mass. It also, similarly, represents a wish to blur specific, various times into a global monotime. (2004, p. 76)

Now, it's the synchronization, aka standardization (and ownership) of data and information, starting at pre-K and following us through adulthood that will be the colonizing instrument dujour. As Griffiths states, "The West's dominant attitudes to land and time are—still—the will to enclosure, a desire for private ownership and empire building" (2004, p. 46). One might suppose that now that most non-Western cultures have been controlled, subsumed, or simply obliterated, the corporate empire turns inward, colonizing the United States and other Westernized countries; not by time management and land control, but through a "data-palooza." All we know, *or can know*, via our educational system, will be mediated by and managed by corporate powers.

In this invisible ideology, those in power in the corporate world have more recently been colonizing education by defining their curriculum and modes of evaluation—the Gates, Waltons, Broads, and ALEC—and using their definition of what counts as important learning as a tool to (their) power; the data collectors seizing the knowledge and information of the children; Teach For America strangling teacher education programs in schools past and present; corporate-driven agendas overruling developmentally appropriate and meaningful learning; charters colonizing noncharters (formerly known as public education); everyone taming children's time.

The standardization and control of data will do for the corporate global paradigm what the standardization of time did for the colonizers of centuries past, and we operate as if they were laws of the universe and not the social constructions that they are. Let's identify the greatest cheerleaders for this educational data frenzy: technology moguls Bill Gates and Rupert Murdoch, The World Bank, global management consulting firms like McKinsey and Co.,[10] and Pearson publishing. Not as visible but equally important are the behind-the-scenes organizations like insurance companies, RAND (the data collection and analysis nonprofit), the Bradley

Foundation, the Council for Foreign Relations and the U.S. Department of Defense (McDermott, 2013c).

Books like *The Education of Sam Sanders* (Poetter, 2006) saw it coming. Sadly, it was intended to be a work of *fiction*, set in 2029. We're ahead of schedule. Requiring parents and children *no choice* but to give up their child's private records in the name of standardized tests, which are themselves highly questionable and objectionable, is a different story. Second, just because *some* technology brings us convenience, efficiency, and pleasure does not always mean more is better. Standardization, with the aim of data ownership via technology "innovations," has the potential to be quite harmful for generations of small children. Just because we *can* put learning online for school age children, where they stare at screens all day inputting data and calling this "learning," doesn't mean that we *should*—or at least not in the record numbers that are cropping up in classrooms all over the country. Organizations developed and pushed for a Common Core of learning, and have done so wholesale across more than half the states and in every classroom *without even knowing yet if it's even good for children*, because "standardization" and more efficient "data tracking" are beneficial to their own pocketbooks.

Such a movement is not merely vying for profit and control within the existing paradigm, *it will completely change our global paradigm of reality.* "While once you could say that time was so local that for every *genius loci*, a spirit of specific place, there was a genius temporis, a spirit of specific time" Griffith's suggests, "the history of Western timekeeping has been one of standardization and of globalization" (2004, p. 43).

Soon we will be saying, "Once, you could say that learning, knowledge and meaning were so local, that education embraced the situated, lived meaningful processes enabling individuals to think creatively and divergently about their world(s). Once, there was a time when learning had a *genius temporis*, a time of its own beyond the universal clocks of testing weeks and pacing guides. Once we had a public education system that was not wholly owned and dictated by the mood swings and interests of the corporate elite. Once, we had something called childhood."

And in this historical moment, where resistance seems both necessary and futile, I will take Griffith's advice:

> The given choice is either look forward to the future as progress (and who could refuse?) or look backward as only backward ... it is an utterly false choice; believing there are only two choices is putting oneself at the mercy of a mere construct. Someone else's construct, at that. When you're given a choice of only two roads, an old saying goes, take the third. In this case, the third choice is one of neither moving forward or backwards but of looking around, not accepting that time need be a straight line at all. (2004, p. 263)

Predatory Reform

Shutting down public schools and handing them over to private organizations is not a "turnaround," it is a heist.

—Sabrina Stevens (2014)[12]

"Reformers ... *what are they?*" We have examined how reformers are modern-day colonizers. But what are modern-day colonizers but *predatory reformers* (also see predatorial policy or predatory policymakers). This term aptly describes both the who and the what in a proverbial nutshell. The name comes from the use of the term to describe immoral, unethical, and illegal lending practices which bubbled over and exploded around 2008. Predatory lending. AskHow[13] (a guide for economic theory novices like myself) describes it in simplest terms as follows:

> Predatory lending is the unfair, deceptive, or fraudulent practices of some lenders during the loan origination process.... The office of inspector general of the FDIC broadly defines predatory lending as "imposing unfair and abusive loan terms on borrowers. The practice of a lender deceptively convincing borrowers to agree to unfair and abusive loan terms, or systematically violating those terms in ways that make it difficult for the borrower to defend against."

Let's (re)define this now in more analogues terms. The "lenders" are the U.S. Department of Education, certain politicians, and billionaires (or the think tanks they fund) who "lend" monies to push (using unfair, deceptive, or fraudulent measures) for certain polices or practices in exchange for self-serving or profitable benefits. Who are the borrowers? Children, teachers, taxpayers, schools, and communities who are convinced they need to agree to unfair or abusive terms.

The most painful parallel is how predators as lenders and as education policymakers started with those who they perceived as the easiest "prey": lower income, largely Black and Brown communities—hard working and struggling individuals who are deceptively led into believing that here is the answer to their prayers, the salve for their struggle. They too can "have the American Dream—no really, it's easy ... just sign here." Predatory lenders often target senior citizens and people of color to place them in unnecessarily expensive loans.[14]

So how are "reformers" and reform policies predatory? Too many ways to count. But we'll focus on the top few.

Race to the Top

RTTT is a primary example. The federal government promises to loan monies to cash-starved states in exchange for a few "terms of agreement." These terms of agreement include new accountability systems (data collection), new tests (PARCC or SBAC), adoption of Common Core, new methods for teacher evaluation, alternative teacher education programs (TFA), school turnaround policies (charters and vouchers). In exchange for the RTTT monies, states in essence are forced to comply with unsustainable and downright abusive policies. "Sure we'll help you get that new house … just sign here."

The Latest Round of ALEC Legislation is Also Excellent Example of Predatory Policy

As part of their new "student achievement backpack" launched at their 2013 Policy Summit,[15] essentially the proposed changes would enable private entities (online and edu-tech companies) to serve in public schools as LEAs,[16] thus enabling them to not only get paid to replace experienced professional public school teachers, but they'll get oodles of data in return (remember: this predator feeds on money and data). Through the "robust and comprehensive data collection," ALEC aims to allow predatory behaviors into your child's classroom, where they will be seen not as learners but as "consumers" of the goods and products being sold via these companies (McDermott, 2013d).

Parent Trigger

This is the greatest heist foisted upon parents in many years. It is the ultimate in deceptive advertising; spawned in the bowels of ALEC and promoted by many think tanks such as the Heritage Foundation (Cohn, 2013). Parent Trigger sold many communities into believing that this policy would place education decision making back in their hands, locally, where it belongs. They were used as patsies to do the dirty work for corporations who, once the public schools were closed, swooped down and claimed their rightful space as colonizers of their brave new world. While many parents across the country have begun to fight back, still many other states continue to see this policy as "empowerment" for communities.

Co-location, Charters, and Turnarounds

Remember, "Predatory mortgage lending practices strip borrowers of home equity and threaten families with foreclosure, *destabilizing the very communities that are beginning to enjoy the fruits of our nation's economic success*" (author's emphasis).[17] Similarly, lending agreements with RTTT funds require that more schools be co-located with charters, the expansion of charters, and higher rates of "foreclosure" on schools which were never equitably funded in the first place. The hedge fund managers finance the giant charter chains, and charter CEOs profit handsomely by bilking millions from taxpayers, for which they are rarely held accountable. As a result of these measures, communities are becoming destabilized and are faced with the loss of community schools and increased race and class resegregation (see Alexander & West, 2012).

Common Core and PARCC/SBAC

The standards and the tests have always been seen as intertwined—because they are. Common Core uses deceptive advertising terms like "world-class standards" and "state-led" to lure buyers into a bad deal. And with the agreement to use PARCC or SBAC, the terms of the loan will prove impossible to repay. The costs associated with the new standards and the testing require technological infrastructures, monstrous loads of data collection, endless need for training and retraining, and new and shinier curricular materials. For example, as of 2013, California taxpayers are looking at "a $1.25 billion bill to prepare the way for the Common Core" (Kittle, 2013, para. 12).

Once the federal funding runs out in 2014–2105, who will pay for all this new stuff? How will we pay for the metaphorical new garage, the built-in pool, or the roof (which, when we bought the place, didn't know it had huge leaks …)? Corporations like McKinsey and Co.—king of the predator food chain (McDermott, 2014)—will step in and "take over" PARCC and SBAC in many states, funneling millions to their bank accounts to help "fix the pool, the garage, and the roof"—for a small fee of course.

Additionally, when children "fail" to meet the expectations (via cutoff scores and value-added measure: VAM) of the new tests, it's like not being able to "make the payment." Time to kick them out and parcel them out to private interests. Public into private, school to prison, public educator into TFA … the list goes on. Both the feds and the free-market corporations are predators it seems. It's a blend of capitalism and federal overstep at their worst. After a few drinks, they mated. And they've bred a strange beast. Don't try to feed it. It'll bite your hand off. It's a predator.

And you can see the effects of predatory policy coming to fruition. The terms of agreement in each instance are deceiving, unfair, and impossible to meet. Or we realize we've been duped and refuse to meet them. Our public education system, our schools, our children, and our democracy are on the foreclosure auction block, for sale to the highest bidder. And we're left out in the cold. So the next time someone asks you what "reform" can be called, call it what it is: predatory.

> *"I've been assured by a very knowing American of my acquaintance in London, that a young healthy child well nursed and at least a year old is a most delicious, nourishing, and wholesome food, whether stewed, roasted, baked or boiled: and I make no doubt that it will equally serve in a fricassee or a ragout."*
>
> —Jonathan Swift, "A Modest Proposal" (1729)

And that we will take it from them.

THE ACTIVIST WORKBOOK

1. Reformers are clever about disguising their real agenda behind glossy "research" papers and projects. When you see a new program or initiative coming to your school or community, visit their website. Make sure to click on "Our Funders" or other key terms like "Our Supporters" or "Our Partners." Make note of who the Board of Directors are and read their biographies. This information will tell you a great deal about who or what this program or initiative really supports.

2. Research!!! There are numerous activists out there who have done tremendous research in the area of corporate reform, including but certainly not limited to Susan Ohanian (www.susanohanian.org), Mercedes Scheinder (www.deutsche29.wordpress.com), Alan Singer (www.huffingtonpost.com/alan-singer), and numerous bloggers available at www.atthechalkface.com.

3. Find ways to make your research and findings publicly available. The corporate connections are rarely publicized in mainstream media and therefore remain unknown to most parents and teachers. Create flyers, Listservs, Facebook sites, and hold meetings where vital information can be made more public.

NOTES

1. For a full account of "who's who" in corporate reform, see M. Schneider (2014) *A Chronicle of Echoes: Who's Who in the Implosion of American Public Education.*
2. As of 2015 inBloom is defunct and no longer in business.
3. http://www.parcconline.org/governing-board
4. http://www.classsizematters.org/inbloom_student_data_privacy/student_privacy_inbloom_timeline/
5. www.alecexposed.org
6. http://www.dailykos.com/story/2011/04/12/966046/-Education-the-ALEC-Way
7. http://fairtest.org/exposing-myths-high-stakes-testing
8. See "model" bills proposed by ALEC at http://alecexposed.org/wiki/Privatizing_Public_Education,_Higher_Ed_Policy,_and_Teachers
9. http://www.alecexposed.org/wiki/ALEC_Exposed
10. http://www.ed.gov/blog/2013/01/education-datapalooza-unleashing-the-power-of-open-data-to-help-students-parents-and-teachers/
11. http://www.mckinsey.com/insights/business_technology/big_data_the_next_frontier_for_innovation
12. http://integrityineducation.org/choice/
13. http://www.ask.com/wiki/Predatory_lending

14. http://www.responsiblelending.org/mortgage-lending/tools-resources/8-signs-of-predatory-lending.html
15. http://respriv.org/wp-content/uploads/2013/11/ED_2013_SNPS_35_Day.pdf
16. Local Education Agency is an entity which operates local public primary and secondary schools in the United States
17. http://portal.hud.gov/hudportal/HUD?src=/program_offices/housing/sfh/pred/predlend

REFERENCES

Alexander, M., & West, C. (2012). *The new Jim Crow: Mass incarceration in the age of color blindness*. New York, NY: New Press.

Bernstein, K. (2013, February 15). So why do hedge funds so favor charter schools? *Daily Kos*. Retrieved from http://www.dailykos.com/story/2013/02/15/1187346/-So-why-do-hedge-funds-so-favor-charter-schools

Bower, J., & Thomas, P. L. (Eds.) (2013). *De-testing and de-grading schools: Authentic alternatives to accountability and standardization*. New York, NY: Peter Lang.

Brown, J., & Dianis, J. B. (2014, May 16). With charter schools, the education business is more separate and unequal. *CNN Opinion*. Retrieved from http://www.cnn.com/2014/05/16/opinion/brown-separate-unequal-schools/index.html

Charen, M. (2010, June 11). Wanting to abolish the Department of Education is not radical. *National Review Online*. Retrieved from http://www.nationalreview.com/articles/229936/wanting-abolish-department-education-not-radical/mona-charen

Cohn, A. (2013, April 4). Public schools, billionaire agendas: The threat of the "parent revolution" campaign. *AlterNet*. Retrieved from http://www.alternet.org/education/public-schools-billionaire-agendas-threat-parent-revolution-campaign-0

Gardner, D. (1983). *A nation at risk*. Washington, DC: National Commission on Excellence in Education.

Griffiths, J. (2004). *A sideways look at time*. New York, NY: Tarcher.

Guggenheim, D. (Writer & Director). (2011). *Waiting for "Superman"* [film]. Paramount Home Entertainment.

Kittle, M. D. (2013, April 4). How much will the Common Core cost you? *Watchdog.org*. Retrieved from http://watchdog.org/104325/how-much-will-common-core-cost-you/

Kliebard, H. (2004). *The struggle for the American curriculum, 1893–1958*. New York, NY: Routledge.

McDermott, M. (2013a, July 1). *The Pearson follies part I*. Retrieved from http://educationalchemy.com/2013/07/01/the-pearson-follies-an-ongoing-saga/

McDermott, M. (2013b, Oct. 31). Four important mythbusters about the Common Core. *Educationalchemy*. Retrieved from http://educationalchemy.com/2013/10/31/four-important-mythbusters-about-the-common-core/

McDermott, M. (2013c, Nov. 27). "Big brother" has an ugly corporate "stepsister." *Educationalchemy*. Retrieved from http://educationalchemy.com/2013/11/27/big-brother-has-an-ugly-corporate-big-stepsister/

McDermott, M. (2013d, July 25). A labyrinth of corporate interests in the Common Core. *Educationalchemy*. Retrieved from http://educationalchemy. com/2013/07/25/a-labyrinth-of-corporate-interests-in-common-core/

McDermott, M. (2014, January 14). The global powerhouse designing our ed reform landscape: McKinsey and Co. *Educationalchemy*. Retrieved from http:// educationalchemy.com/2014/01/04/the-global-powerhouse-designing-our-ed-reform-landscape-mckinsey-and-co/

Manyika, J., Chui, M., Brown, B., Bughin, J., Dobbs, R., Roxburgh, C., & Hung Byers, A. (2011, May). Big data: The next frontier for innovation, competition, and productivity. *McKinsey & Company*. Retrieved from http://www.mckinsey.com/insights/business_technology/big_data_the_next_frontier_for_innovation

Mirel, J. (2010). *Patriotic pluralism: Americanization education and European immigrants*. Cambridge, MA: Harvard University Press.

Ohanian, S. (2009). Race to the Top in education. *Susan Ohanian.org*. Retrieved from http://susanohanian.org/outrage_fetch.php?id=614

Poetter, T. (2006). *The education of Sam Sanders*. Falls Village, CT: Hamilton.

Ravitch, D. (2013). *Reign of error: The hoax of the privatization movement and the danger to America's public schools*. New York, NY: Knopf.

Schemo, D. (2006, Aug 23). Study of test scores finds charter schools lagging. *New York Times;* Retrieved from http://www.nytimes.com/2006/08/23/education/23charter.html

Schneider, M (2013). The Common Core memorandum of understanding: What a story. *Deutsch29*. Retrieved from http://deutsch29.wordpress.com/2013/10/14/the-common-core-memorandum-of-understanding-what-a-story/

Schneider, M. (2014). *A chronicle of echoes: Who's who in the implosion of American public education*. Charlotte, NC: Information Age.

Swift, J. (1729). A modest proposal. *Quotidiana*. Retrieved from http://essays.quotidiana.org/swift/modest_proposal/

Thomas, P. L. (2012, March 16). Charter schools are not the answer. *Daily Kos*. Retrieved from http://www.dailykos.com/story/2012/03/16/1074948/-Charter-Schools-Not-the-Answer-Especially-if-We-Fail-to-Identify-the-Question

Zinn, H. (2003). *A people's history of the United States: 1492–present*. New York, NY: HarperCollins.

CHAPTER 2

WHO WE ARE

Morna McDermott

It Started on E-mail and a Listserv

From: Peggy Robertson [writepeg@juno.com]
Sent: Thursday, August 11, 2011 6:40 PM
To: tln@listserve.com
Subject: creating a campaign to opt out …

Okay fellow TLNers …

I know that there are tons of campaigns out there to opt out. For example, http://www.thecbe.org/Pages/issues.html. However, I think there are some key components that are missing …

–killer marketing slogan

–factual information that actually hits a cord. Knowing for example, that your child has lost her music teacher but has gained 52 new standardized tests … yay!!!

–actually knowing that when you opt out, there is someone standing next to you … holding your hand and doing the same thing-an incredibly simple list of basic facts that make sense … in other words, if someone were to question a parent and try to put them on the defense they could simply say (in response to any question).… For me, it's more important to.… My catch all answer here in Colorado could be … "seriously … you want my kid to take the CSAP

An Activist Handbook for the Education Revolution:
United Opt Out's Test of Courage, pp. 17–38
Copyright © 2015 by Information Age Publishing
All rights of reproduction in any form reserved.

to the tune of 25.9 million dollars while you've cut pretty much anything meaningful from the curriculum? And my child is now supposed to attend a test prep school instead of a public school? No thanks. I want a public school that provides a whole education for a whole child, so we will be opting out." If they say, our school would will lose funding ... well then, quit making tests.

I would like to create a simple pamphlet that a parent could download from a Facebook page and begin to spread the word. And somewhere within the slogan I would like something comparable to the concept of passing the relay stick. For example, this is no flipping race to the top ... we are in this together ... take the stick from me and pass it on ... one by one. A parent would hang on to the symbolic stick until s/he had found another parent to give it to (in other words, getting another commitment to opt out).
  Please brainstorm with me. Our Facebook page needs a good name. This should cost nothing except time and commitment from each parent to share with the next parent ... and perhaps a team of dedicated educators willing to post information and answer questions ... almost like group therapy ... on the Facebook page as parents join and ask questions. Opting out of standardized testing solves many problems quickly. It pretty much says no to all the systems that are allowing corporate reform to stay in force. I'm cc'ing this to Susan Ohanian on fb (one of her latest posts discusses mass opt out). If we can focus on one thing, perhaps we will make headway. Who is in???? And if you disagree ... it's okay ... I need to know what the potential downfalls are!!! Peg :)

www.pegwithpen.blogspot.com

---------- Original Message ----------

From: "Mcdermott, Morna M." <mmcdermott@towson.edu>
To: The Learning Network <tln@listserve.com>
Subject: Re: [TLN] creating a campaign to opt out ...
Date: Fri, 12 Aug 2011 01:33

i'm in sister ...
even though I know little about the how of opting out although i am fully aware of the WHY
will help in any i can—let me know what i can do Peggy
m–
Morna McDermott McNulty

> Peggy and Morna had never met except over the TLN listserv. Peggy, at the time was an educator who was taking time off to stay at home with her young sons, and Morna was a university professor at Towson University, with two young children of her own. But over e-mails, a friendship had blossomed.
>
> We are now two.

---------- Original Message ----------

From: "Mcdermott, Morna M." <mmcdermott@towson.edu>
To: Peggy Robertson <writepeg@juno.com>
Subject: RE: creating a campaign to opt out ...
Date: Tue, 16 Aug 2011

Hi Peggy

I am up late here at the beach on my computer—feeling badly that i cannot generate any helpful ideas for how to navigate the FB problems on the page you have worked so hard to create already!!! I wish i knew more about FB and other social media—it seems that between all the other FB and websites devoted to antitesting what we are doing differently is trying to create a communication network in and across states for parents and others to communicate our collective efforts to opt out or other forms of protest—so whatever format we use needs to sustain that somehow ...

i did add more to the flyer we might be able to use-trolled a bunch of sites and research to get some solid data (i referenced things so that for example if i present this to parents I know they'll see it is not just my opinion or personal ranting that undergirds these problems)—the draft is attached-needs a lot of cleaning up—too wordy still but i want to see if you like the talking points i picked and/or if you have better data or examples to include in addition or in lieu of what i have included
—wish we could meet somehow!!!!!!!!!! :)

morna

From: Peggy Robertson [writepeg@juno.com]
Sent: Tuesday, August 16, 2011 11:30 AM
To:Mcdermott, Morna M.
Subject: RE: creating a campaign to opt out ...

Okay now I am totally getting the giggles. I can't flipping open your document because I don't have the right software. My husband says he can send me a link to download that will allow me to open it. OMG all this computer savvy shit makes me crazy!! So then, Shaun Johnson, writes on that high stakes fb page that we can link a fb page to twitter and to docs and blog ... you work with him right? Maybe he would help us? Maybe we do a blog and place the documents there as well as on an fb page? I really appreciate all you are doing to create this brochure—I haven't helped at all!! Don't let it detract from your lovely vacation on a beach?? Seriously? I want to be on a beach!!!!!!!

Peggy Robertson

www.pegwithpen.blogspot.com

Peggy also connected with Tim Slekar, who had blogged on *Huffington Post* regularly about opting his son out of PSSA testing in PA, and was a vocal university professor opposed to education reform. He had created a facebook site critiquing high-stakes testing. Meanwhile, Shaun was becoming very involved with the newly forming UOO FB site, offering suggestions for possible group names. Peggy invited him to become an administrator. He said yes. We were now four.

From: Peggy Robertson [writepeg@juno.com]
Sent: Tuesday, August 16, 2011 8:48 PM
To: Mcdermott, Morna M.
Subject: RE: Goals!!!!

I literally was just cleaning the house ... doing laundry and thought ... hum. let's get the group listed and get the fifty states on there. And then ... people started joining so then I figured what the hell and started adding everybody from my fb. Okay ... goals look good ... it's a start. This movement is meant to happen and just needed an avenue to jump on it seems ...

Our goals: Inform teachers, parents, students on options for opting out in each of their states. Develop a support network which includes one or two contact people per state to support those opting out. Develop district goals —X number opting out to gain parent commitment. (idea from Deborah Meier)

Peggy Robertson
www.pegwithpen.blogspot.com

From: Peggy Robertson [writepeg@juno.com]
Sent: Tuesday, August 17, 2011 10:36 A.M.
To: Mcdermott, Morna M.
Subject: RE: Goals!!!!

okay cool ... I will send Ceresta questions ... want to do an interview with her because I think her story (laying it all out) especially in FLORIDA will be fucking awesome. Okay ... we have one computer ... now Darrin needs it for his work ... may try to check in later!!!!! Thank you thank you thank you Morna for all your incredible ideas, your time helping with all this and your guts to do this with me!!!!

---------- Original Message ----------

From: "Mcdermott, Morna M." <mmcdermott@towson.edu>
To: Peggy Robertson <writepeg@juno.com>
Subject: RE: Goals!!!!
Date: Wed, 17 Aug 2011 02:08:39

cannot keep up ... yes i really like the questions for Ceresta! she is so amazing

Morna

Ceresta had been active in efforts in the opt out movement through her involvement with the *Save Our Schools* (SOS) March on Washington in July 2011, where she and Morna met. She was also vocal in her stance as a nationally board certified FL teacher and opted her own daughter out of FCAT in Florida. Peggy reached out to interview Ceresta for *Pegwithpen* and then invited Ceresta Smith to become part of *United Opt Out*.

We are now five.

---------- Original Message ----------

From: "Mcdermott, Morna M." <mmcdermott@towson.edu>
To: Peggy Robertson <writepeg@juno.com>
Subject: RE: Goals!!!!
Date: Wed, 17 Aug 2011

yes ...
1) support people for each state (maybe 3)
2) let each district establish their district goals maybe?
3) and generate a move for action--petitions to opt out-local parent meetings--staging protests in front of DOE's—legal fronts—seems like a lot of parents in certain states have already done this—so it will vary from state to state or district to district—i am doing my homework FAST! didn't know enough going into this and thought i would have more time :)

i have NEVER seen anything like this is my life—massive movement here!!!!!!!!!!!!!!! look what's been started~!!!!
WHAT CAN I DO TO HELP???????
threw my husband under the bus to do bedtime so i can catch up with all this info!!!

Morna

By late August, Laurie Murphy, who was active in organizing the *Save Our Schools March* of Washington in July 2011, was invited to join *United Opt Out National* SOS leader Bess Altwerger had recommended her after Morna shared with Bess that UOO needed help with social media and strategy. Laurie had met both Ceresta and Morna at the SOS March.

By September 2011, we were six, six pissed-off radicals.

Six Pissed-Off Radicals

From left to right: Ceresta Smith, Laurie Murphy, Morna McDermott, Tim Slekar, Peggy Robertson, Shaun Johnson. Occupy the DOE, 2012.

It took us over one full year to finally arrive at a short but accurate description of "who we were" as *United Opt Out*. Given two pages—20 minutes, or reading from our website statement—it is easy to articulate. But really, when you're standing on an elevator and you've got 20 seconds and someone asks you, "Who is *United Opt Out*?" and the elevator doors are about to slide open, you have to be to the point: *We are six pissed-off radicals fighting for public education.*

Let's break this down.

Part I: We Were Six (Now Seven)

We began in August of 2011 following on the heels of The *Save Our Schools* (SOS) March on Washington. As a group, we had never formally met one another. During the collaborative and planning phases of the SOS event, in which many of us were involved, we began to cross paths in cyber working groups and listservs. Ceresta, Morna, and Laurie were all working on various facets of the SOS campaign and had "met" on a few Skype calls. Tim and Shaun had begun working together on *At the Chalkface*. Shaun and Morna both (in 2011) were working at Towson University College of Education (but Peggy was not aware of that when they each joined). Peggy reached out to each of us and said, "I'd like to form a Facebook group that addresses the issue of high-stakes standardized testing and promotes opting out." We all said yes.

In spring 2013, Laurie decided to step down from the *United Opt Out* (UOO) team and Ruth Rodriguez joined in the summer of 2013. The original five had come to know Ruth when she attended the first UOO Occupy the U.S. Department of Education event in spring, 2011, and shared our commitment and vision ever since. By spring 2014, we realized the workload was becoming increasingly too much for six of us to manage and Rosemarie Jensen, an active member of the UOO actions since the beginning, joined the team.

Part 2: Pissed-Off Radicals

It became increasingly apparent as the months passed that what we were advocating for *was* radical. Opting out was more than a personal choice, like breastfeeding versus bottle feeding. The radical nature of our efforts was made apparent by the backlash we were receiving from education reform proponents. The concept was far more edgy and provocative than any of us realized. It was advocating for individual into collective actions that would entirely dismantle corporate-driven education policy. Opting out was refusal. It was a call to civil disobedience. It was a large-scale boycott of the takeover of public education. We were making people (and testing companies) nervous. And we were pissed. As individuals and as a group, we were fed up with what we were witnessing in public education. As 2011 rolled into 2012, and 2013—and Race to the Top heralded a whole host of new policies including Common Core and new nationalized tests (PARCC and SBAC), the rage grew thick, the battle more tenuous, and our resistance more necessary.

We launched the Facebook site in August of 2011. Within 48 hours, we had 500 members. Holy shit. What had we gotten ourselves into? Within one week, we had our first trolls. And this forced us to examine more deeply the question: *What are we for?*

Part 3: Fighting for Public Education

September 2012: *A Letter to our Supporters* **(posted on our website[1])**

Supporter of Public Education:

Thank you for your interest in opting out of high-stakes standardized testing and for your bravery in taking this very important step in the defense of public education. You may be a parent, teacher, student, para-educator, higher education faculty, or community member. Your role may be a combination of these. Whatever the case, we are all responsible for preserving a system of high-quality education as a public good for all young persons in this country. The central mission of *United Opt Out* is to eliminate the threat of high-stakes testing in public K–12 education. We believe that high-stakes testing is destructive to children, educators, communities, the quality of instruction in classrooms, equity in schooling, and the fundamental democratic principles on which this country is based.

We are inundated with the false narrative that our public schools have completely and totally failed. But continued public opinion surveys and reliable data from the annual National Assessment of Educational Progress (NAEP) show two things: one, that confidence in our community schools is still very high; and two, our achievement as a nation is higher than ever in all subgroups.

High-stakes testing is not supported by educational research as a measure of student learning and progress. It is, however, the crucial information needed by groups who seek to privatize public education and run it for-profit.

Lip service is certainly paid to students, teachers, and parents about the necessity of a good education. Yet, predominant reforms ignore the wishes of those working within our schools. Reforms also ignore the overwhelming evidence against test-driven mandates.

As a result, *United Opt Out* believes that our trust has been violated. It is dubious that test data is collected innumerable times throughout a school year to close schools, fire teachers, and ruin communities. If we cannot trust the decisions made with test data, then those who make the decisions should no longer have it. We own that data. It is ours and we do not have to give it up.

With Our Warmest Regards,

United Opt Out National

How We Got Here

CERESTA SMITH: Dr. Wade Nobles defines power as, "the ability to define reality and to convince other people that it is their definition" (1986).[2] About 5 years ago, Dr. Nobles' definition for power became very real to me as I entered a world that was fabricated from pure fiction and sold to the black community as their new reality. The world was that of Miami Norland Senior High, a predominantly African American school in northwest Miami-Dade County that was under Florida state sanction for low performance on state standardized testing for reading and math. The school functioned like a 21st century plantation, with the economic and social rot of *Gone with the Wind's* Tara, the infamous plantation won from an all-night poker game that fell into dysfunction and disrepair. At Norland, the white power structure ruled from the periphery while particular chosen "Negroes" acted as administrative plantation overseers with little to no autonomy. And, out of politeness, political correctness, fear, or just plain ignorance, those caught up in that horrific narrative chose to wallow miserably in this powerful and nightmarish fiction passed off as reality.

PEGGY ROBERTSON: I became a teacher in 1990. My first job started in January in a fifth-grade classroom. Teaching at that time was like I expected it to be. I tried new things. Some succeeded. Some failed. I individualized my teaching for each student and still tried to juggle the organization of a classroom full of students on the brink of middle school. When I look back, I can see how easy it would be to watch a classroom such as mine and assume the worst. Assume chaos, lack of learning, and assume that someone needed to step in and take control. This concept of control has never set well with me. I always believed in watching and listening to my students in order to determine the curriculum based on their needs, their strengths, and their attempts.

TIM SLEKAR: As an elementary educator involved in teacher education for 14 years, I have been tirelessly advocating and, literally pleading with my future teachers, to refuse to carry out inhumane orders (teaching to the test). Before I go any further, I want to state up front that I am an ardent supporter of teachers and public schools. However, some of what I'm about to say might be taken as anti-teacher or anti-public school. This is not the case. In fact, it is the current position that teachers and public schools are in, that I believe, push them to do things that they would not do if it weren't for the pressures to be "adequate."

MORNA McDERMOTT: I love the quote from *Who Framed Roger Rabbit* (Zemeckis, 1988), that cheesy animated film from the 1980s, in the scene in which the beautiful villainess, Jessica Rabbit, says, "I'm not bad, I'm just drawn that way." When it comes to activism, I believe I was just "drawn that way"—starting as a child eager to write letters like one to the President (it was Jimmy Carter I believe) about the environmental woes of our country.

LAURIE MURPHY: I am often asked how a woman from a conservative, rural county in the dead middle of Florida became involved with the movement to support public education on the national level. I laugh. It wasn't intentional. Early on, I had learned that diversity of beliefs was not something that was always honored or respected in my community. As a matter of survival, I had learned to keep my beliefs about politics and society locked safely inside.

ROSEMARIE JENSEN: My journey into full-on activism started the moment Jeb Bush became governor in Florida. This was right after I had my first child, I was a first-grade teacher on leave and was reading everything that he was going to do to hold schools "accountable." The FCAT and school grading that was going to accompany it sent my blood into a boil because I *knew* what it meant for schools that were underresourced and in low-SES communities. My former colleagues and friends were already complaining about the test prep they were being required to do, but of course, they believed if they shut their doors and continued to do what they had always done, provided a child-centered and developmentally appropriate curriculum, they could fly under the radar. Or they could just move to a better-resourced school west. The exodus had begun.

PEGGY ROBERTSON: I wrote a letter to President Obama, which got picked up by Anthony Cody's *Living in Dialogue* blog. After that, I created my own blog, *PegwithPen*. I began to research how to fight this madness.

RUTH RODRIGUEZ: I became active in *Citizens for Public School* (CPS), a grassroots organization that began in 1992 with a campaign for equitable school funding. In 2009, I was elected co-president with Barbara Fields. CPS works closely with *FairTest*, and together we have been collaborating in attempts to end high-stakes testing, school closings, and charter conversion. I testified at the State House and at school committees; we held forums with speakers such as Diane Ravitch, Jonathan Kozol, Deborah Meier, and many others. We joined many groups across the state that are working as we are to end the corporate reforms.

CERESTA SMITH: Prior to arriving to Norland Senior High late fall 2009, I taught at Dr. Michael Krop High School. Less than 5 miles away, Krop served an economically and racially mixed population in contrast to Norland, which was 98% black with a majority low-income student body population based on numbers of those qualifying for reduced price or free lunch. The first disturbing fact that was shared with me was that the school constantly faced staff turnovers similar to the same disturbing dismantling and dysfunction of 18th century slave families often broken apart by sales, murders, and escapes. I asked the question, "How can the school ever progress if there is such a huge instability in staff?" And I got no response.

LAURIE MURPHY: With most reluctant activists, something happens to crack that protective seal. For me, that something was Senate Bill 6. The year was 2010. I was working as the Resource Development Director for a nonprofit agency. However, my husband and two of my children were teachers, as were countless others on both sides of our family.

ROSEMARIE JENSEN: Fast forward to around 2008, and now I had seen firsthand the destructive effects of the hyper focus on testing. By this point I had realized going back to the classroom wasn't going to happen, I could be more effective as an advocate as a parent, I could be the mouthpiece for my former colleagues, and I had the time to call, write, and hound my representatives. I observed in my children's elementary school, School Advisory Council meetings centered around nothing more than improving test scores, specials like computer literacy and Spanish cut, recess shortened, teachers being told what to teach and how to teach, and, then, in a true cosmic slap to the head, my own son recommended for third-grade retention based on his FCAT score. My daughter, in a self-contained gifted program, was spared test-prep curriculum. My son, who was diagnosed at 2½ with language processing issues, was not so lucky. The disparate curriculum he received floored me. I could only imagine how narrow the curriculum was for kids in schools where parent support was scarce and the income level was depressed.

MORNA McDERMOTT: When I was 7, I created a *Save the Seals* club in my living room and donated all my earnings culled from parents' change purses and my allowance, to the *Ranger Rick Club*. Becoming a K–12 teacher for social justice beginning with my teaching career in 1989 was a "gimme." I needed little convincing or evidence to approach my pedagogy that way.

CERESTA SMITH: I designed a literacy plan that did not compromise our contractual academic freedom, and to the dismay of the "powers that be," the educators, the students, and I did create success in building overall literacy at Norland. In my search for like-minded activists, I discovered that Norland was one small part of a greater scheme to dismantle public education in an effort to channel tax dollars into the hands of private profiteers.

TIM SLEKAR: I have been a second-grade, fifth-grade, seventh-grade, and eighth-grade teacher, teacher educator, and administrator in higher education. I know the research. I have worked with children. I have worked with new teachers. I frequently visit the local schools as part of my job being Coordinator of the Education Program at Penn State-Altoona. I work with public school administrators. I have seen firsthand the slow and steady dismantling of the public school system. I finally said to myself, "No more. You will not use Luke as a pawn to produce test scores that will be used to eventually punish his school."

MORNA McDERMOTT: I spent 6 years working with students who had various severe to moderate special needs, ages pre–K to seventh grade. Words like "average" or "normal," whether they pertained to my students or my approach to teaching, were nowhere on the radar. There were no tests. I wrote my own curriculum. I enjoyed radical freedom.

PEGGY ROBERTSON: In my first job in 1990, I was left alone to do as I saw fit for my students because it was clear that my students were always engaged, happy, and motivated to learn. Later on, the TLN schools I worked in were also exciting, progressive, and always on the brink of learning more. Students were engaged and helped to develop their own learning plans. Assessment was student-centered and valuable to teachers as they determined next steps for their learners. I worked with TLN in several capacities for the next 5 years.

CERESTA SMITH: The level of principal autonomy and academic freedom was abundant at Krop, whereas both were badly compromised at Norland. I was asked by the newly appointed administrator, disadvantaged because the transfer occurred after the school year commenced, to serve as a reading coach, teacher mentor, first National Board Certified Teacher, and peer to the staff of educators who taught remedial reading to eleventh- and twelfth-grade students who failed to demonstrate reading proficiency on the Florida Comprehensive Assessment Test for Reading that was issued during their 10th-grade year. I, a 20-year veteran educator at the time, assented and arrived at Norland ready to help create success.

ROSEMARIE JENSEN: Connor's third-grade FCAT score was more of a test of his disability than his ability. My husband, a licensed psychologist, is very knowledgeable about test construction and protocol. He asked to see the test because how did we know if Connor missed a bubble, how did we know if he got all the first passages correct but then experienced neural fatigue and just stopped answering, how did we know which types of questions were difficult … we were told we weren't allowed to see the test. *We* both knew right then and there this entire thing was a joke and we put him in a private school for fourth grade and brought him back for fifth. *We* knew we would face the FCAT again, but this time we knew there were alternatives and it wasn't a mandatory retention year. And we toyed with the idea of keeping him home, opting out. I had no idea if anyone had done it, but it was there in the back of our minds.

TIM SLEKAR: Since late in August of 2011, my son has been subjected to a system of indoctrination that has essentially squashed his inner desire to learn—the Ruinous Culture[3]—5 entire months devoid of intellectually stimulating classroom experiences. He was forced to complete worksheets in language arts and mathematics. He can alphabetize spelling words and find the main idea of a paragraph. He's had practice in sequencing. He can round numbers. He can add, subtract, multiply, and divide with fractions and decimals. And he has mastered the scripted art of estimating (Who knew there were incorrect estimates?). He had multiple PSSA practice tests, and according to these tests, my son was ready. He had been trained for 5 months to produce scores that would help his school achieve Adequate Yearly Progress (AYP). I'm sure his school was counting on him.

LAURIE MURPHY: Senate Bill 6, introduced by Florida GOP Chair John Thrasher, mandated that teacher retention, certification, and compensation be based on the test scores that students received on standardized tests.

ROSEMARIE JENSEN: After the major fight of Senate Bill 6 in Florida, which I was immersed in, I met other Florida activists on FB. They were telling me I needed to go to the SOS MARCH on Washington, D.C. to start pushing back on the testing juggernaut. Being so disappointed in Obama and his complete reversal on testing and teacher support, I knew I had to go. It was the light that started the fire and from there I met other Florida activists, including Laurie Murphy, who put me in touch with Peggy Robertson and the Opt Out team. Holy cow, I found people who supported opting out and now I didn't feel alone. I discovered the first action was happening in Washington, D.C. and with Peggy's urging in e-mails, off I went. Alone, knowing nobody, but I knew it was what I needed to do. I came home energized and prepared to opt out Connor. I became more outspoken at SAC meetings, PTA meetings, FB, and so on. I warned people only 5 years ago that this whole testing movement was about destroying public education, firing teachers, and privatizing schools for profits, and was told I was a "chicken little" and I needed to "calm down."

PEGGY ROBERTSON: I was working in schools in Colorado and discovered that the teachers I was supporting could no longer teach based on the needs of their children because now the Reading First[4] coach said they needed to be on the same page every day. Skills were being taught in isolation and were not embedded back into authentic text and learning experiences. Kindergarten students were being red-flagged as failing at the age of 5 due to their inability to meet the expectations under Reading First initiatives.

CERESTA SMITH: Reared in Iowa by a political guru and respected African American female who had leadership roles and an African American man whom was loved and respected by all in my community, I knew nothing about compromising my democratic voice or my ethics. I was not going to learn how to at Norland Senior High.

MORNA McDERMOTT: The desire to advocate was there. By 2001, I had received my doctorate and had begun my journey as a professor in teacher education. Once introduced to the ideas of liberation and equity inspired by the scholarship of Paulo Freire and Maxine Green among others, my teaching was on fire. I felt little fear in sharing these ideas with my undergraduate students who were beginning teachers. But No Child Left Behind (NCLB) was just getting started.

TIM SLEKAR: My wife and I went to my son's teacher in early October of 2011 when we noticed some problems. This was when the reality of the situation smacked me in the face. When I asked his teacher what my son was doing that was contributing to some of his difficulties, his teacher looked puzzled. According to her, he wasn't having any major problems. But when I said, "He is not looking forward to language arts class, so there must be something going on that he is reacting to," again she looked puzzled. When I asked for some examples of what he was reading, his teacher did not provide any real literature. "What about writing?" Nothing except spelling words five times each week with a Peterson's Handwriting Guide. Not a very rich language arts experience. I asked his teacher the big question, "What is your goal?" Her response, "To get them ready for the state test." Big fat smack of reality to the face!

PEGGY ROBERTSON: I loved my work. I loved learning, and when NCLB began to infiltrate the schools I worked in, I was taken off-guard. I had never been political. I had never been stopped in my tracks as I advocated for what was best for children. But during NCLB, everywhere I turned I began to see that I was being silenced.

CERESTA SMITH: Having been raised in Iowa, as one able to develop a critical intellect and one never taught Southern humility, I was unable to fall in step with the sanction process that, to me, undermined any and all opportunities for success. In other words, I was the rebellious Negro on the plantation. And rebel I did. Not only did I rebel, I began to walk an education activist path that I continue to walk today.

LAURIE MURPHY: We decided to fight. I learned to post on Facebook, made protest posters, and write letters. Together, we cheered when the bill was vetoed by Governor Crist.

RUTH RODRIGUEZ: In 2008, Massachusetts governor, Deval Patrick, launched his Readiness Project, an initiative that gathered citizens from across the state to advise him on issues affecting the well-being of the citizens in areas ranging from health and education, to name a couple. I was invited to serve on this project and was appointed to the subcommittee, "Massachusetts Comprehensive Assessment System" (MCAS). Our task included looking at systems of assessments and to make recommendations on the state's high-stakes standardized test. We spent 11 months working on the project, which was to look at alternative assessments; and in the end, we presented the recommendations to the governor. Sadly, our recommendation was turned down; and Paul Reville, who was the chair of the project and a friend, took me aside and said, "Ruth, we have been friends for some time and work on many educational issues, but this is one issue you just have to live with, because MCAS is here to stay."

TIM SLEKAR: The consequences for schools are pretty straightforward. According to NCLB regulations, 95% of student populations (minority, English language learners, special education students) in a school must participate in testing programs. If 6% of a student population does not take the tests, the school automatically fails to make AYP. Failure to make AYP in consecutive years results in mounting sanctions—eventually closing the school. This is where "opting out" gets a little tricky and people get confused as to our motives. On the surface, "opting out" appears to be directed at public schools. However, as I stated earlier, opting out is the only form of action that can save public schools from high-stakes testing. Teachers and administrators that actively work against the system can be reprimanded or worse. Politicians on both sides of the aisle won't listen. Therefore, when a parent opts out, it is the ultimate action in support of public schools.[5]

PEGGY ROBERTSON: As a teacher, I had always simply refused to do what was not in the best interests of children. I refused to do mindless worksheets, lockstep basals—I refused anything that did not meet their needs. And therefore, taking the leap to consider refusing the tests was simply common sense in my opinion.

CERESTA SMITH: I set about to accomplish two tasks: first, design a plan to begin the systemic changes needed to build literacy for Black students, and second, find like minds that understood the need for organization and activism, as it was apparent that the systemic racist practices I saw implemented in Norland were happening to Black people all over America.

RUTH RODRIGUEZ: Some members of the subcommittee of the Governor's Project, myself included, expressed disappointment with the governor's position to retain the MCAS assessment system, contrary to the committee's recommendation. This decision to refuse the recommendation of the grassroots team assembled was unfortunate, especially with the governor indicating that the MCAS and graduation requirement would remain. As a subcommittee member, I was very unhappy that the final report did not reflect the letter and spirit of their subcommittee's recommendations. I made it clear to the governor that, "For the sake of educating students of color to their full potential, the sink or swim method of teaching and assessing must be replaced by one that takes into account the difference in learning styles." At a subsequent meeting with the governor, I challenged him, "to immerse himself in Spanish for one year, then take the MCAS in Spanish, for this, Governor, is what you are asking English Language Learners to do."

MORNA McDERMOTT: I live by a double-edged sword. Education, which has always been an immensely political issue for me all these decades, has also become a deeply personal one beginning in 2005 with the birth of my son Conor, and 2 years after that with the birth of my daughter Molly.

PEGGY ROBERTSON: While I stayed home with my youngest son over those 6 years, I attempted to strip my experience as an educator from my life. I gave boxes of teaching books away. I wanted out. I felt that there was no way to work in the system called NCLB. I didn't understand it. I didn't know how to fight it. And I didn't like what they wanted me to become within the system.

LAURIE MURPHY: The very next month, an Illinois teacher, Chris Janotta, created a Facebook page, The Million Teacher March. Chris's goal was to have teachers gather in Washington to demand more respect for the teaching profession and for public education in general.

TIM SLEKAR: It is my belief that the most effective way to start a national "opt out" movement is by enlisting parents and children (locally) and actually "opt out." As I have said in the past, parents are the only ones with the power to stop high-stakes testing and take our schools back from the corporate reformers.

MORNA McDERMOTT: There is a lot at stake here. The term *high-stakes testing* is aptly named indeed. I have heard stories of and know a few parents around the country who have been brave enough to opt their children out of testing. Where I live in Maryland, testing is attached to a high school diploma. So in essence, if I opt my children out after eighth grade, they may risk not receiving their high school diplomas. That is a very high price to pay to prove a point. In the meantime, I have other fears. If I make a big issue out of this and fight the tests, which will begin for them in third grade, what will other parents think? Will my children be treated differently by their teachers and school administration? I imagine the glares and whispers when I attend the PTA meetings.

ROSEMARIE JENSEN: In the past 2 years alone, here in Florida, I have been involved in fighting every single bad reform idea that Jeb and his merry band of privatizers have tried to implement. Despite defeating SB 6 during Governor Crist's tenure, with the election of Rick Scott, SB 736 was implemented, which tied teacher evaluations to test scores. This has ramped up the narrowly focused curriculum and has tied teachers' hands in terms of meeting the needs of the students in front of them and having professional autonomy. Charters are opening (and closing) in every neighborhood they can get into and most recently, I had to advocate for stopping Jon Hage and his Charters USA outfit from buying my former hometown city's performing arts center. It seats about 2,000 people and provides an affordable entertainment option for families and elderly alike. It's a performing arts center along with an art museum and art classes. It also sits next to one of the largest parks in the city, with baseball, football, soccer, and a swimming pool that Mr. Hage could use, for free! I have been involved in the fight to stop the illegal and unconstitutional voucher program that recently passed in the 13th hour once it was attached to an omnibus bill.

PEGGY ROBERTSON: After researching this concept and seeing that others were also attempting to "opt out," I began to examine how I might support opting out in a way that would help organize grassroots movements across the country.

TIM SLEKAR: In 2010, I decided to send an email to the building principals and let them know now (4 months before March Madness) that there would be more children opting out and that the school should plan alternative activities. On Sunday evening, I received an e-mail from the school superintendent. According to his terse e-mail, Michelle and I were "premature" to think that more parents would join the opt out movement. In fact, according to the superintendent, the district would "educate" (frighten) parents about the "consequences" associated with opting out—the district might not make AYP. Also, the superintendent was adamant that any issues I had with PSSAs in the future would only go through his office and he made sure that the school board was copied to the e-mail.

LAURIE MURPHY: Within a month, I was helping Chris with the planning of a rally and march on the White House, as well as an educational conference. Over time, others with similar interests also joined in with the planning. Chris eventually dropped from the group, but plans continued under the name, *Save Our Schools March* and National Call to Action. I served on the Executive Committee as the National Organizer

CERESTA SMITH: It was via *Save Our Schools' 2011 March* on Washington and activists workshops at American University in July that I publicly announced that since high-stakes testing is the key to the market-based reformers effort in dismantling public education, I would no longer allow my 14-year-old daughter to participate in state-mandated testing. I also stated that I would be willing to encourage others to do so as well. Those statements were published by an education reporter. I had no idea how I was going to carry this promise beyond my own family, but I knew somehow that I would.

RUTH RODRIGUEZ: As a result of this unfortunate experience, I decided to put my energy into something productive. I worked to try to convince school administrators that they should join us in combatting this regressive measure and to see if we could convince the governor to end this destructive measure.

PEGGY ROBERTSON: I could not be true to myself and to what I knew was best for kids. I thought it would be easy to walk away from public education. But it wasn't. I began to research what was happening. While my youngest son napped, I spent my time reading about the billionaire boy's club and NCLB, and finally, Race to the Top. I had voted for Obama and was waiting on pins and needles for Linda Darling-Hammond to get appointed as Secretary of Education. Now, in retrospect, I have reservations about her appointment as well, but at the time, the appointment of Arne Duncan sent me into a spiral of despair. I knew exactly where we were headed. And at that point I became very angry. I remembered the children I had taught in southern Missouri who lived in poverty, and I imagined the havoc these mandates were now having on their lives. I thought about my oldest son, who was currently enrolled in a private Waldorf school in Denver, where children learned much like the children of Finland—learning to read at age 7 and being allowed to thrive and grow without the fear of high-stakes testing. I knew that Sam had not learned to read until second grade and he was now an avid reader.

ROSEMARIE JENSEN: And last year I was involved in the campaign to stop the Parent Trigger law from being passed. What I see as integral to all this is denying these reformers the data—data that is used to close schools in favor of for-profit charters, fire teachers, retain students, and track them for dropping out and the school-to-prison pipeline (and my county, Broward, the sixth-largest school district in the country, had the highest arrest rates (Armario, 2013) for minors committing transgressions in schools).[6] I am in this fight until the bitter end, as I know how wonderful and joyful learning can be and should be for *all* children, regardless of their zip code.

TIM SLEKAR: I think there are a number of people involved in public schooling (parents, teachers, even some administrators) who are finally realizing that the standards movement and high-stakes testing is not helping. In fact, I talk to more parents and teachers that are outright critical of the entire process. Parents see the time wasted on test prep and the shrinking curriculum. Teachers are tired of being treated as low-level technicians and being labeled as "crappy." And some communities see the damage a full-fledged "reformation" of public schools has on local neighborhoods—closing schools hurts communities.

LAURIE MURPHY: The group held weekly web-based planning meetings. While the schedule was brutal, what I learned about organizational development, strategic planning, and group relationships was incredible.

RUTH RODRIGUEZ: In 2011, I attended the national *Save Our Schools March* (SOS) in D.C. From this point on, I have been totally immersed in the fight against the corporate takeover. I was voted into the steering committee of *Save Our Schools*.

MORNA McDERMOTT: And then the time was ripe. It was 2011. I met Peggy through a listserv I had joined at the same time that I was working on the *Save Our Schools March* and *National Call to Action* campaign. It was during the march that I met Ceresta, Laurie, and Ruth.

PEGGY ROBERTSON: I discovered that I could create a Facebook group page and create a file for every state in order to organize information on opt out per state, therefore organizing local communities to take action. Again, it seemed very common sense to me. A simple action. And a simple way to pull together information in a way that was accessible to the local communities who currently were searching for a way to take down corporate education.

PEGGY ROBERTSON: I knew clearly that no data meant no profit. I e-mailed my friend Morna McDermott, whom I had only thus far corresponded with via a lovely relic of the Learning Network, the TLN listserv, which was still alive and well despite the harm NCLB and RTTT had done to our work at TLN. Morna and I had been corresponding for quite some time about public education. She was an associate professor at Towson University and I was currently a stay-at-home mom. Together, we decided to launch a Facebook group page. I titled it, OPT OUT OF THE STATE TEST: The National Movement. I e-mailed Morna to let her know it was up and running and together we watched the madness begin.

MORNA McDERMOTT: I had never met Peggy personally. But through a series of e-mail conversations, I knew I liked her and I somehow intuitively knew I could trust her. I shared personal frustrations with her on a regular basis. And then one day in August she asked if I was interested in helping start a new Facebook site dedicated to testing resistance. Not being very tech savvy, or appreciating the power of social media, I thought" "Oh how nice ... sure I'll help you." I agreed as if I were signing on for a hobby. I had no idea what was to transpire from this.

TIM SLEKAR: By opting out of corporate reforms (high-stakes testing), you are demonstrating your disdain for the reformers' approach to the dismantling of public schools and demanding that neighborhood schools be given back to the local communities. Politicians aren't listening. The media isn't listening. Therefore strong acts of civil disobedience are the only tools left in this battle to save public schools.

PEGGY ROBERTSON: It was like our computers had exploded. We couldn't keep up with the requests from parents. The questions. The stories. Hour after hour our membership at our Facebook page grew. We began to research states and e-mail departments of education as we looked for loopholes to make the opt out process as painless as possible.

LAURIE MURPHY: A month after the event, a person I had worked with during the march (Morna) contacted me to ask if I could help a new group with which she had become involved, *United Opt Out*. While I was unable to resolve their technological problems, I was eventually asked to join in as one of the six administrators of the group.

RUTH RODRIGUEZ: It was at this time that I began to use the information from the UOO website. I attended and presented at Occupy in D.C., both 2012 and 2013. I was energized and gained confidence that this was a winnable fight. I used the information to help me organize with the community whose students were marginalized—English language learners and special needs—by translating some of the information and by providing teachers with data and tools to help their students.

ROSEMARIE JENSEN: After attending the first *United Opt Out* event in Washington in 2012, I came now armed with the knowledge and support to opt out Connor from the sixth-grade FCAT testing. Rick and I crafted our letter and sent it to the principal based on the sample letters on the UOO website. We have since sent one every year of Connor's middle school experience. He has not taken an FCAT since fifth grade. With his accommodations and support from the ESE staff, he has been wildly successful in school. The test would never show that or show how hard his teachers work with him. But as I have continued to explain to friends and teachers, it's never been about the students, it's been about failing teachers and public schools. It has been making a dent as several people chose to opt out in both the elementary school and middle school. I have since attended the 2013 and 2014 UOO events in D.C. and Denver, and each time I come away more informed, educated, and affirmed in my resolve to continue to fight the reforms coming from both the federal DOE and Florida's DOE. I have increased my networks of support both nationally and in my state. I continue to educate and advocate for public schools and for teachers here, who despite the state's best efforts, continue to try to do what is in the best interests of all children.

PEGGY ROBERTSON: And so *United Opt Out National* came to be. We soon added Ceresta Smith, Tim Slekar, Shaun Johnson, and Laurie Murphy to the UOO team, and our work began to take form. We learned a lot. We discovered that social media is a powerful animal on its own, and we learned to fine tune our messages and build relationships with other like-minded groups and individuals. We learned that not all folks could be trusted. We discovered that ego was to be avoided. And together, we formed friendships across miles as we Skyped every Wednesday night. We became our opt out family in a way. And that first year, we began to formulate a plan that had clarity and vision.

LAURIE MURPHY: From the beginning, I knew that there was something very special about *United Opt Out*. Never before had I met a group so diverse yet so bound together by a sense of mutual respect and belief in the cause. By September of 2013, however, my duties at my day job shifted and I was forced to step back from my activities with *United Opt Out*.

CERESTA SMITH: Early August, I was contacted by Peggy, and in discussing taking opting out to a whole new level, I did not hesitate to agree to work on that mission. The rest of the story is history unfolding as we collectively work to bury the plantation mentality that is so much a part of the market-based reforms, work to disempower those in power who, as according to Nigerian author Chimamanda Adichie (2009), use power "not just tell the story of another person, but to make it the definitive story of that person." Collective togetherness is what we have, and with our collective togetherness, we will accomplish much.

From left to right: Morna, Tim, Shaun, Peggy, Laurie, Ceresta, Occupy the DOE, 2.0.

"Sister" Support

There are numerous groups and individuals who were central in the early weeks and months of the creation of *United Opt Out*, but none as central as *Save Our Schools* (SOS). Morna, Ruth, Laurie, Tim, and Shaun were all in attendance at the SOS march and rally, and it was where many of us had met for the first time. The march in 2011 hallmarked a convergence of efforts from around the country which is still growing. Additional support from SOS national leaders, including Bess Altwerger and Rick Meyer, was instrumental in the opt out movement. Since our beginnings in August 2011, in addition to SOS, we have partnered (for various campaigns and events) with numerous other national organizations including *FairTest*, *Bad Ass Teachers Association*, *Change the Stakes*, *Parents Across America*, *Teacher Resistance*, and *Action Network*, *Edu4*. *United Opt Out* is only seven. We are only as strong as the solidarity we have with others. We are grateful that the resistance is many—and growing.

ACTIVIST WORKBOOK

1. Taking Laurie's advice, ask yourself the following questions and be able to respond: What makes a team work well? Identify clearly what you are for. Be prepared in advance for complex alliances with other groups. Determine what the guiding principles are so that when you need to, you can refer to them for deciding when you can or cannot work with other groups who may not share your end goals or values.
2. What is a good number of people to serve as central organizers and decision makers? More than 8–10 individuals makes it easier to distribute labor for various actions and efforts, but makes it more difficult at times to make group decisions that require democratic dialogue and voting. Also, the more folks you have as decision makers, the far more likely, just given the higher numbers, that at certain times you'll find that the group "divides" on an issue. It's easier for 4 people to share the same view of left/right political alliances and to vote on how to handle them than it is for a decision making body of 20 people. There's no magic number. But streamline for efficiency and solidarity, and branch out for active participation and distribution of tasks.

NOTES

1. http://unitedoptout.com/about/letter-from-us/
2. http://www.library.wisc.edu/EDVRC/docs/public/pdfs/LIReadings/Power%20and%20Privilege%20Definitions.pdf

3. http://slekar.blogspot.com/2011/01/is-boycotting-tests-solution-to-ruinous. html
4. http://www2.ed.gov/programs/readingfirst/resources.html
5. Originally quoted in http://blogs.edweek.org/teachers/living-in-dialogue/2011/09/the_slekar_family_stands_up_an_1.html
6. http://bigstory.ap.org/article/florida-agreement-reduce-student-arrests

REFERENCES

Adichie, C. N. (2008). The danger of a single story. *Ted.* Retrieved from http://www.ted.com/talks/chimamanda_adichie_the_danger_of_a_single_story

Armario, C. (2013, November 5). In Florida, agreement to reduce student arrests. *AP/The Big Story*. Retrieved June 8, 2014, from http://bigstory.ap.org/article/florida-agreement-reduce-student-arrests

Zemeckis, R. (Producer and Director). (1988). *Who framed Roger Rabbit?* [film]. Touchstone Pictures.

CHAPTER 3

CHANGING THE NARRATIVE

Ceresta Smith

Ole Master bought a yaller gal,
He bought her from the South; My name's Ran, I wuks in de sand,
I'd rather be a nigger dan a po' white man.

—as cited in Brown (1985, p. 416)

Ceresta Smith

An Activist Handbook for the Education Revolution:
United Opt Out's Test of Courage, pp. 39–56
Copyright © 2015 by Information Age Publishing

Opting Out in the 21st Century

The History

If one is able to get past the use of language to look at the insight and inherent wisdom of this simple ditty, it speaks volumes of a genius insight into the social dynamics of life in America during the days of chattel slavery. Slaves, who spoke with their own dialectical nuances and operated in a system that forbade developing their intellects past those necessary to function enough to serve "Ole Master," were always characterized as dumb and stupid, slow and ignorant. More than not, slaves had no choice but to accept the most often false characterizations and act accordingly. With all the restrictions that were leveled against slaves, and the insurmountable odds against a slave who was literate, it is a marvel that slaves, in their own free time, as a form of entertainment (*Dave Chappell Show* on the plantation of sorts) could come up with the aforementioned clever ditty. It is brilliant on many levels: short and concise like a Japanese Haiku and likewise possessing of a sense of beauty. It is filled with spot-on social commentary as it subtly hints at the social hierarchy and sexism among the slaves by reference to the "yaller" gal in contrasts to "I wuks in de sand." Moreover, it shows how classism was just as distasteful, if not more, than the racism that had the slave in bondage in the first place when it targets the social hierarchy of White America with its insinuation that a White man who does not capitalize on the privilege afforded his white skin is worse off than a slave.

This is a classic piece of satire, and one has to have an appreciation for the sense of humor of Black folk in bondage because, after all, what did a slave have to laugh about? And sadly, through the laughter, many will agree that this ditty is still relevant today. Interestingly enough, nothing has changed. The dialectical nuances of Black folk still exist. The social hierarchy among Black folks still exists as the "yaller gal" remains the desired sex symbol for status seekers and lighter-toned Blacks are afforded privileges that darker-skinned Black people are not. The distaste for, but unwillingness to, eradicate poverty still exists in the form of a class system that perpetually places people of color at the bottom. Restrictions continue to exist on intellectual development via a separate and unequal education system that a significant number of Black folk know only enough to serve "Ole Master." And in a more pronounced and more documented way, supports are put in place to continue the stamping of dumb and ignorant on Black folk, Brown folk, and poor folk via an accountability that perpetuates an oppression akin to that of the social structure and hierarchy of the plantation system that depended on chattel slavery to exist. All this continues and is perpetuated by a system of public education accountability wrought with ethnically and racially biased high-stakes testing that hands down, puts the slave master and his plantation system to shame in a head-to-head competition during a period of history where slavery is supposed to be outlawed.

After teaching in Miami-Dade County Public Schools for over two decades, I drew the conclusion that there is a concerted effort to keep the American populous ignorant and devoid of the critical thinking necessary to fight back against oppressive laws that serve to enslave most, some more than others, and keep the masses working to enrich an elite few. Moreover, I would be remiss if I failed to acknowledge that some segments of American society are forced to be more ignorant than others. Corporate elites along with the public officials they put in office—both liberal and conservative—use the achievement gap between Black, Brown, and impoverished children and their White counterparts to create a distorted narrative that America's public educational system is failing the entire American populous.

The resulting education reform policies created under the guise of facilitating the closing of the achievement gap between non-White and impoverished students and their White peers have failed to close gaps that evidence shows are based on opportunity and economic realities that will continue to exist as long as classism and racism persist. And sadly, laws are actually enacted to destroy the critical thinking ability of the majority of people. Ignoring and/or distorting reality, the market-based reformers' use of documented evidence consists of various "data": lower performance outcomes on standardized, multiple choice tests for reading and math, lower rankings on international scales for standardized testing, and lower high school graduation rates.

The 21st century plantation patriarchs collected the "data," used it to put their propaganda machine in motion, and forced upon public education reform policies created under the guise of closing the achievement gap while paying no attention to expanding opportunity beyond what is extended to a select few. The rather controversial movie *Waiting for "Superman"* (Guggenheim, 2011), filled with extreme pathos, brought to big screen a pathetic portrait of inner city children—mostly of color—whose parents sought quality education for their children in order to escape the gap of low test performance outcomes and to avoid adding to the scores of students who fail to matriculate through high school and higher education. Outright pitiful, it focused on the many losers and the few winners. More importantly, its corporate backers (Singer, 2010) financed a project that promoted market-driven reforms, charters, vouchers, and teacher accountability while denigrating teachers' unions.

Essentially, it was a well-funded piece of propaganda which evidenced the proliferation of neoliberal private foundations and neoliberal policymakers as the architects and directors of education reform that serves to keep most of us ill-informed. It also inspired a host of celebrity liberals of color such as Oprah Winfrey and John Legend to pick up the whip and crack it in synchronization with the reformers.

What this film *did not do* was present the major reasons that Black, Brown, and impoverished students do not perform as well as their White, middle- and upper-class counterparts on standardized achievement tests. What it *did not do* is present the grand design to keep a majority of colored and poor children largely ignorant and devoid of opportunity to excel in a society that continues to need institutionalized racism, sexism, and classism to continue an economic exploitation that serves a select oligarchy. What it *did not do* is present how the lucrative nature of a failing culture has caused the oligarchy to extend the failure to middle-class White America by using a contrived set of national standards designed to make equal opportunity failure that transcends racial and class barriers to ensure that all children fail to some extent, if not completely. What it *did not do* is present the identity of the oligarchs who financed the film or their role in heisting billions of tax dollars of money that is set aside to support public education in order to facilitate a redistribution of wealth that serves to undermine the economic advances previously made by Black, Brown, and impoverished communities that benefitted from quality public education. And last, what it *did not do* is present how compromising educational opportunity and quality results in a shrinking middle class.

Who Are the Plantation Patriarchs?

But who are these people, these oligarchs, these patriarchs? According to former Assistant Secretary of Education, author, and historian Diane Ravitch, as told to *Democracy Now!*'s Amy Goodman and Juan Gonzalez in an interview, they are members of the "Billionaire Boys Club":

> The "Billionaires Boys Club" is a discussion of how we're in a new era of the Foundations and their relation to education. We have never in the history of the United States had foundations with the wealth of the Gates Foundation and some of the other billionaire foundations—the Walton Family Foundation, The Broad Foundation. And these three foundations—Gates, Broad and Walton—are committed now to charter schools and to evaluating teachers by test scores. And that's now the policy of the US Department of Education. We have never seen anything like this, where Foundations had the ambition to direct national educational policy, and in fact are succeeding. (2010, para. 30)

Other academics cite them as those that are participants and perpetrators of White supremacy and patriarchal control. Legal scholar Frances Lee Ansley provides an academic definition in which White supremacy is a political, economic and cultural system in which whites overwhelmingly control power and material resources, conscious and unconscious ideas of white superiority and entitlement are widespread, and relations of white dominance and non-white subordination are daily reenacted across a broad array of institutions and social settings. (1997, p. 592)

Author, educator, and feminist scholar bell hooks takes it a step further as she states that the:

Imperialist white-supremacist capitalist patriarchy is a political-social system that insists that males are inherently dominating, superior to everything and everyone deemed weak, especially females, and endowed with the right to dominate and rule over the weak and to maintain that dominance through various forms of psychological terrorism and violence. (n.d. p. 1)

hooks (n.d.) sees it as a force operating beyond the individual and functioning very much as a collective force with strata and layers put in place and supported by a complicit collective inclusive of all races, ethnicities, and social classes.

Who Are the Overseers?

In other words, the patriarchs exist, but they also exist because of those who allow it, particularly those who function as the overseers to the system. And who (and what) are they, the overseers? The White supremacist social and economic structure has always been willing to scrape the cream off the top of the ranks of the colored populace and the impoverished White hard worker, educate it, and assimilate its genius into its well-manufactured social fabric. Literacy specialist and Chair of Illinois Township High School District 214, Gerri K. Songer, explains how top cream skimming works in the realm of education:

ACT and PARCC are standardized assessments that are inaccessible to most students, using text that is too complex and requiring a level of cognition that is completely inappropriate. They are designed as a filter and used to skim the "cream" off the top of the bell-shaped curve. Students who fall into the category of "cream" are admitted into the best colleges and are eligible for scholarships based on their "academic merits." (2014, para. 3)

Waiting for "Superman" (2011) chronicles how this particular methodology functions too, and to its credit, albeit unintentional, it points out the inequity of such a system that has operated under the radar for far too long. In the movie, one sees the lucky lotto winners of the "choice" charter. And it is no doubt that those children, if they maintain the required academic and behavioral requirements, will prosper while the numerous scores of losers will struggle in a very exclusive society. Our United States President Barack Obama, media mogul Oprah Winfrey, Florida's Federal Congressional Senator Marco Rubio, and the current Congressional Speaker of the House John Boehner are all top cream, are beneficiaries of top cream scraping, and all are proponents of this corporate-based education reform. Not all made it due to academic prowess, but they represent those with the perseverance, determination, and a willingness to serve a master that is not so kind to those communities of folks they left behind.

In a rather scathing and somewhat embarrassing speech I made during our 2011 *United Opt Out* occupation of the Department of Education, I referenced those who are in that select group of "top cream." I cited how many people of color in positions of power, maintain those positions by willingly undermining the various communities from which they come.[1] During the speech, I harshly criticized President Obama, entertainer John Legend, former Newark Mayor Corey Booker, the legendary Oprah Winfrey, Senator Marco Rubio, Superintendent of Miami-Dade County Public Schools Alberto Carvalho, and former Chancellor of the District of Columbia Public Schools and current organizer and spokesperson for Students First Michelle Rhee for their culpability in embracing and promoting market-based reforms that serve to undermine as opposed to build. I addressed this in an interview with retired teacher and blogger for *Ed Week* Anthony Cody:

> My greatest concern is [that] the implementation of Dept of Ed policies has many accepting fiction as true fact. High stakes test scores do not indicate that students have learned deeply, claimed ownership to knowledge and learning, obtained the ability to work with others, or developed the ability to think creatively. Nor do they really reflect the quality of a school or a teacher. They suggest trends in regards to cultural practices, social class, and the ability to learn test taking strategies. And to a certain extent they reveal aptitude based on assimilation and cultural bias. The Department of Education promotes these misnomers. The student who scores high on a single math test is going to receive more respect and validation than the young man who scores poorly on a single math test but is able to create a practical and stunning fashion design using recycled materials. Consequently, we are wounding instead of empowering students, teachers, and the overall academic culture. All of us need validation, not a fictitious grade stamped on our school, a misleading number stamped into our consciousness, or a bonus check for a random number that we may or may not have had something to do. (2012, paras. 2–3)

I continued,

Another concern is the huge racial and economic divide that the standardized test culture is fostering. Many great teachers are backing away from teaching in minority and impoverished communities, and others are being tossed out of these communities. Schools are very segregated by class and color, and the divide is filled with inequity. Sadly, there seems to be a trend in that the different groups are becoming insensitive and discriminatory toward each other in very harmful and non-progressive ways. (2012, paras. 2–3)

The resulting harm is of no consequence to the non-White people and the formerly impoverished, the "top-cream" of their ethnic, racial, or low-socioeconomic groups who hold and foster the moral values (or lack of) of a patriarchal and supremacist system. They are ultimately beholden to the money-driven method of systemic exclusion and exploitation that maintains today's bipartisan attack on public education, collective bargaining, democracy, and egalitarianism overall.

Who Are the Victims?

Where would have any of the "top cream" ended up had they not been so complicit? Good question, but one that is not all that easy to answer. Conversely, it can be answered where most of the "top cream" never end up. Most, not all, avoid ending up in communities that are predominantly Black or Brown, working class, and/or poverty class. Most do not have their children attend schools like Miami Northwestern High School, a school with a history in which many former graduates take pride, and a school where in 2007 pride was compromised by a racist and unfair Florida state school grading system that continually labeled it and other Black and Brown high schools in the city as "failing." Located in Miami, Florida, about 1,600 non-White students attend Northwestern. In 2007, my husband, an excellent math teacher who was later involuntarily transferred from this school due to the replacement of good, veteran educators with *Teach for America* novices, was the offensive coordinator for Northwestern Senior High's football team who played a team in Southlake, Texas, in a prearranged football match that was televised on *ESPNU*. The two teams were competing for the National High School Football Championship.

While Northwestern is located in an inner-city community, Southlake Carroll is located in an upper-middle-class to upper-class suburban neighborhood in the Dallas/Ft. Worth area of Texas. A teacher friend and I went to visit the Southlake Carroll High School campus and discovered it was more like a college, spread with two campuses—one for freshman and sophomores, the other for juniors and seniors. They had a million dollar aquatic complex right on the campus, and the high school had a multimillion dollar athletic stadium. The students had a 98% pass rate for standardized testing and almost a 100% higher education admission annually:

> The Carroll Independent School District serves families in Southlake and Grapevine. In a few weeks, 575 Carroll graduates will accept their high school diplomas at this stadium, and 97 percent of them will go on to college. Thirteen of these students will be honored as National Merit Semifinalists, a record number for Southlake Carroll. In fact, for the last nine years, Carroll Senior High School has received an "exemplary" rating from the Texas Education Agency. (Kix, 2007, para. 29)

On the other hand, Northwestern Senior High was under state sanction for low performance on standardized testing and at the time had approximately a 46% high school graduation rate.

> Northwestern does not take top honors academically. It gets an "F" rating from the state of Florida. The grand jury report that examined the Easterling case alleged the school has been more interested in athletics than academics.... Laurence Axtell, who teaches African-American history at Northwestern, says the school's academic failings have more to do with institutional racism in the way education is funded in this country than with failings on the part of many of its teachers and students.
>   We're a powerhouse of athletic talent, and we shouldn't be punished for that.... People say, "Oh, you're an F school, the one with that sex scandal." Yes, but we're also the oldest continuously open, historically Black high school in Dade County. That says something. It's very disheartening to have to defend yourself to people who don't know anything about you. (Brady, 2007, paras. 52–56)

For clarification of the "Easterling case," referenced above, team member Antwain Easterling was charged with lewd and lascivious battery on a minor 2 days before the state championship game December 9, 2007 for engaging in consensual sex with a minor. He completed a diversionary program instead of going to trial.

The Southlake Carroll community was very showy in their wealth, but the people that my friend and I encountered as we toured the town were very pleasant and kind. Sadly, we did encounter a very hurtful incident that changed our opinion of the community—the insensitivity displayed as the Northwestern players entered the football field on game day. These folks who had all the advantages afforded to their race and class began chanting: "SAT, SAT, SAT," indicating the seemingly poor academic performance of the students from Northwestern High. The commentator stopped it with his hearty rebuking of the rudeness of the Carroll fans. But it was too little to alter our opinion that the town was filled with a bunch of insensitive people that fed into systemic racism. Needless to say, we took special delight in the fact that the Northwestern Bulls defeated the Southlake Carroll Dragons 29–21 and ended their 49 game winning streak. It was an unfortunate loss for them, and it is unfortunate that this community, well aware of the "White and economic privilege" pointed out in the media prior to the game, chose to insult the Northwestern team and fans in such an offensive way. And that single act punctuated how "the perfect world" in contrast to "the other" that was wrought with social problems, complete with a player who faced charges and possible jail time, characterizes life in America and the role that public education, very much separate and unequal, plays in facilitating systemic racism and classism. Author and educator, Tim Wise (2014) said it well:

> As W.E.B. DuBois noted, over time, white supremacy invested white folks with a "psychological wage," which allows them to feel superior to people of color, even if they ultimately pay a price for their indulgence of white privilege … what is often ignored is the way that white privilege, relative to people of color, has served as the transmission belt of false consciousness. By investing white workers with a sense of their whiteness as property—albeit an inadequate form of property, relative to real material well-being—white privilege and racism provide to whites an alternative sense of their own self-interest. As such, the ability of working people to form effective cross-racial coalitions (which would be needed in order to fundamentally challenge or alter the current class arrangements in the U.S.) is itself made less likely precisely because of white racism and institutional racial inequity and privilege. To the extent whiteness confers certain relative advantages to whites, it makes it less likely that those whites will join with people of color to alter the class system or even push for reforms that would benefit all working people. (para. 18)

And this plays out as a major problem when trying to fight education reform policies stemming from neoliberalism that stretch across racial and class boundaries to stop the massive disenfranchisement and all inclusive oppression of non-White, White, immigrant, second language, and special needs. Author and theologian Rev. Osagyefo Sekou quotes Audre Lourde in his article titled "The Master's House Is Burning: bell hooks, Cornel West and the Tyranny of Neoliberalism" (2014) where he provides an appropriate metaphor which characterizes the bondage we all face:

> As Audré Lourde so eloquently wrote—a now often-quoted refrain—"The Master's Tools Will Never Dismantle the Master's House." Neoliberalism is the master's house and tool. It limits discursive space, subjugates radicality and seduces the othered into defending its existence. (para. 8)

This age-old reality continues to persist as we watch a world that is becoming more and more unfair in its treatment of those who are the

"Others," who are not the real beneficiaries or a part of the corporate class of patriarchs who continue to manipulate a redistribution of wealth via control of government and policy.

Today, as we face this redistribution of wealth firmly rooted in neoliberalism and facilitated by the bipartisan political attack on public education and collective bargaining, it is right to fear for the future of both. What has been passed off as a friendly and symbiotic merging of public and private is actually a hostile takeover by a systemic force that has never acted in the best interest of people of color, women, or laborers. The use of the achievement gap between non-Whites and the impoverished and their White counterparts coupled with this pseudo-philanthropic market-based reform effort utilized to take over public education completely via the erroneous notions of "accountability" and "choice," is driven by them.

Accountability, data-driven instruction, value-added measure, merit pay, choice, national standards attached to high-stakes testing, and even the absurd electronic bracelets pedaled by Bill Gates to monitor student engagement support the corporatist and political figures, and to support those who push them is to co-sign the death certificate of equity and quality in public education while placing a strangling choke hold on collective bargaining.

Which leads to the next question: Why would a largely female profession with organized labor institutions be held responsible as the major reason why America's educational system fails its children of color and poverty? Most of those children attend schools that suffer with at least one, and in most cases, most of the following problems: inadequate funding ranging from the inequities of neighborhood tax bases, whims of conservative budget-slashing, corporate tax-breaking state legislators, to the exclusionary Race to the Top method of funding. Furthermore, they suffer with a chronic, reeling flux of constant staff turnover resulting in inexperienced staffs short of skilled "veteran know-how" teachers and administrators, absentee parents and absentee parental involvement, integrated schools that have classrooms segregated by race and class, compromised curricula that stress test prep while largely ignoring how short- and long-term memory banks store and retrieve data and how critical thinking and problem solving are nurtured. *None of this is coincidence or accident.*

Many questions arise such as why are *we*, the "others"—people of color, women of all colors and ethnicities, impoverished and oppressed peoples of all races and ethnicities—so complicit in this patriarchal system of control? Why are *we* not fighting these forces? In other words, why are *we* not opting out of a system that is so harmful for democracy, sustainability, and the moral cause? When I said, in my speech on the floor of the National Education Association Representative Assembly in campaigning for an NEA Executive Board position in 2012, that White supremacists have conducted a hostile takeover of public education in lieu of a reciprocal relationship between public and private, I know I shocked many of the delegates, and I could almost hear, "Why does she have to mention race?"

Not surprising to me, it is being mentioned more frequently as overt racism is replacing that which had gone covert. At a 2011 Selma Jubilee Workshop in Selma, Alabama, during the annual commemoration of Bloody Sunday,[2] Whites, Blacks, indigenous, Latino/a, and Asian folks were all referring to the "White supremacy" as a force in which we all have to reckon. Aligned with the thinking of bell hooks, we, as exploited Americans, have to understand the systemic nature of the terminology and move past thinking that it is terminology that is directed toward or targeting a specific individual, racial, or ethnic group or viewing it as a prejudicial rant when used. Instead, we have to understand the term for what it is: a systemic and powerful force that serves to oppress all people as it pulls a major ruse on many who buy-in to the notion that America is a democracy that functions under democratic principles.

Once we understand the full ramifications of how it works, as a powerful and oppressive system bought in to by most of us and not as an old White man or White people collectively behind a curtain, we can begin to identify how we must work to become disengaged from this powerful force that serves to create an oppressed cabal of victims, who just happen to be the "others," the majority who live in America, in the world. We can and will need to work together across the ethnic, class, racial, and gender strata to create a movement that changes the current patriarchal paradigm that really fails to serve the greater interest of productivity and sustainability for all. And more importantly, we can create a movement that is powerful enough to end the deliberate abuse and destruction of the child mind, body, and spirit via the oppressive policies that are well on the way to destroying the freedoms and rights gained by people of color and well on the way to destroying a public education system that facilitates a vibrant and diverse working class and middle class that is able to exercise a democratic voice.

What Does it Mean to "Opt Out?"

In response to these questions posed above, most do not have an answer. Nor do they have the time or attention span to figure out an answer. Some, however, *want* answers and are willing to work for them, create them, and implement them. That is the motivation that brought our initial six pissed-off people together to start *United Opt Out National*. All of us were driven by a need to right wrongs that we see occurring in public education that have greater implications when it comes to the preservation of democracy and social justice in America. But what exactly does that mean, opting out? For me, it means opting out of the supremacist, patriarchal notion boosted by neoliberal ideology that the elite can completely revamp public education to meet their selfish and money-grubbing needs, and this is done by refusing to give them the high-stakes test-driven "data" they need to perpetuate the false narrative that allows them to conduct a heist on taxpayer money, social justice, and the principles of democracy. Others have their own definition or explanation. Let's see: **Catie Shafer**: "That as a parent and as a taxpayer I actually have a say in my child's education" (personal communication, May 2014). **Erin Contino**: "That I am advocating for my children by exercising my constitutional rights and taking charge of their education and not blindly handing them over to the state" (personal communication, May 2014). **Peggy Robertson**: "Opting out is a vote for public schools. Opting out is declaring our independence from those who wish to oppress us. Opting out allows us the freedom to move forward as we shift the narrative and reclaim and improve public schools for all children" (personal communication, May 2014). **Sarah Duvall**: "It can mean a lot of things: you don't feel that taking the test is a good use of your child's time or your taxpayer dollar. You don't know who wrote the test, and since you aren't allowed to see the test after its graded in order to find out which questions your child missed, you can't be sure it was graded correctly— therefore, why take it? You hear that your child's test data will be shared with unnamed third parties (you don't know when, why, how many, nothing), and you don't want to share it without signing a consent form" (personal communication, May 2014). **Cindy Hamilton**: "Since I am not doing the opting out, the kids are, my responsibility is to gather the most accurate information and instructions to lessen the blow and pushback. Once the pushback starts, I do my best to remain calm until the student is out of harm's way, with a successful opt out, and then I aim to bite the heads off the SOBs doing the pushing" (personal communication, May 2014). **Alison Hawver McDowell**: "Exercising my power to advocate for meaningful education in opposition to the corporate model espoused by Pearson et al." (personal communication, May 2014). **NekoGatoKatze Cat**: "Resistance and solidarity! We do it not just for the kids in my family, but for all kids everywhere, and for the future of public education in this country!!" (personal communication, May 2014). **Kristina Lozada**: "Refusing the test for my child is a way for me to protest the wrong direction that American Education is heading. As a teacher I have to accept a lot of things that I don't agree with, but as a parent through the power of refusal I can try to influence change" (personal communication, May 2014). **Tooty Taah**: "Opting out means I would rather our school-focused tax dollars go toward teachers in classrooms and school programs than testing companies. I would rather curriculum and assessment decisions were made and created by actual K–12 educators. I would rather educators be evaluated by their actual planning and teaching than by my child's performance on a test. I would rather school districts/teachers/students were not held accountable for the deficits created by poverty and other societal ills—institutionalized racism, stagnating middle class, lack of health and mental health care. I would rather my children's whole self be nurtured, including the arts, as opposed to just reading and math. I would rather we didn't use assessments for reasons they were not intended, and that we didn't overrely on such invalid assessments. For my children, for my children's school, for my children's school district, and for all children in public schools, I opt out" (personal communication, May 2014). **Kate Skinner:** "Opting out means exercising parental discretion over educational matters, even in areas where the school has more expertise in a particular field. Parents have the expertise in their child and what is best for the family. Opting out is a way for individual families to coexist in a system built for the general public" (personal communication, May 2014). **Heather Berger:** "That they are MY children NOT the government's and that I have the final say in their lives and education!" (personal communication, May 2014). **Tasha Pascucci Wolcson:** "That as a parent who cares about my children's education I must stand up for them and do what is right. I must act as their advocate and do what is best for them. That I believe they are not going to be 'college ready' if they are spending all of their class room time preparing for a test that is not age appropriate or even created by educators. That I will not have my children treated as test subjects as the creators of the test don't believe their children need to take that very test. Opting my children out of the test is one of my many ways of showing my kids just how much I love them and that they will always know that I'm here for them—no matter what anyone says!" (personal communication, May 2014). **Sandy Stenoff:** "It means that I do not give my consent, either implied or express, and that I do not agree that the test does what they purport it does. It also means that I do not consent to the way the test and results are used" (personal communication, May 2014). **Jennifer Proseus:** "Opt out = refuse the test" (personal communication, May 2014). **Amanda Rattray-Bywater:** "To direct my children's education in a manner that will allow them to be and feel successful" (personal communication, May 2014). **Kim Zito:** "I did not opt, I refused" (personal communication, May 2014). **Ed John:** "In the current education language it means to decline to take high stakes tests. Particularly those tests that don't actually measure anything except how much money a state department of education has available to pour down a rat hole" (personal communication, May 2014). **Marla Kilfoyle:** "To my family it means we are not asking permission we are TELLING you we, as a family, will not take part in a scheme and a lie!!! We will NOT take part in testing that isn't used to help kids or inform instruction PERIOD" (personal communication, May

2014). **Denisha Jones:** "To me it means to remove myself from the chaos" (personal communication, May 2014). **Lesa Aloan Wilbert:** "Choose not to participate—but if you are talking about the awful tests … it means stand up for what you believe, refuse to participate in crap testing, and have a voice in some way when the 'powers that be' won't listen" (personal communication, May 2014). **Mark Naison:** "Opting Out to me means refusing to participate in an education system hijacked by the very wealthy and insisting students, parents and teachers' voices be put front and center in revitalizing public education" (personal communication, May 2014). **Shaun Johnson**: "Opting out can be understood in multiple ways. It is a boycott of a product. It is refusal to participate in our own oppression. Opting out is withholding power from the oppressors. It is a method of recapturing our conscience. Opting out may be the only tool left in the arsenal of the oppressed to break the chain that yokes us to the struggle for freedom that is imposed upon us. We know that education is freedom. To opt out, or in our case to refuse tying our own hands to testing, is to redefine education and therefore usurp the means to which we seek our freedom" (personal communication, May 2014). **Ruth Rodriguez**: "Child protection laws are meant to be applied to ensure that children are not abused or neglected. As a kindergarten teacher I was mandated by law to report any sign of abuse that I detected, or suffer facing the criminal courts if harm befall upon a student that I failed to report. Opting out for me means that families have chosen to take on this responsibility of protecting their children from the abusive measures of pervasive testing. It means taking a moral stand against a system that has used the for-profit testing industry complex to instill fear on the children of the disenfranchised and on their teachers. It also means that families understand that the testing madness that has taken over our public institutions is just another scheme to create unequal schools, it is the present day 'bell curve' if you please creating unequal schools" (personal communication, May 2014). **Morna McDermott:** "Opting out is a refusal to believe, or be complicit, in perpetuating a corporate-run system of education that hurts children. It means to refuse, to advocate against or to engage actively against that which you believe to be wrong. We opt out by not participating IN a destructive harmful system of oppressive behaviors or attitudes. To opt out is to take any and all actions to end corporate reform of public education. It is a way of being, a way of being done. We believe that the quickest and most effective way to END the harmful practices being forced upon our children and our teachers, and to disrupt the corporate takeover of public education, is to refuse the tests. Opting out sounds the end of destruction and invites a new beginning for more humane, sustainable and necessary educational possibilities" (personal communication, May 2014). **Rosemarie Jensen:** "Opting out is choosing to protect students, teachers, and schools from the abusive use of high stakes tests, the test prep that supports it, and from the scripted one size fits all curriculum demanded by it. It means standing up to the corporate interests that have co-opted true learning and teacher autonomy at the expense of individual needs and interests of students and communities. It means demanding a high quality, well rounded, student centered education, full funded and equitable education for all children and respecting teachers as the experts in the classroom" (personal communication, May 2014). **Tim Slekar**: "Opt Out—a simple act of physically and intellectually removing yourself from a toxic situation. It is also the ultimate act of love because it reclaims the boundaries of the conversation. It recognizes when a conversation is being controlled by those in power and is a refusal to participate and an act to redefine the conversation within the boundaries as defined by those that support public schools and refuse to even acknowledge the failing schools narrative. Instead it forces the conversation to recognize that failing social, economic, and political systems are destroying America's system of public education" (personal communication, May 2014).

Taking Action

Creating resistance to laws that serve to oppress and exploit is never easy. It always involves pushback from the opposition that can be frustrating, disheartening, and sometimes filled with reprisal that can be costly. Options 1 through 4 (as outlined below in the Activist's Workbook section of this chapter) can be done with very little or no reprisal for parents and caregivers or little reprisal for students. However, parents and caregivers and students who select option 6 (refusing the tests), can be and have been victimized by schools and or local school districts that engage in various punitive actions in an effort to deter folks from opting out: Forcing students to sit and stare for hours during testing, excluding children from school, field trips, and or extracurricular activities, mandating remediation for math and or reading by attempting to force parents to accept enrollment in summer school or remediation classes regardless of the student's proficiency, denying school grade promotions, denying opportunities for student placement in higher-level classes, denying diplomas, and denying opportunities for scholarship opportunities.

Each parent has to become familiar with the individual state and district polices that can negatively impact the child if he or she is opted out of testing. Parents or caregivers who are firm in their resolve to opt their child out must know that the law is on the side of the parent in that the parent has the final say in the education of their child. Therefore, all the punitive measures leveled against caregivers and their students can and should be fought. But it is still wise to know what might be a recourse taken by the school if the child does not sit for standardized testing.

Employees of public schools and institutions of higher education can be met with punitive measures that range from verbal reprimands to getting fired if they engage in any of the options. Often when engaging in activities even as simple as joining Facebook groups, they are forced to do so incognito. Every educator, administrator, or support staff member must know down to the smallest details what contract protections are afforded to them if they choose to become public education activists who engage in opting out on some or all levels. Most districts allow for activism that does not occur during contract hours, but there are those that do not. Other districts allow for activism inclusive of all the options, which has been demonstrated in Seattle and Chicago, where large numbers of educators refused to administer tests with impunity. Again, it is important to know the individual contractual obligations to avoid costly reprisal.

Often people caution that it is disingenuous to compare what is going on in the privatization of public education to slavery and the plantation hierarchy of existence. They have a point in that the horrific lifestyle of the slave on a plantation filled with forced bondage; chattel status; beatings; rape and misogyny; subpar housing, food, and clothing; restrictions on literacy and intellectual development; restrictions on cultural practices, and continual destruction of the nuclear family does not equate to what we deal with in the 21st century with regard to social, political, economic, and living conditions. And they are right—for the most part. But when one takes a good look at the underlying neoliberalistic social, political, and economic hierarchy—those who are running the market-based reform effort and those who act as their agents, those who are victimized and those most victimized by the market-based reform effort, the legislated limitations on curricula and academic freedom, the resegregation of public schools, the lack of teacher quality in schools populated with Black and Brown students, the sanctions placed on Black and Brown schools that do not meet the proficiency standards, the lack of equity in curricular materials and funding, the sexist manhandling of a female-dominated profession, the emotional beatings and brainwashing to accept inferior status via school grading and ranking of schools and their educators, the nationwide standards that serve to enlarge the failing culture, and the economic exploitation—there are startling parallels, parallels that we should not ignore because the same force that created and implanted chattel slavery is still at work today as prisons that are direct parallels to chattel slavery fill up with Black and Brown people, and the middle class shrinks due to the rather massive and rapid redistribution of wealth. Simple ditties like the one used as a preface will be the standard fare for far too many to sing while "Ole Master" walks away from the market with most of the goods. However, with well-organized resistance that starts with empty test chair by empty test chair, the market-based reformers and their policymakers will get the message that enough is enough.

THE ACTIVIST WORKBOOK

So ... How Does One Engage in "Opting Out?"

Everyone has their own unique concept of what it means to opt out, and within the wide lens of various perspectives there is a narrow set of concrete steps that one can take to opt out. First and foremost, individuals should educate themselves as to what market-based reform is, who is driving it, and what its impact is on their state and local school districts, their tax dollars, and most importantly on their individual children. This includes knowing the federal, state, and district polices. Once a thorough understanding is gained, individuals can proceed with opting out on various different levels.

1. Advocate for a change in laws that negatively impact public education, teachers, students, and the taxpayer by using the political voice: campaign for or support public education-friendly politicians, run for political office, write letters to elected officials, sign petitions and resolutions.
2. Partake in demonstrations, marches, town halls, forums, public education advocacy groups, school board meetings, and share information with others.
3. Join Facebook groups that advocate for public education, join in Twitter campaigns, and join national and or local organizations that advocate for public education.
4. Write blogs, letters to the editors, articles for publication, and call in to talk radio programs.
5. If a member of AFT, NEA, state union affiliates, and local union affiliates of NEA, AFT or both, become active in or form a social justice caucus.
6. Opt a child or children out of standardized testing using the guides posted on the *United Opt Out* website.
7. Refuse to administer or proctor standardized tests.

The *United Opt Out* website[3] includes guides for each state and provides the federal laws that protect a parent in the decisions they make for their child. Parents and caregivers can also find on the website the "Get Tough Guide" that speaks to possible scenarios and what options parents can take in the face of school or district pushback to complete the opt out process.

NOTES

1. For more on this, see Chapter 7 of this book.
2. On "Bloody Sunday," March 7, 1965, some 600 civil rights marchers headed east out of Selma on U.S. Route 80. They got only as far as the Edmund Pettus Bridge six blocks away, where state and local lawmen attacked them with billy clubs and tear gas and drove them back into Selma. See http://www.nps.gov/nr/travel/civilrights/al4.htm
3. See www.unitedoptout.com

REFERENCES

Ansley, F. L. (1997). White supremacy (and what we should do about it). In R. Delgado & J. Stephanicic (Eds.), *Critical white studies: Looking behind the mirror.* Philadelphia, PA: Temple University Press.

Brady, E. (2007, September 14). Carroll-Northwestern match shaped by contrasts. *US Today.* Retrieved from http://usatoday30.usatoday.com/sports/preps/football/2007-09-13-carroll-northwestern_N.htm

Brown, S. (1985). Negro folk expression: Spirituals, seculars, ballads and work songs. In R. Long & E. Collier (Eds.), *Afro-American writing: An anthology of prose and poetry* (p. 416). University Park: Pennsylvania State University Press.

Cody, A. (2012, March 22). Teachers and parents prepare to occupy the Department of Education. *Education Week Teacher.* Retrieved from http://blogs.edweek.org/teachers/living-in-dialogue/2012/03/teachers_and_parents_prepare_t.html

Goodman, A., & Gonzalez, J. (2010, March 5). Leading education scholar Diane Ravitch: No Child Left Behind has left us schools with legacy of "institutionalized fraud." *Democracy Now!* Retrieved from http://www.democracynow.org/2010/3/5/protests

Guggenheim, D. (Writer & Director). (2011). *Waiting for "Superman"* [film]. Hollywood, CA: Paramount Home Entertainment.

hooks, b. (n.d.). Understanding patriarchy. *Imaginenoborders.com.* Retrieved from http://imaginenoborders.org/pdf/zines/UnderstandingPatriarchy.pdf

Kix, P. (2007, September 1). Southlake: Welcome to perfect city, U.S.A. *D Magazine.* Retrieved from http://www.dmagazine.com/publications/d-magazine/2007/september/southlake-welcome-to-perfect-city-usa

Sekou, O. (2014, May 19). The master's house is burning: bell hooks, Cornel West and the tyranny of neoliberalism. *truthout.* Retrieved from http://truth-out.org/opinion/item/23792-the-masters-house-is-burning-bell-

Singer, A. (2010, October 12). No longer waiting for "Superman." *The Huffington Post.* Retrieved June 3, 2014, from http://www.huffingtonpost.com/alan-singer/no-longer-waiting-or-sup_b_755781.html

Songer, G. (2014, May 14). Standardized testing does not produce good education. *Diane Ravitch's blog.* Retrieved May 30, 2014, from http://dianeravitch.net/2014/05/14/gerri-k-songer-standardized-testing-does-not-produce-good-education/

Wise, T. (2014, January 1). F.A.Q.s. *TimWise.* Retrieved from http://www.timwise.org/f-a-q-s/

CHAPTER 4

OCCUPY THIS

Peggy Robertson

Peggy Robertson

An Activist Handbook for the Education Revolution:
United Opt Out's Test of Courage, pp. 57–77
Copyright © 2015 by Information Age Publishing

How It Started

United Opt Out (UOO) has had an event every year since we founded our group in 2011. It's hard to look back and remember every detail of each event. So when I was tasked with this chapter, I became a bit overwhelmed. Adding to that overwhelmed feeling was the fact that this year, 2013–2014, our website was hacked and destroyed during the final day of our annual event. Therefore, gathering and locating the necessary documents to discuss our work has become even more of a challenge. I want to begin by saying that these three events (Occupy the U.S. Department of Education in 2012, again in 2013, and our workshop in Denver in 2014) have been crucial to our work, to our ability to organize, to build relationships, and to develop a better understanding of who we are, why we are here, and how we can best utilize our strengths to take down corporate education reform and reclaim public schools.

Our first event, Occupying the U.S. Department of Education in Washington, D.C., in the spring of 2012 was an "experiment" of sorts. I recall being on the phone with Morna one evening in which we were discussing strategy and actions that might catch the attention of the media and at the same time bring together like-minded folks who needed an opportunity to talk, strengthen our work, and further solidify our efforts to save public schools. Morna and I have some sort of sixth sense. She calls when I think of her. I call when she is thinking of me. We tend to work in tandem, and our strengths play off one another very well. Occupy Wall Street had begun in September of 2011, and we were watching this carefully, thinking through how public education could be brought to the forefront through social media and Occupy. We contacted folks at Occupy Wall Street. We were each beginning to attend our own local Occupy events to see how we could get the message out that public education was being dismantled. At the time, there was so much else going on with bank bailouts and foreclosures that it was incredibly challenging to bring the education issue to the forefront. As Morna and I continued to talk, she said, *"Why not occupy the Department of Education?"* Remember, we were still very new at this. Very green to be quite honest. In some ways our innocence served us well because we took risks that others who were more experienced might have immediately turned down. We were just beginning to learn about long-term planning and short-term strategic actions. Yet we clearly recognized that the momentum Occupy was gathering all over the country was indeed a chance to get our message to a greater audience. So, when Morna asked, it seemed like the perfectly logical thing to do. Who wouldn't "occupy" the Department of Education under these conditions? It seemed like common sense. And so the planning began.

Occupy the DOE, 2012
Poster created by Jay Rivett from Occupy ART: Indiana.

It is time to end Wall Street Occupation of Education.

We asked—they said NO. We wrote—they said NO. We sent them research—they said NO. We say NO. We opt out. We will put a screeching halt to corporate education by saying NO to the test.

We will occupy the Department of Education in D.C. from March 30th to April 2nd. Ongoing planning can be found at our Facebook Occupy the DOE page.

It's time to put the public back in public education. Occupy the DOE and show them who education REALLY BELONGS to.

Join *United Opt Out National* & #OCCUPYDOE in Washington D.C.

April Fools!

No Child Left Behind—Fool Me Once.

Race to the Top—We Won't be Fooled Again.

Join us. In solidarity with Occupy Movements everywhere.

Organizing and Messaging

One thing I have learned over the last 4 years of being an activist is that strategic planning is crucial, and the messaging must be tight. But when you are new to this, there are many bumps along the way. The permits required for this event were ridiculous: permits to be on the ground at the U.S. DOE, off the sidewalk, on the street, and so on. On the front patio of the U.S. DOE we needed a permit from the Government Services Administration (GSA), and if we walked 4 feet to the left onto the sidewalk, we needed a D.C. Metro Police permit to do so, and when we marched to the White House, we needed yet another permit from Parks Services. Morna handled all of that. She spent many a day in D.C. organizing these permits and getting us "legit." We decided that while we were indeed occupying, we wanted to occupy legally so that teachers, who already lived in fear of losing their jobs, could easily attend. The group decided early on that while arrests can be a powerful tool for resistance, in an instance where we wanted to remain present, to speak, and to plan, being arrested would be an obstacle to our goals.

We titled our event Occupy the DOE. We took our cue from the Occupy the DOE event in New York. Little did we know that many folks would think we were occupying the Department of Energy. Numerous e-mails from folks across the country ensued as they attempted to explain to us our error with the acronym. We held our ground and stayed with our title; if folks showed up to occupy the Department of Energy, so be it! They could meander over to the Department of Education after checking in with our website.

We aligned ourselves with Occupy Wall Street, whose members, like Margaret Flowers, supported us by sharing our event with their own membership, and created the following demands to be presented to Congress on our first day of the occupation:

> We, administrators of *United Opt Out National* (www.unitedoptout.com), wish to collaborate with the Occupy Wall Street Movement and offer our vision for CORPORATE-FREE PUBLIC SCHOOLS.
>
> We believe that QUALITY PUBLIC EDUCATION is a democratic right for all persons. It is through vibrant and fully funded school communities that all children have the opportunity to develop and grow into happy, successful, free, and active citizens. High stakes testing functions in opposition to QUALITY PUBLIC EDUCATION, as it is used to punish children, to malign educators, and to provide financial gain for testing corporations and their political sponsors.
>
> THEREFORE, WE DEMAND AN END TO THE FOLLOWING:
>
> ALL high stakes testing and punitive policies that label schools, punish students, and close public community schools
>
> ALL high stakes testing that ties teacher evaluations, pay, and job security to high stakes test results
>
> Corporate interventions in public education and education policy

The use of public education funds to enact school "choice" measures influenced and supported by the corporate agenda
Economically and racially segregated school communities

"Model" legislation that provides special rules to charter schools that are forced upon public schools

Corporate run for-profit charter schools that divert public funds away from public schools

Mandates requiring teachers to use corporate approved, scripted programs that sublimate and negate authentic and meaningful learning experiences imparted by varied and rich curricula

FURTHERMORE, WE DEMAND RESTORATION AND/OR IMPLEMENTATION OF THE FOLLOWING:

Libraries and librarians to all schools and communities

Teaching force educated through accredited college teacher education programs only

School buildings in ALL neighborhoods that meet health codes including clean drinking water, heat and air conditioning

Developmentally appropriate, problem-based, literacy-rich, play-based and student-centered learning, with the return of nap, play, and snack time for kindergarteners

Smaller student-to-teacher ratio (25 or fewer to one)

Wrap around services for schools that offset the effects of poverty and social inequality, including but not limited to: school staff such as nurses and health providers, social workers, community organizers, family counselors; free quality community daycare and preschool programs, healthy food availability, safe and healthy housing options, community social facilities, and after school programs to enhance learning and provide safe recreational spaces for all students

Fully funded arts and athletics programs

Recess and adequate time allotted for lunch

New national funding formulas that ensures EQUITY in funding to ALL public schools regardless of zip code

Requirement that a significant percentage of textbook or testing company PROFITS go BACK TO public education

Requirement that all DOE positions are filled with qualified and experienced educators

Requirement that superintendents and school administrators have exceptional, extended teaching and school-based experience

Community and Truth

There were two things we hoped to accomplish over our 4-day action at the Dept. of Ed. We wanted to create a national community of activists who would build relationships, connections, and further expand our impact across the nation. We wanted to spread the word of opt out in order to shut down corporate education reform. But we also wanted experts from all over the country to come speak and share the research and truths that could be used to educate the public and create action across the country. Our *Who's Who List of Speakers*[1] included citizens who had stayed committed to the goals of public education. Bluntly put, we did not want any sellouts—those who had been negotiating with children's lives in order to profit and/or gain political or career milestones. We wanted our speaker list to include folks who play hardball, those who were willing to take risks—folks who do right by our children.

Our list included Bess Altwerger, Don Bartalo, Liza Campbell, Dave Greene, Jim Horn, Brian Jones, Mike Klonsky, Stephen Krashen, Bob and Yvonne Lamothe, Barry Lane, Mark Naison, Linda Nathan, Ann O'Halloran, Tom Poetter, Ruth Rodriguez-Fay, Dov Rosenberg, Ira Shor, Jesse Turner, and of course, the UOO crew: me (Peg Robertson), Tim Slekar, Morna McDermott, Ceresta Smith, Laurie Murphy, and Shaun Johnson.

Our event[2] was a true occupation in the sense that we were parked right outside the doors of the Dept. of Ed. Throughout the day teaching ambassadors, teachers who have received a fellowship to work with the Dept. of Ed., would stop to speak with us. D.C. locals would walk through our event to examine our posters and our displays, as well as to listen to our speakers. Our event was well rounded with a visit to Bernie Sanders, educational assistant; a march to the White House; a visit with Arne Duncan's civil rights assistants; and time to meet, talk and figure out how we could support one another when we left D.C.

Stories

It was also crucial to share our stories. We had mic checks intermittently throughout each day. Teachers, students, parents, and citizens all came to the mic to express their concerns with the corporate reform that is dismantling our public schools. One of the most powerful aspects of the occupation was the opportunity for individuals to find their voice. So many of us have been silenced over the years, and then, to be handed a bullhorn and given the right to speak freely—let's just say that a moment like that can send chills up your back and a roar comes forth that you previously did not know existed. This empowerment of individuals is one of the most successful outcomes of our first occupation.

When we took the knowledge, relationships, and empowerment back to our respective local communities, we each became a force with which to be reckoned. There were lots of folks who shot us down, saying that the turnout was low in numbers. I believe that on our best day we had 50 folks in attendance. Was that a hard pill to swallow? Yes. Did it make us stronger for it? Yes. And we recognized that we were building the base; the solid, core base that would grow throughout the country. And it did. Videos of the event were created courtesy of Vincent Precht (aka CaliFather).[3]

Occupy the DOE 2.0

Occupy DOE 2.0 (2013) came about as a natural next step following our success of Occupy the DOE in 2012. We were gaining allies and friends, and momentum for ending the privatization of our public schools was increasing. We had opt out leaders popping up all over the country. Requests for opt out support had reached such extensive levels that we were spending every waking moment outside of our day jobs trying to assist individuals as well as opt out groups that needed organizational support. We honestly could not meet the needs of everyone. The grassroots movement was growing, and we were beginning to make solid contacts in many states to support parents and citizens who were fighting back.

I suppose I could relay the entire story of Occupy DOE 2.0, but I think the more important story is understanding the depths of organizing and the relationships and the power behind this event, even if, historically, this was not recognized or acknowledged in the media as a turning point in favor of the masses.

It's important to remember, at least for me, that our event organizing was mainly the work of six people. Six people. **I want to state that loud and clear because it is crucial that readers of this book understand what is possible in this world**. We must understand the power we hold, if indeed, we are willing to harness it and take action. While the first occupation was empowering, the second occupation was, where we, as the UOO team, came to recognize our strengths, but also, our weaknesses. We became wiser and also perhaps, more jaded. We realized that our work was truly just beginning. The second occupation was a wake-up call. We were no longer new to activism, we were now in the thick of it—the harder, at times brutal, and life-changing work.

As we gathered momentum for the second occupation, we jumped through the same hoops once again. We got the permits. We created our sound bites, our logo for the event, our theme, and we creatively circumvented obstacles like no electrical outlets for sound systems, and regulations galore about tables, banners, and trash removal. We truly had, once again, a "Who's Who" list of educators and citizens who stood on the right side of history. We sent out the following press release:

OCCUPY THE U.S. DEPARTMENT OF EDUCATION 2.0 The Battle for Public Schools

Administrators of the public education advocacy group *UNITED OPT OUT NATIONAL* are hosting the second annual event on the grounds of the US Department of Education in Washington, D.C. on April 4–7, 2013. We ask all of those in support of teachers, students and public schools to attend. The third day will include an organized march to the White House.

The event is a four-day gathering of progressive education activists endeavoring to resist the destructive influences of corporate and for-profit education reforms, which began in previous administrations and persist with the current one. We cannot and will not stand silent as the threats to dismantle our system of public education continue. These threats include the erosion of the teaching profession, excessive use of standardized testing, mandated scripted curriculum, the absolute disregard of child poverty, and reforms which disproportionately impact minority communities.

We ask that you join us, stand tall, and meet your responsibility as citizens to be heard above the din of corporate influence. You will have the opportunity to hear speakers and converse with public school advocates from across the country, including Diane Ravitch, Nancy Carlsson-Paige, Chicago Teachers Union President Karen Lewis, Stephen Krashen, Brian Jones, Deborah Meier, and many other students, teachers, and community members.

Do not miss this free and unique opportunity to connect with like-minded public school advocates. Come gather information and strategies that can be used to fight corporate education reform in your own community. Join us and make your voice heard.

And so once again we headed to D.C. to occupy. We kept our fingers crossed for good weather. We did our best to accommodate the needs of students, speakers, and citizens who were traveling at their own expense to attend this event. We dealt with the same naysayers who told us that if it wasn't well attended, the event could harm us in the long run. We tried to think of new ways to garner the attention of the media. We continually strategized, planned, and built our resources in order to make the event success. This time around we had more than a bullhorn, we had an full-on sound system. We felt ready. Our website announcement framed the effort this way:

Our goal this year is to share successful actions that we can take back to our communities and implement immediately to fight corporate education reform. Also, we are committed to our belief that the narrative must change— we must reclaim public education and preserve and improve real teaching,

Poster created by Jay Rivett from Occupy ART: Indiana.

real learning and acknowledge the importance of social and civic education as a right and a necessary component to caring communities within public schools. The business model of education is cold and defined by numbers. Education is messy. Teaching and learning are messy and involve human beings who must be nurtured and supported as individuals *who will be the future citizens of our country.* We cannot minimize them to "numbers" or "data" and we cannot attach high stakes to these numbers; this is harmful to our children, our educators, our schools, our community and our democracy. We are much more—come to D.C. and hear us roar.

And so the first day of the occupation came around. We lugged the speakers, the pamphlets, the art displays, the trash cans, the books—we set up "camp" with the help of other attendees, and found our home in front of the Dept. of Ed. in D.C. once again. There is a bench at the Dept. of Ed. in D.C. where we always stood to launch our day. Shaun was unable to attend the first day so the five of us: me, Tim, Laurie, Ceresta, and Morna lined up to give our greetings and begin the event. We each had planned short speeches, and this time we would be holding a microphone. I looked out at the crowd and once again, saw the low numbers. Low in numbers, I reminded myself, but not low in commitment. Here were folks from all over the country coming here to show their passion for public education. I swallowed hard and reminded myself why we were here. We were here because we had been silenced, we were here because someone had to speak up for the children. And we needed to speak up in a way that agitated and made the corporate reform leaders uncomfortable. Petitions, letters, and asking for a seat at the table wasn't working. We at UOO knew this, we knew that hardball had to be played. And now, once again, we were going to play it in their front yard. I grabbed the microphone, and this is what I said:

My name is Peggy Robertson. I am a parent, a public school teacher, and one of the founders of *United Opt Out National*. Welcome to Occupy DOE 2.0: The Battle for Public Schools. We are here for the next four days to collaborate, create action, build relationships, inspire, inform, and to tell the world the truth—and the truth is this. Our public school system, the cornerstone of our democracy, is being dismantled. Are you listening mainstream media? Our public school system—the cornerstone of our democracy— is being dismantled. And who's doing it? Here are a few names. ALEC, the corporations, the politicians, the billionaire boys' clubs, Michelle Rhee, McKinsey, Pearson, President Obama, and Secretary Arne Duncan. Our president's policies are privatizing our public schools. You'd think that the dismantling of our public school system would be the news scoop of the year wouldn't you? But when cash is involved, when billions of dollars can be made off the backs of those who cannot speak for themselves, and that would be OUR young CHILDREN, it seems that our message falls on deaf ears. We are here today to demand that this message be told. Parents everywhere must know that their children are now attending test prep schools. Our children with the highest needs, our children living in poverty—which is close to 25% now, suffer daily in schools stripped of resources, void of real teachers—our children are often kicked out of these charter schools or are denied entrance. These policies are racist and require our schools to Race to the Top and compete for resources. Our children are not learning how to be citizens who can problem solve and help a democracy thrive. They are being tested. One test ends, another test begins. Talk to the teachers here today. They will tell you. We have no time to teach because we are continually testing. These tests are high stakes tests—which means teaching to the test is the mantra, so when you are not testing, you are preparing for the next test. The goal under Race to the Top is more tests tied to scripted curriculum—all created by the corporations. The corporations are now teaching our children, our teachers have no autonomy. We do not need these tests. Teachers already know how to assess their learners. We are professionals. Mainstream media, end the mass amnesia, tell the public that teachers know how to assess their learners. And I must ask, do President Obama's children take these tests? Do Bill Gates children take these tests? No! Do their children's schools have the common core NATIONAL standards? Does their children's data get placed in a database which shares student data with for profit corporations? Oh no. These tests are not for their children. The common core NATIONAL standards and scripted curriculum that comes with it are not for their children. The InBloom database is not for their children. Their children enjoy creative learning; they enjoy art, music, PE, libraries, recess and beautiful buildings. Our children are fed tests purchased using our tax dollars. Here's another news scoop mainstream media. We don't have to take these tests. We can refuse these tests. We can refuse common core curriculum. You see, we can opt out. We can demand that our children receive creative learning experiences. We can demand that our children are assessed by teachers using portfolios, projects and presentations. And when we opt out of these tests and curriculum—the money trail ends. These are our schools. We pay for them. These are our children. We decide what is best for them. This is why we are here today. We at *United Opt Out National* will continue to tell everyone that we can end the dismantling of our public schools. We can reclaim our public schools and improve our public schools by refusing to play their game. We call for a nationwide opt out of all high stakes testing. Game over. We call for parents to refuse the common core curriculum. Game over. We must halt the harm being done to our children now. These people privatizing our public schools do not care about our children. This is about one thing—profit—profit using other people's children. We have one thing they don't have. We have numbers. There are many of us. And we are organized. We are smart. We are brave. And we do not negotiate with our children's lives. We call for a mass opt out. We WILL SHUT YOU DOWN.

And so, each of us spoke in turn. The crowd was small, but dedicated and strong. We had not all shared our pieces ahead of time. It had been such a rush to get into D.C. and to meet and greet many of the folks that had already arrived. When Ceresta got up to speak, we did not know what she planned to say. A portion of her speech was directed to the wrong-doings of the corporate reformers. And within that portion she referred to Michelle Rhee using words that angered many folks. I share this event because, as activists, sometimes we create very large bumps in our road as we move forward, and it's important to be prepared for such bumps, if indeed one can ever be prepared. While we are passionate individuals, we are far from perfect.

As organizers, activists, and friends, we found ourselves dealing with a complex situation that could easily have torn the UOO team apart. It did not. However, Ceresta's words soon became the focal point for the reporters and many who watched from afar, eager to criticize and ready to pounce. Our energy, which we needed, to focus on the 4-day event, soon became redirected to handle this situation. In retrospect, I recognized that part of our planning should have clearly included an opportunity for each of us to read one another's opening speech to see that we were all in agreement. However, we had each been rushing to get to D.C., we had no assistants to help us lug all of our gear to the site, nor did we have a press secretary to advise us on how to speak at the launch of our occupation. In addition, there is never a fully predictable lived moment; in a live speaking situation any of us is capable of deviating from a script. We were learning on the go, and sometimes that learning can be painful. In many ways, this was bound to happen in some shape or form. The press was chomping at the bit to find a way to discredit us. And as a team, we had to come together and find our way back to our roots, even when the honeymoon was over.

So I view the second occupation through a different lens than the first. The first occupation was exciting and we were green. The second occupation was where we, as a team, were forced to put everything on the table and see if we could continue to be a team. This is that moment when you look around and wonder, *is it worth it?* Why are we lugging these 50-pound speakers down to the Dept. of Ed. every day, only to meet a crowd of max 100 on our best day? Why are we spending our own money, sacrificing time with our family, and taking risks within our own careers, *for this?* **Is. It. Worth. It?**

And, then it hits you. The UOO team could break up. What if we are no longer friends in 10 years? Will every Skype meeting away from my family, in order to plan with the UOO team, indeed have been worth it? Or, on my dying day, will I look back and say, "That was a mistake. I wasted my time." Ultimately, I know I have done the right thing. I have done right by America's children. But the second occupation is where those questions began to lurk in each of our brains. And the sweet innocence of the new activist had been replaced with a wiser (sometimes wary) and honestly, better activist, because now we truly knew what was at stake. Activism is complex. For me, it is important to do what is right and true. It is important to be a good role model for my children, my community, and my country; but, doing so also comes with great sacrifice to those who are closest to you. And attempting to find that balance between the personal life and the activist life is forever a challenge. This moment for UOO is a moment every activist experiences; this is the moment when you move forward, or you take your ball and go home.

We moved forward. And the occupation continued. We announced speakers that should have been heard by thousands. Our speakers list included Bess Altwerger, Sam Anderson, Philip Arnold, Phillip Cantor, Nancy Carlsson-Paige, Chris Cerrone, Anthony Cody, Lauren Cohen, Matt Farmer, Alexia Garcia, Dave Greene, Nikhil Goyal, Michelle Strater Gunderson, Leonie Haimson, Melissa Heckler, Jim Horn, Jessica Hochmann, Sherick Hughes, Brian Jones, Denisha Jones, Alex Kasch, Stephen Krashen, Kevin Kumashiro, Barry Lane, Karen Lewis, Pamela Lewis, Malcolm London, Barbara Madeloni, Deborah Meier, Rick Meyer, Helen Moore, Mark Naison, Linda Nathan, Kris Nielsen, Dani O'Brien, Katie Osgood, Tom Poetter, Susan Horton Polos, Jessie Ramey, Diane Ravitch, Stephanie Rivera, Ruth Rodriguez, Stephen Round, Kim Runyon, Faye Rose Saunders, Sue Schutt, Jean Schutt-McTavish, Ruth Powers Silverberg, Ankur Singh, Diayu Suzuki, Henry Taylor, Lois Weiner, and Pam Zich.

And of course, the UOO team: Ceresta, Tim, Morna, Shaun, Laurie, and me. And finally, we were joined once again by Vincent Precht, who livestreamed the entire event. We requested that speakers send us their speeches; many of the speeches can be located as archived documents on our website.[4]

The second occupation was a bit different than the first in the sense that we did not even attempt to engage with legislators or any individuals at the Department of Education. Our attempts were futile the previous year so this year we decided to focus our attention solely on the individuals attending our event. Over the four days, we made more connections and strengthened our base, which, by the way, was growing bigger by the day. The event ended with a march to the White House. We had approximately 300 in attendance for this event.

Activists at the Occupy the DOE march on Saturday, April 6th, protested education reform measures including high-stakes standardized testing, school closures, and defunding. Photo by Dave Madeloni.[5]

Many ask us why we weren't able to gather a larger audience. We don't really have an answer for this. We contacted every media outlet at our disposal. We contacted the D.C. Teachers Union. I believe there are many reasons for the lack of attendance, but ultimately, speculation wastes energy that is better spent looking at the facts and planning our next steps accordingly—so that's what we did. We planned our next event and we watched to see the impact of our second occupation, which soon became clear.

The power of Occupy DOE 2.0 was evident in what happened after the event. While our event was indeed a powerhouse of activists gathering and organizing, the four-day event was instrumental in empowering individuals to head home and forge ahead in their own communities. As we hunkered down over the summer to plan our launch of the 50 (state by state) opt out guides, we watched as opt out groups continued to be created in states, cities, and in districts. The opt out movement was growing and it was clear that our occupation was the catalyst which allowed many to move forward. We listened as individuals e-mailed, called, and messaged on Facebook to tell us how the event was the launch pad for their own local events. According to one report by *The Nation* (Brown, 2013),

> Although it was small, the Occupy event revealed spaces of hope in the fight against corporate-style education reforms. A growing network of Facebook pages, blogs and Twitter feeds has given teachers that lack a local activist network or a supportive union a way to draw strength from a counter-movement. (para. 17)

While we, as a group, might have been battered and worn down, we recognized that it was worth it—and we stuck together and we moved forward, as always—with our eye on the ball. Our belief has always been that no data means no profit for the corporate reformers. We believe that together, the masses can take down corporate education reform. Now, as the opt out message began to spread, we could see it happening.

Protestors, including Francine Huckabey [front/center] march to the White House, Occupy 2.0, 2013.

And we began to rethink strategy. For two years, we really targeted build-ing relationships and sharing information in order to educate and create action. We also were a bit wiser at this point. We were now in our third year of activism and we were a family in our own way. We Skyped every Monday night and we now knew one another quite well. We watched with sadness as Laurie Murphy moved on in 2013 due to work reasons, but we welcomed Ruth Rodriguez as our newest addition to the UOO family. We had changed as a group. We didn't see any benefit in returning to D.C. with a bullhorn. It was time to leave D.C. and attempt a new approach—an approach that was targeted locally and very concrete in its actions. It was time to peruse the landscape and find a community in desperate need of support. That community happened to be mine.

Next Stop: Denver

UOO in Denver **poster by Shaun Johnson**

Denver had been a hotbed for corporate education reform for many years. We had multiple districts in need of help. Each district's needs were unique in their own way, yet we had commonalities that could bring the districts together in order to fight harder, stronger, and smarter. It was time to unify Colorado on one front. And we realized that we were ready to take our activist skills and our organizing skills to support one community as they created a hard-hitting campaign to reclaim public schools specific to the needs of one state. Because this was my community, I felt like a gift had landed in my lap. Also, because it was my community, I recognized that a lot of the organizing and planning would be my responsibility, so it was time to get busy.

We were no longer occupying, we were now creating an event with a focus on planning for action. We began by asking the Coloradoans what they wanted. I reached out to community members, students, teachers and parents to determine Colorado's specific needs as we structured the 3-day event. After many conversations, six key areas of need stood out clearly: reclaiming unions at the grassroots level, reclaiming school boards, understanding the basics of corporate education reform, creating a civil rights campaign, creating a legislative plan, and finally, determining solutions as we toppled corporate education reform.

It was a tall order. We knew that our skills as educators would be a strength in supporting the needs of Colorado. We knew how to create a democratic classroom, and so that is what we did. Our 3-day event in Denver was truly a democratic classroom in action. We created a facilitator's guide and brought in national activists from across the country to support the facilitation of each working group. This new organizational format was a great departure from our previous work as occupiers with bullhorns. But it was the right thing to do. As activists, we had always kept an eagle eye out and our hound's nose to the ground to be certain our work would lead to action on our departure. Colorado was prime for this—parents had been opting out all year, and citizens were ready to move and reclaim public schools for all children. They simply needed a base from which to begin. Just as we had created a space for a national base, we now were creating a space for a local base. The difference was that the local activists were already organizing and creating action. What they needed was a chance to unify as one—as Colorado. They needed time and space to create strategy as a state in dire need of support for those on the right side of history. It was time to quit reinventing the wheel in each district; it was time to recognize that each district could learn from one another as we shared experiences, built relationships, and formulated a plan of action.

Our three-day event was a time for each of the six working groups to plan and prepare their strategic timeline of action. We interspersed the work with some keynotes who we believed had a powerful message and the experience needed to push forward the work occurring over the three-day event.

We kept our schedule short and sweet, as summarized here:

United Opt Out National Spring Action March 28th to 30th Schedule

The minimalist schedule is intentional, as we want to be sure that the working groups are able to organize their time based on what they need to accomplish in order to have an action plan prepared for Colorado at the completion of our event. This three-day event is designed to create an action plan for parents, students, teachers and citizens to follow in order to reclaim our public schools with a keen focus on the following six areas: School Boards, Legislation, Corp. Ed. Reform 101, Civil Rights, Unions, and Solutions.

Our keynote speakers included: Sam Anderson, Angela Engel, Alex Kasch, Ricardo Rosa, Pasi Sahlberg, and Lois Weiner.

The facilitators had an immense job. Just as teacher must do, they needed to support the group but also allow the group to take the lead. We had many local and national activists support this process. They included Bess Altwerger, Sam Anderson, Tracey Bowen Douglas, Angela Engel, Stefanie Fuhr, Michelle Gunderson, Jeremiah James Henderson, Jim Horn, Rosemarie Jensen, Denisha Jones, Alex Kasch, Larry Lawrence, Rick Meyer, Monty Neill, Kris Nielsen, Susan Horton Polos, Becca Ritchie, Pasi Sahlberg, Carmen Scarfaro III, Rachael Stickland, Jocelyn Weeda, Lois Weiner, and Pam Zich. And of course the UOO team: me, Tim, Ceresta, Ruth, and Morna. Shaun was unable to attend and was sorely missed.

As a team, UOO had learned a lot over the last three years. In our fourth year of activism, we came to this event as a more mature, seasoned team. It paid off. Our intense planning worked. We began each morning and each afternoon with a keynote, and the remainder of the time was spent creating a plan of action with a keen focus on each group's target area.

We had some bumps along the way. As Pasi Sahlberg began his keynote, our venue's fire alarm suddenly went off and we all stood waiting to see if it was real. It was. For those of us who have become jaded due to sabotage in various shapes and forms over the years, it was hard for us to take the "an omelet caught on fire" story from our venue's contact person as legit. But after standing outside with a fire engine pulled up among the approximately 80 folks attending that day, we had to let things be and quickly get back inside to our event and Pasi's impending speech.

It is interesting to watch a community come together to do more than simply protest or listen. To watch districts with very different demographics, different views on politics, and varying reasons for fighting was a moment in Colorado history that only a few of us were privy too. It was ignored by the majority of news outlets. We did receive coverage from Fox News TV and *Chalkbeat*[6] online news coverage. Other than that, the Denver Post was clearly MIA as was NBC and CBS and everyone else. However, we are accustomed to being met with silence, but this in no way deterred us from firmly moving forward. We used social media to get the word out, and we planned to blog and blast the world with the news of Colorado's amazing work, until another very large bump, or should I say mountain, blocked our path.

On the final day of the Colorado effort, our website was inaccessible to any of the administrators of *United Opt Out*. We arrived early on Sunday to our venue and got online to post something on our website at www.unitedoptout.com. When we typed in our username and password, we were unable to access our own site. We had been locked out. After doing this several times in disbelief, I suddenly felt a bit queasy. Something wasn't right. I called our hosting site to determine what had happened. I was placed on hold while they did a little research. Not only was I unable to log in, I was also unable to see the site. They assured me that they could go back 24 hours and retrieve the site should anything be wrong. So I waited. When they got back on the phone the message had changed. They were sorry. The site was hacked. They could not help us. *The website was gone.*

I stood there in disbelief. Our website was gone. I really wasn't sure what that meant at that point. Was it gone, but still retrievable? Could we log in again at some point and fix it? What did that mean? We were also told that multiple user names were logging into the site. We had only one username and password. Based on our research into the destruction of our website, the hack job was not a typical hack job. It was an intentional and deliberate attempt to destroy our website—our public source of opt out guides and resources that were used daily by individuals and organizations across the country. As I stood there trying to process this, all I could think was, "*Someone has broken into our house and they have locked us out.*" My hair stood on end and I felt the anger rise in my body, as I knew that I was trapped. I was trapped outside while they wreaked havoc inside, and there was nothing I could do. And the day had to move forward. It was the final day of the conference. I had to get off the phone, acknowledge defeat at this point in time, and patiently wait for our moment to regain our website and our power to educate. Someone attempted to halt our work to inform and create action. It is our belief that they strategically planned the destruction on the final day of our conference, when we were full of ideas, energy and action—and of course right in the heat of the testing season. It was an attempt to take a pin and burst our bubble.

It did the opposite. We shared what had happened immediately with the attendees at our conference. We shared with Diane Ravitch and anyone else who we felt might get the message out. It went viral. Soon we had more publicity for our work than ever anticipated. But back to the conference, where the real work was happening, amidst the chaos that someone, or some entity, created in an attempt to halt our work.

The final day of the conference was each working group's opportunity to share their work and their next steps. When we planned the event, we had concerns about our ability to pull this off; the big question was, would each working group have enough time to form relationships, organize, and work together to plan next steps? We honestly didn't know, but that is the power of the democratic process—being okay with disequilibrium and being okay with not being in control. The people were in charge, and we were simply there to support them as they worked together, soon to be a force to be reckoned with in Colorado.

That final day is a historical moment in the history of public education in Colorado. As each group came forward to present, I couldn't help but smile at the many creative ways they shared their thinking. Some had created websites, others had PowerPoints, others had timelines, and all groups were prepared. I thought about what we wanted to see in our public school classrooms—and this was it. A true democratic classroom empowered, engaged, and action-oriented. Each group had worked through problems over the last few days, some more volatile than others. But they had done it. They had come together and Colorado's children and Colorado's communities were soon to reap the benefits. I also looked at the national activists who had come to Colorado's aid; we had approximately 30 national activists who had come in to provide support—not dictate or tell. Again, this is what democracy looks like. It's messy, it's unpredictable, and it makes everything possible.

When the three-day event ended, we in Colorado had a new family. An activist family. *United Opt Out's* goal had been accomplished. While Colorado moved on with their work, we at *United Opt Out* moved on with the rebuild of our website. Because I am in Colorado, I have been privy to both experiences. I can attest to the success of the UOO event because I am part of the activism that is now occurring here. It is action oriented, it is messy, it is strategic, it is well planned, creative, and full of heart, determination, and passion.

Our work at *United Opt Out* continues amidst the loss of the website. We raised money to rebuild the website within 48 hours. The media attention that our website hack job received could be considered positive, in the sense that our website was obviously regarded as a powerhouse if it was necessary to take it down. Realizing our impact simply fueled our fire to come back stronger. And as of May of 2014 (as I am writing this), that is exactly what we are doing.

There is something about an event that is needed in order to solidify relationships and determine future plans. Just like an event with relatives, many times well-planned activities go astray. Many times random happenings create new opportunities. The key is being there together, at the same time, to work through these pieces. Together, we can grow stronger. Together, we can solve problems. *United Opt Out* has gathered much strength from these events. We take this strength, and we send it back out, back home to the communities who can use it to topple corporate education reform.

And onward we push.

ACTIVIST'S HANDBOOK

1. Plan an event. Big or small—makes no difference. Planning an event will give you a sense of purpose and create relationships. It could be a house party where you simply share information. It could be a rally on the capitol steps. It could be a panel discussion at a library. Perhaps you organize an opt out letter-writing open house where you support individuals in completing their letters.
2. Organize the event carefully, whatever that event might be. Make sure you have a clear message and that the message is visible and understandable to the general public, via a pamphlet, a poster, or a speech. Make sure your team agrees on the message to be shared.
3. Have others help you organize—working alone can be challenging and honestly, less productive and creative. Make sure the work is dispersed evenly amongst the team. Remember, we empower one another. A strong team will make it much further than one who does it all.
4. Don't worry if the numbers are low at your event—whatever the numbers, be happy with the results and make sure you get every-one's contact information. Remember, you are building a base. If you are ready for it, call the media to attend. If you are ready, plan a social media campaign to publicize your event.
5. Make sure your event has a follow-up action. That action could be as simple as planning to communicate with the base that was cre-ated. Perhaps you all agree to write letters to the editor. Perhaps you go big and target an area to canvass and educate the community around opt out. Remember, the sky is the limit.
6. As your activist base grows, consider planning an event that occurs at the same time in multiple locations. Get louder.

NOTES

1. See Appendix for full bios of all speakers.
2. Our full schedule for the event can be seen here: http://unitedoptout.com/archived/occupy-the-doe-march-30-april-2-2012/

3. Videos from the event can be seen here: http://unitedoptout.com/archived/occupy-the-doe-march-30-april-2-2012/videos-from-occupy-doe-in-dc-2012/
4. http://unitedoptout.com/archived/occupy-the-doe-march-30-april-2-2012/speeches-from-occupy-doe-2-0-the-battle-for-public-schools-april-4-7-2013/
5. Original article and photo published in The Nation (Brown, 2013) http://www.thenation.com/article/173728/occupy-doe-push-democratic-not-corporate-education-reform

REFERENCE

Brown, A. (2013, April 9). At Occupy the DOE, a push for democratic, not corporate, education reform. *The Nation.* Retrieved from http://www.the-nation.com/article/173728/occupy-doe-push-democratic-not-corporate-education-reform

CHAPTER 5

TAKING ACTION

Shaun Johnson, Ceresta Smith, and Morna McDermott

Shaun Johnson

An Activist Handbook for the Education Revolution:
United Opt Out's Test of Courage, pp. 79–106
Copyright © 2015 by Information Age Publishing
All rights of reproduction in any form reserved.

Broadening the Conversation

Shaun Johnson

If the actions of *United Opt Out* (UOO) could be described in one word, then that one word is *responsive*. Our small organization, from its inception, always took a national view of the assaults on public education. We focused initially on the concept or action of "opting out," or boycotting high-stakes tests. But as we became more involved in the broader conversation on education reform, this turned out to be too myopic. This is not to say that the pivotal act of opting out was less important over time. Test refusal was now a significant part of a larger arsenal of resistance to corporate-style education reform.

In recognition that opting out was one of many methods of protest, perhaps one for which some public school supporters were not ready (namely, the large national unions like the NEA or AFT), UOO responded to numerous national crises in support of public schools. The UOO response took many forms and offered various suggestions, but we eventually stayed true to our origins by recommending a refusal or boycott of corporate reform mandates, whether it was implementation of scripted curricula or the administration of standardized tests.

Our métier as an activist group, so to speak, is withholding participation in the demise of public schools. Consenting to the apparatus of standardized testing, handing over student data, or narrowing teaching and curriculum that only prepares students for tests all feed into the potential for the privatization of public education. Disobedience of disagreeable mandates is key to asserting the professional autonomy of classroom teachers. Thus, for any issue to which UOO has chosen to respond, and there have been many, opting out of mandates, particularly standardized tests, is of paramount importance. Once the testing process is compromised, or held hostage, negotiations can begin over what is meaningful teaching and learning that preserve public schools and solidify the professional integrity of professional educators.

Our initial objectives for UOO were to provide information for opting out of standardized tests and to respond to various national education crises, or those that, in our view, were a threat to public education. Threats fall under a broad banner of "privatization," which to us means the infusion of economic (read: "for profit") ideals in what should be maintained as a public service. Market competition, school choice and school closures, and favoritism of charter school models fall under the purview of these economic ideals.

These objectives dovetailed rather serendipitously; that is, before we even chose the name UOO, we had no idea what we were going to do. In the very beginning, we were simply six individuals with an equally passionate disdain for high-stakes standardized testing. We were and are firm in our conviction that a boycott of standardized testing, very similar to an economic or consumer boycott of a certain product, is one of the only maneuvers left available to grassroots activists when up against very wealthy philanthropic organizations, like the Bill and Melinda Gates Foundation. Collectively, we did not believe that opting out of testing was impossible, nor a difficult concept to understand. The only thing missing was providing the information necessary to encourage parents, students, and ultimately teachers to give it a shot.

The first task was, therefore, to gather and publish the information. We did not just post the work of others or link to external reports or studies. UOO uploaded fresh content to our website. Under various tabs on the UOO website, we generated documents such as the "Get Tough Guide," brochures for dissemination at events and workshops, and lists of talking points for parents and teachers on important topics like the Common Core State Standards, of which UOO is vehemently opposed. Perhaps more than information alone, the documents also endeavored to give parents, for instance, the courage of their convictions. The information in our documents offered a vocabulary of sorts, words and phrases that convey strength. For example, in response to perceived threats, the "Get Tough Guide" states:

> The goal here is to demonstrate proficiency, and as a parent I have the legal right to request the use of a portfolio or alternative assessment to demonstrate, my child's ability. I will be the one to decide along with your expertise if remediation is necessary.

UOO also created numerous templates to encourage direct action with resisting standardized testing. These included documents on writing editorials in local newspapers, generic and customizable opt out letters, and parent flyers for distribution. Ultimately, we wanted to eliminate the possibility that inaction could be excused for lack of information. We provided the facts as we saw them, as public school advocates. It was thus up to communities and individuals to put that information to good use. These documents speak for themselves in terms of outlining the exact composition of our efforts.

We by no means concluded our goal of disseminating as much as information as possible in support of our cause. UOO is constantly revising and adding documentation as conditions on the ground change with new laws, mandates, or procedures. Our corporate reform opponents are adapting to the efforts of grassroots activists, so we must adapt as well. In time, however, our information gathering and communication coalesced into various campaigns against major education reform initiatives. These campaigns were largely waged on social media and online, with the exception of our "Occupy the Department of Education" and "Opt Out-Denver" rallies, which are detailed in another chapter.

United Opt Out believes that an effective strategy to redirect our nation's narrative around education reform, and to eliminate harmful policies and practices is to engage (a) in an *ongoing* manner, (b) actions that can be taken at *local and national* levels, that (c) are *open-ended* enough for all people to participate within their level of ability and circumstance.

What needs to be done in the aftermath of these campaigns is some honest reflection. What was their impact? Did UOO move the needle, so to speak? These are very difficult questions to answer, and maybe we will not necessarily like what we discover. Many of us fancy ourselves activists when we are passionate about a perceived injustice. An obsession with our own work puts those blinders up, shutting us off from the reflection necessary to judge our impact and adjust accordingly. No one can accuse UOO of lack of passion about public education. But our reflections here will certainly help the authors understand their own work, and we hope it aids the readers in considering their own efforts on behalf of public education.

Action: Boycott Pearson (Spring, 2012)

Morna McDermott

One of the first campaigns we launched was our Boycott Pearson campaign. This came about as the result of research we were doing, and others had been doing[2] (Ravitch, 2013; Schneider, 2014) on Pearson's far-reaching tentacles into every facet of education policy and practice. How does one stop the influence of a corporation so powerful and so ... *wealthy?* We decided that the best way to diminish Pearson's influence was by public exposure,[3, 4] which would affect their public image, and hurt them where it counts: their pocketbooks. We decided to call for a boycott of Pearson products, Pearson Boycott Part I. Soon after, Boycott Part II came about as Pearson's tentacles reached further—into teacher education and a new form of new teacher evaluations called edTPA.

Pearson Boycott Part I (Spring, 2012)

Pearson, ALEC, and the Brave New (Corporate) World Take a Stand Against Pearson Now!

Dear Supporters of Public Education,

A great deal of much-needed attention has been given recently to the role that ALEC has played in dismantling our democratic rights in favor of corporate profit. The institution of public education has not escaped the interest of

ALEC. In fact, ALEC has taken a seat at the head of the educational table, and is helping itself to an enormous piece of the educational pie, the key ingredients of which consist largely of citizens' federal and state tax payer dollars.

ALEC writes model legislation in educational policies that lend themselves toward privatizing public education and channeling money into the pockets of for-profit corporations. And where does all that money go? Aside from going toward the corporate-model charter schools in the forms of vouchers, per pupil funding and other special financial packages, a lion's share of the monies are going directly into the coffers of large textbook and testing publishing companies, including Pearson.

While the Pearson profit motive has been well-documented and is evident from a mere glance at their stock portfolio, one has to dig a little deeper to see the insidious ideological ties between Pearson, the largest provider of education related materials (read: textbooks, testing materials, test preparation materials, National Common Core materials and teacher training workshops ...), and ALEC. Some of Pearson's associations with ALEC **and/ or** other organizations with a **similar corporate-based educational reform agenda** include the following:

- Connections Academy—Mickey Revenaugh is a co-founder and executive vice president of the Baltimore-based Connections Academy, which operates online classes in numerous states.[5] She is the **co-chair** of the **ALEC Education Task Force. Pearson recently acquired Connection Academy.** Connections Academy was, and University of Phoenix still is, a subsidiary of the Apollo Management Group. CEO of **Apollo,** Charles, (Chaz) Edelstein, was Managing Director of Credit Suisse and Head of the Global Services group within the Investment Banking division, based in Chicago. He is also on the Board of Directors for Teach for America.
- America's Choice[6]—also recently acquired by Pearson. America's Choice is directly associated with Lumina, and the Broad and Walton Foundations, all active members of **ALEC.** They each promote educational "innovations" that favor corporate-model reform.
- University of Phoenix—According to Pearson's website: "Pearson Education and the University of Phoenix, the largest private (for profit) university in the United States announced **a partnership** which will accelerate the University's move to convert its course materials to electronic delivery" (May 18, 2001).[7]
- Bryan Cave LLP is the lobbying firm for Pearson.[8] Edward Koch is currently one of the partners at Bryan Cave. Edward Koch also conveniently sits on the board for StudentsFirst of NY, a state-level branch of **Michelle Rhee's** brainchild StudentsFirst initiative.
- Pearson also has a business agreement with Stanford University to deliver the Teacher Performance Assessment (edTPA) to more than 25 participating states. The edTPA is a subject-area-specific, performance-based assessment for preservice teacher candidates, centered on student learning. The edTPA was created by Stanford University faculty and

staff with substantive advice from teacher educators. The edTPA is led by Stanford University, American Associations of Colleges for Teacher Education (AACTE), and Pearson. The edTPA is supported by Pearson's electronic portfolio and electronic scoring (http://www.pearsonassessments. com/products/100000025/tpa-teacher-performance-assessment.html#tab-details). Pearson provides the administrative management skills and broad-based technology and delivery systems that will support the edTPA and bring it to **national scale**. Stanford University's Office of Technology Licensing (OTL) selected Pearson to provide these needed services for the edTPA.

- Sir Michael Barber[10] is the current Chief Education Advisor for Pearson. Research shows that Barber is a **powerful advocate for the free-market approach** to education including union busting, merit pay, and turning public schools into privately run charters.
- Pearson contracts with Achieve[11] to manage the PARCC assessments. Achieve is funded by Lumina, State Farm (both are members of ALEC), and The Alliance for Excellence in Education (AEE). AEE chairman Bob Wise is a regular contributor to and participant with the **ALEC** educational agenda. PARCC awarded Pearson a contract in January to develop a new Technology Readiness Tool which will support state education agencies to evaluate and determine needed technology and infrastructure upgrades for the new online assessments.
- The Tucker Capital Corporation[12] acted as exclusive advisor to The American Council on Education (ACE) and Pearson on the creation of a ground-breaking new business that will drive the future direction, design, and delivery of the GED testing program.
- The Council of Chief State School Officers (CCSSO)—CCSSO partners with a whole cast of other "nonprofit" organizations who promote a cor-porate anti-public education reform measures. CCSSO central "partners" include (among others) McGraw-Hill and Pearson. CCSSO Director Tom Luna (as of 2011)[13] works closely with Jeb Bush, whose associations with ALEC and corporate-reform are too numerous to mention.
- GradNation—GradNation[14] is a special project of America's Promise Al-liance, sponsored by Alma and Gen. Colin Powell. Grad Nation sponsors include State Farm (ALEC), Walmart Foundation (ALEC), AT&T (on the corporate board of ALEC), The Boeing Company (ALEC), the Pearson Foundation, and Philip Morris USA (ALEC). The GradNation Summit list of presenters reads like an ALEC yearbook.
- Gen. Colin Powell sits on the Board of Directors for The Council for Foreign Relations who issued an "Education Reform and National Security" report[15] (led by Joel Klein and Condoleeza Rice) which states, among other things, that: "The Task Force believes that though revamping expectations for students should be a state-led effort, a broader coalition—including the defense community, businesses leaders, the U.S. Department of Education, and others—also has a meaningful role to play in **monitoring** and supporting implementation and creating incentives to motivate states to adopt high expectations. **The Defense Policy Board,**

which advises the secretary of defense, and other leaders from the public and private sectors **should evaluate the learning standards of education in** America and periodically assess whether what and how students are learning is sufficiently rigorous to protect the country's national security interests." According to Susan Ohanian[16]: "In the introduction to the report Julia Levy, Project Director, thanks 'the several people who met with and briefed the Task Force group including the U.S. Secretary of Education Arne Duncan, Mary Cullinane formerly of Microsoft [Philadelphia School of the Future] [now Vice President of Corporate and Social Responsibility for Houghton Mifflin Harcourt], Sir Michael Barber of Pearson and David Coleman of Student Achievement Partners....' They were briefed by Houghton Mifflin Harcourt, Pearson."

- Pearson has partnered with the Bill and Melinda Gates Foundation to create a series of digital instructional resources. In November 2011, the Bill and Melinda Gates gave **ALEC** $376,635[17] to educate and engage its membership on more efficient state budget approaches to drive greater student outcomes, as well as educate them on beneficial ways to recruit, retain, evaluate and compensate effective teaching based upon merit and achievement (although we must note that Gates Foundation recently withdrew its support for ALEC under the heat of public pressure). However, their billions of dollars still flow to other far-reaching organizations dedicated to dismantling public education.

- The National Board of Professional Teaching Standards (NBPTS) is a private-sector member of **ALEC**. Bob Wise (Chairman, of NBPTS) and Alliance for Excellent Education presented on "National Board's Fund Initiative to Grow Great Schools" at the Education Task Force Meeting at the 2011 ALEC Annual Meeting.[18] According to the NBPTS website[19] they, "announced that it has awarded Pearson a five-year contract for the period 2009–2013 to develop, administer and score its National Board Certification program for accomplished teachers. Pearson will collaborate with NBPTS to manage its advanced teacher certification program in 25 certificate areas that span 16 subject areas" (para. 1).

- Pearson has also acquired partnerships with companies to deliver PARCC, SAT testing, GED testing, and was the central player (through Achieve) in the design of the National Common Core Standards. The GED Testing Service, while wholly owned by American Council for Education, entered into a joint venture with Pearson to transform the GED to turn services to some 40 million adult Americans (one in five adults), who lack a high school diploma, into huge profits.

We must make note that Pearson, while the biggest, is not the only bully on the block. McGraw-Hill is the other publishing giant that will benefit from its association with SBAC and made billions as the publisher of sanctioned and promoted reading programs (Open Court, SRA Reading Mastery) associated with the Reading First provision of NCLB. Of course, after billions spent on Reading First and the McGraw-Hill materials, the federally funded evaluation of the program showed no increase in reading comprehension by third grade (Shanahan, 2011). McGraw-Hill is also one of the biggest test publishers in the U.S. and publishes the CTBS, the main competitor of Pearson's SAT 10.

The legislation forced upon states to adopt the Common Core and associated testing measures essentially eliminates the power of consumer choice (supposedly a darling concept of the free market ideology) and requires that tax payer dollars for education be handed over to Pearson and McGraw-Hill as key providers of nearly all educational resources available to the schools. We find it frightening and ironic that Pearson, who profits off of public education to the tune of billions of dollars, is simultaneously run by and sponsors organizations that promote the destruction of public education. We are in essence paying for our own demise.

We are calling on all university and college professors to take a stand against the use of all Pearson and McGraw-Hill related materials. Please see our sample letter at the end of this document, which you may share to encourage others to refuse to buy their products and services.

Sincerely,

The administrators for *United Opt Out National* (Morna McDermott, Peg Robertson, Tim Slekar, Ceresta Smith, Shaun Johnson, and Laurie Murphy (with research support from Bess Altwerger, Professor of Education)

Boycott Pearson was a national campaign which we promoted across Facebook, Twitter, any social media site we could find. We received an e-mail from that Pearson employee, which led us to revise the original Boycott Pearson paper, though we contend that the majority of the "errors" and "corrections" required little more than a mincing of words or tweaking of phrases. This e-mail contended that we perpetuated many "falsehoods" about Pearson. Our favorite is this: (*United Opt Out*) asserts the organization (Pearson) is actively lobbying by drafting model legislation. Pearson has no other relationship with ALEC other than as a **non-voting member of their Private Sector Education Task Force**.

Oooohhhh.... That's all!!! Just an innocent "non-voting member?" Well, I guess that puts them in the clear. Whether they partner with, own, or are simply in cahoots with other corporate interests, the results are the same. Pearson cannot extricate itself from the implications of its involvement no matter how it chooses to clarify the details. That's where the devil resides, right?

Boycott Pearson Part II

We had come to know Barbara Madeloni when she invited us to interview with her on her radio show. We liked each other immediately. Then we were informed that she was in jeopardy of losing her job because of her refusal to participate in the UMASS edTPA program (see Winerip, 2012), largely because of its connections with Pearson and corporate reform. So we campaigned once again against Pearson. We crafted and promoted another letter and action campaign in support of her courage.

Dear Education Activists,

Continue the Pearson Boycott and defend Barbara Madeloni, a faculty member at UMass-Amherst, who is fighting to keep her job. She had the temerity to ask critical questions of the Pearson juggernaut, this time regarding student teacher performance evaluations. As a result, her contract with the university may not be renewed.

As the reader may already know, Pearson endeavors to control every piece of the public school pipeline, this time with the evaluation and certification of new teachers earning their degrees in education. Pearson wants all national tests based on its curriculum, taught by teachers their way. Enter the Teacher Performance Assessment (edTPA), a pre-service educator evaluation system assembled by the American Association of Colleges of Teacher Education (AACTE), the Council of Chief State School Officers (CCSSO), and Stanford University. While the edTPA was designed at Stanford University with teacher educator and K–12 teacher input, we raise our eyebrows at how quickly this initiative has moved in with a for-profit publishing company, one which conveniently also micromanages the SAT, the GRE and the National Common Core. Maybe Pearson doesn't "own" these enterprises (technically)—ALEC doesn't technically "own" congress either … right? Sure. It seems as if, given that Pearson is a British company, that we've taken to outsourcing our public schools.

While we might support a university-led initiative to improve how universities prepare future teachers, we cannot sit silently by and watch Pearson build a for-profit monopoly at the expense of quality education and institutional autonomy via their well-financed lobbying efforts.

Pearson's political, economic, and ideological ties go way deep with the corporate reform agenda: facilitating the privatizing of K–12 public education, increasing mandatory high stakes testing that has had negative impact on the quality of teaching and learning, and promoting the eliminating of collective bargaining for educators and support staff. Now, they have purchased the rights to co-pilot teacher preparation nation-wide and mandatory for many colleges of education.

Charter schools were once a teacher/student led initiative that had great potential.[20] Corporate reformers, their political allies, and their corporate entities such as Pearson, love to co-opt great educator-inspired ideas and twist them into forms of social engineering and profit making machines. With Pearson at the helm, what future awaits edTPA?

The edTPA will likely become an AACTE requirement for certification of programs to be permitted to educate new teachers. The Pearsonization of the American mind is nearly complete. We demand, therefore, that the edTPA's implementation and manipulation operated and controlled by

Pearson be questioned, as it (and thus Pearson) will be shaping what and how universities scholars and academics will be "free" to teach, and more important, what they will now be told by the corporate agenda NOT to teach.

So we pose some questions that we think must be considered and discussed:

- What research is being used to evaluate the usefulness of the edTPA, and research by whom?
- If a state adopts edTPA as a state-wide initiative and requires it for all state universities, why are universities required to use Pearson to evaluate their students' performances? Why can't the evaluation piece be kept in house? In other words, why MUST universities use Pearson?
- Is it ethical to give the reins of teacher preparation (nation-wide for all state universities for accreditation and teacher certification) to one sole for-profit publishing company? Don't we call that a monopoly? And is it right?
- Who is ultimately profiting from the administration and scoring of the edTPA?
- What do student-teachers have to say about being evaluated with a edTPA?
- What permissions and informed consent have been given to permit the current pilots of the edTPA in various states?
- Are there any opt-out provisions in place if students or faculty members do not wish to work with Pearson?
- What bearing will Pearson have on determining teacher education curriculum, what and how teacher educators are free to teach?
- Will edTPA's tight alignment with Pearson as a piece of state legislation tied to university accreditation lead to silencing genuine educational critiques of EdTPA by university faculty?
- What options can be used other than Pearson to implement and control edTPA?

This week, and in subsequent weeks, we ask all education advocates to send e-mails to Christine McCormick, Dean of School of Education at UMass, at cmccormick@educ.umass.edu and James Staros, Provost at UMass, at jstaros@provost.umass.edu. Ask them the above questions or your own. Forward us any answers you may receive.

It is our contention that Barbara Madeloni's potential non-renewal as a faculty member within the UMass system is not a mere coincidence. This is a direct assault on academic freedom and spreads a culture of fear across the educational landscape.

We may not have all the information; moreover, the jury is still out on the ultimate effectiveness of the edTPA. Before we ruin the livelihood of Barbara Madeloni and others, let's ask those in positions of authority to hold on a moment, slow down, and ensure we have all the information on this week's next greatest thing in education. We may soon realize that the edTPA is really not all that special and a newer, brighter, and shinier object will attract attention. Yet, while attentions are ephemeral, ruined careers and educations are not. They are permanent.

Work with us and ask Christine McCormick and James Staros to simply slow down and gather all the evidence before a corporation is allowed to ruin the lives of caring educators nationwide. It's time to get all education related polices and measures out of the hands of for profit corporations who have a conflict of interest. History shows that when people compete with profits that profits win out at the expense of social welfare. Educational policies and practices must remain in the hands of educators, both K–12 and higher education. We believe edTPA belongs in the hands of those who do not use education for profit. It belongs in the hands of professional educators whose only interests are in serving the needs of students.

Sincerely,

United Opt Out

Back to the Future

Here it is, now 2014, two years after we started the campaign. Pearson is still alive and thriving. Always "earning" (a phrase originally coined by Fred Smith of *Change the Stakes*). The reality is that it would have been nearly impossible for teachers themselves to actually boycott Pearson products in large fashion given that few of them have direct control over the books and curricular materials ordered for their schools. But the campaign did raise consciousness. And a host of actions everywhere were just heating up.

Pearson, Always Earning, phrase by Fred Smith.

We hope that our campaign helped shaped the narrative that would follow. So much has changed: Barbara Madeloni is now President of the Massachusetts Teachers Association. Faculty and students at Columbia Teachers College, in an effort led by UOO advocate Daiyu Suzuki, stepped up and challenged their university president Susan Furhman to cut her questionable connections with Pearson (see Joseph, 2013).

We were amused when "Pineapplegate" (Haimson, 2012) went viral. Campaigns all over the country have been amassing ever since. And most interesting of all, for reasons none of us at UOO can discern, the Boycott Pearson has reemerged in 2014. We are seeing links to our original press release and documents being posted on various social media. Peggy called me on June 1, 2014, and asked, "Did you send anything out about boycott Pearson?"

"No I didn't."

"But people are asking me about it!" she says laughing. "It's being posted in many places."

Well ... I guess it's taken on a life of its own. It's Frankenstein's monster. That's good. Because so has Pearson. And it will take everything we've got in our arsenal to take them down. As a reporter from a South Dakota blog[21] states,

> Getting schools to opt out the testing industry's profiteering won't be easy. Parents applying to exempt their students from the state's tests can face some serious backlash. Keeping the teacher evaluation system from falling into corporate clutches will take action at the ballot box.... But it's worth a shot. (para. 4)

The Union Campaign

Ceresta Smith

It Started in Summer 2012

It goes without a doubt that *United Opt Out National* is a staunch supporter of collective bargaining and the organized labor bodies that engage in this process. After all, it was via the organized labor process that laborers were able to advocate for and earn livable wages, safe workplaces, reasonable work hours, due process in the hiring and firing, job benefits such as paid leave and healthcare coverage, and the right to strike. In the past, public education employees have benefited from the collective bargaining process as the two national organized labor bodies, National Educators Association (NEA), American Federation of Teachers (AFT) and their state and local affiliates navigated through the waters of give and take to help— in the past—to establish state and national polices that served to provide public education employees with the aforementioned rights and benefits.

It only makes sense to maintain leadership that which has served laborers well, but when *leadership* begins to falter, one has to challenge leadership to do the right thing or step aside and let someone else take over. UOO challenged NEA and AFT leadership via a campaign that involved blogging, tweeting, and press releases as we pushed support for pro-public education policies and hard core "unionism."

The National Education Association (NEA) and the American Federation of Teachers (AFT) were engaging in anything but hardcore unionism when they capitulated on a premature endorsement of Obama at a time when he upheld the Department of Education policies that pushed market-based reforms that violated the essence of collective bargaining. These policies also violate sound pedagogy with their support of charters as well as sound pedagogy with its support of charters and money appropriated using a competitive process that designated winners by how much they agreed to destroy collective bargaining, teacher due process, and equity in education.

AFT President Randi Weingarten had spent that year urging local teachers unions to surrender decades of gains in collective bargaining. Her "model or template," as she put it, was an agreement in New Haven, CT, that stripped the contract to a handful of pages, gutted tenure and imposed merit pay that fostered competition rather than collaboration among teachers.

Similar deals ensued in Baltimore, Pittsburgh, and Florida as the AFT sought to prove itself as a "partner" with school officials and politicians who take their marching orders from corporate education reformers. Dennis Van Roekel, president of the far larger NEA, stumbled along behind Weingarten as budget cuts slashed union membership rolls and Barack Obama's Race to the Top legislation, which gave states incentives to pass laws that hit NEA affiliates with harsh new teacher evaluation systems, attacks on tenure and the proliferation of charter schools (Sustar, 2014, paras. 12–13).

Recently, former labor organizer, editor of *Jacobin* magazine, and the author of *Strike for America: Chicago Teachers Against Austerity*, Micah Uetricht, wrote a piece "Nice Unions Finished Last" (2014), in which he pointed out how conciliatory approaches from labor leaders result in tremendous loss. He criticized the labor organization UAW in its recent failure to unionize Volkswagen workers in Tennessee, and for good reason, he championed confrontation as opposed to conciliation:

> Unions must therefore operate with an ethos of confrontation, rather than one of collaboration; anything else renders them totally useless. If workers imagine unions as organizations that exist simply to facilitate collaboration— rather than, say, to engage in battle with employers in a fight for social justice for themselves and other workers—what good would a union do them? As in

this case, workers wouldn't see the point of joining them. When unions give up their combative role, workers lose. (para. 9)

It was unfortunate that both NEA and AFT engaged in and continue to engage in conciliatory behavior that was and is antithetical to the principles of "unionism" and equitable and quality pedagogy. In an effort to maintain an unhealthy relationship with the Democratic Party, many of their corporate benefactors created collaborative vehicles such as "the Teacher Union Reform Network (TURN), started by the American Federation Teachers" which was "later heavily funded by the Broad Foundation and the Gates Foundation" (Derstine, 2014, para. 5).

It begs one to question their legitimacy as advocates and defenders of public education and its employees. *United Opt Out* did just that prior to NEA's 2012 Representative Assembly as we began to publicize and coalesce around the need for both organizations to remember for whom they are working. In doing so, we posted a challenge to the NEA leadership on our website:

> We the administrators of *United Opt Out National*, in order to preserve a free and equitable system of public education in the United States, do solemnly issue the following challenge to the leadership, members, and ultimately President Dennis Van Roekel, of the National Education Association (NEA): We challenge the NEA to terminate immediately the pattern of negotiation and capitulation leading to policies destructive of public education, of children's lives, and representative of a derogation of educational professions. We see the most damaging policies as follows: implementation of an untested set of common standards, punitive high-stakes standardized testing, and the unreasonable evaluation and remuneration of professional educators based on these policies.
>
> We have come to the unfortunate and inconvenient conclusion that a failure of leadership and advocacy on the part of the NEA has led to the consideration and implementation of policies anathema to the preservation of a free and equitable system of public education. In reckless pursuit of profit, corporations and other philanthro-capitalist entities are transforming the educational mission of public schools in favor of training a compliant workforce. In feckless pursuit of compromise, the NEA has unequivocally failed in its mission to advocate for public education in favor of placating a privileged few.
>
> Should the NEA, its members, leadership, and President not accept this challenge, we will be forced to advocate for the erosion of support for the NEA and its mission, ultimately leading to its unfortunate, yet deserved, dissolution. Make no mistake: we do not negotiate with children's lives. Accept our challenge to, at minimum, introduce a resolution to the assembly denouncing high-stakes testing and the impending Common Core. If unaccepted, the NEA's eventual eradication as a legitimate organization in support of public education will be met with a bittersweet jubilation. (Johnson, 2012)

This action was met with a wide range of responses, from both those who supported us as well as those who did not. In hindsight, could we have phrased our call to action better? Maybe ... only to the extent that we did *not* intend to come across as a group who supported the dissolution of unions, and to some, our "call" was interpreted as a hostile threat to unions. In response to one critique of our effort (Klonsky, 2012) we felt the need to clarify our stance:

> The organizers of *United Opt Out* are 100% behind unions who are 100% behind their members! There is a difference between an enemy who WANTS to see our demise as fighters for public ed, and those who criticize or even dare challenge some of the efforts in a desperate attempt to SAVE the things we are fighting for from being sold up the river, or co-opted. Anyone who KNOWS the members of Opt Out knows this difference. I agree with you Mike that unity and coalition building are vital (in spite of misunderstandings to the contrary) but the question looming is—with whom should we build and with whom should we unite? Let us not forget that the push toward corporate reform is being done by corporatists, who have "friends" in their back pockets from BOTH sides of the aisle! The Democratic Party has brought us Michelle Rhee and Arne Duncan. Thanks. Yet teachers are being told from those who claim to have their back that they are being unrealistic in expecting the changes they are entitled to demand, and that we are supposed to be fighting for. Instead of forming official and public unity with groups who have proven their dedication to the elimination of corporate model reform, like Dump Duncan and SOS, and empowering teachers BETTER in their desires to opt out of HST, we are aligning with big powers and big money, neither of which have done anything to earn my trust. As the saying goes, "If you hang around a barber shop long enough you're gonna get a haircut." Solidarity = democracy = transparency. I stand with those who are fighting for public education, teachers, and children as their first and primary goal. (Response to blog post, July 6, 2012)[22]

Further down the comments sections we added more responses to the ongoing dialogue:

slekar July 7, 2012 at 6:37 A.M.

"You obviously don't like it that our union supports Obama. Does that make us a bad union?" I'm glad "your union" supports Obama. The union that I support would have no problem calling out the Democrats that have been complicit in selling out public schools, teachers and kids.

atthechalkface.com July 7, 2012 at 8:17 A.M.

I think it would be reasonable to ask the NEA to support education policies that buttress rather than undermine the teaching profession. So, taking strong stands against HST, common core, and Race to the Top are nice starts. Making out with the air Obama breathes when he's pushing these kinds of policies is not becoming of a so-called activist organization, which is part of the illustrious history of labor and trade unions.

Understandably, perhaps the message we wished to send was interpreted differently by different folks, and it took time and ongoing communication to explain what it was we were intending to say. But it certainly got folks' attention. And let's face it, that's half the battle. It opened up a space to have uncomfortable conversations about complex issues. It was suggested by a few UOO supporters that we "revise" our union statement. We deliberated deeply on this issue. *We* knew what it was we were trying to say. But the message came across to some readers as a threat to solidarity. We weren't sorry that we had called the NEA and AFT leadership out for selling their membership up the river. But did we really intend to alienate supporters or be perceived as "union haters?" No. Those who really *knew us* also knew better. We did *not* wish for the demise of unions, which are (or should be) a stronghold of labor rights. We had to consider that this message wasn't *about us*—it was about a message to, and about, and for *unions*, and we did not want to aid the agenda of Conservative anti-union advocates any more than we wished to endorse union sellouts. Could there be a third option? We wondered, What was the price of backtracking, and what was the price of refusing to amend our position? In the end we crafted a rebuttal of sorts, an addendum to clarify our position and posted it on our website.[23]

Following 2012, advocates for public education seem more willing to be critical and demanding of these large unions than they were in 2012. That 2012 was a presidential election year does not escape us either. I guess we simply spoke a little too soon for widespread acceptance. But since then, new resolutions, and "push back" from NEA and AFT membership is swelling.

The Battle Continues: "New Business Item 24" (Summer, 2013)

The following year for the 2013 NEA Representative Assembly, UOO concentrated efforts on getting a resolution passed that would designate NEA as an organization that supported the parental right to opt children out of testing that conflicted with parental beliefs or was considered inimical to the well-being of the child. Delegate and Bad Ass Teacher (BAT) Linda Myrick and Ceresta joined Delegate Manny Lopez's efforts to get the resolution passed. It did.[24]

NEW BUSINESS ITEM 24 *Adopted as amended*

NEA shall support the rights of parents/guardians to collaborate with teachers in determining appropriate options for assessment of student proficiency if opting out of standardized assessments, and advocate for their right to do so without retaliation.

Furthermore, NEA shall encourage its state and local affiliates to work alongside student and parent leadership groups in promoting opt out options wherever possible.

Lastly, NEA shall inform its members of current student and parent organization effort through existing communication vehicles. (Schmidt, 2013)

This NBI can be accomplished at an additional cost of $2,750.

United Opt Out reached out to NEA on July 31, 2013. We sent an e-mail (and press release) to all the national staff. We did not receive a response. Read here:

Our Letter to the NEA

For Immediate Release—

United Opt Out National Requests NEA to Join in Fight against High Stakes Testing Abuse

United Opt Out National Offers Expertise and Resources to National Education Association after Teachers Vote to Request Union Support for Opting Out of High Stakes Testing

Washington, D.C.—July 31, 2013—*United Opt Out National* announced today that it has offered to collaborate with the National Educational Association (NEA) in promoting and supporting the act of opting out of standardized testing.

This offer was prompted by the passage of resolutions at the 2013 NEA Representative Assembly that addressed the expansion of high stakes testing in public schools. The resolutions called for the NEA to affirm opposition to excessive and inappropriate high stakes tests, promote the opting out of such tests whenever possible, and assist parents and teachers to identify alternate and more appropriate means of assessment.

"For the past several years, teachers have watched as the focus on high stakes testing has impacted curriculum, restricted classroom activities, pulled students from classrooms, and created high stress environments," says Laurie Murphy, co-administrator for *United Opt Out*. "Teachers are finding it increasingly difficult to respond to the unique needs of their individual students or apply what they have learned through their years of education, professional training, and experience. Teachers have now asked the NEA for help. *United Opt Out* is proud to support that request by sharing our expertise and resources with NEA."

Since 2011, *United Opt Out National* has critically examined the impact of high stakes testing on students, teachers, schools, and learning environments, and has assembled a body of research concerning the negative consequences of high stakes testing on its website http://www.unitedoptout.com/.

This month, *United Opt Out National* published Opt Out Guides for each of the 50 states, detailing the current tests being utilized in each state; the impact of such tests on student access to programs, promotion, and/or graduation; the major entities that support or oppose education reform efforts; and the policies and procedures for opting out of testing.

Every day, *United Opt Out* is contacted by a new wave of people anxious to discuss the impact of high stakes tests. They have discovered that the sound bites and political spin used to promote education reform policies do not match the reality encountered in the classrooms. Parents, teachers, administrators, and even government officials—they all have questions. And they want answers. It's time for America to have a real conversation about education reform and its key tool for implementation: high stakes testing. *United Opt Out National* looks forward to working with NEA and its members to lead this important discussion.

For more information about the actions referenced in this release, the State Opt Out Guides, or to schedule interviews with the Administrators of *United Opt Out National,* please contact Peggy Robertson at (720) 810-5593 or via e-mail at writepeg@juno.com.

Now it's 2014. We are still waiting for both NEA and AFT to engage the grassroots effort on one hand,[25] but on other hand, time waits for no one:

The trend toward more militant teacher unionism remains modest, but it is significant. Reformers made inroads in the local in Newark, N.J., and progressive union leaderships in St. Paul, Minn., and Portland, Oregon, won solid contracts in recent months because they followed the CTU example, preparing for a strike with both internal mobilization and building parent-community alliances. Teachers in many other union locals don't hold union office, and won't in the foreseeable future, but they are having an impact on their unions by building militant, activist caucuses. Those groups have established a network that met in Chicago last summer and again at the Labor Notes conference last month. Plus, the emerging alliance of the CTU and UTLA will create a powerful voice for a more assertive brand of teacher unionism. It's noteworthy that Karen Lewis was slated to appear at the LA union's leadership conference in September.

After two decades of corporate school reform, privatization, degradation of educators and obsessive testing of students, there's an emerging alternative to the AFT and NEA leadership's strategy of collaboration at any cost. The challenges ahead for militant teacher unionists are many. But the fight back has begun. (Sustar, 2014, paras. 26–29)

Now It's 2015

Ceresta along with the election of militant, anti-market-based reform leadership in NEA's Massachusetts' state affiliate and AFT's Los Angles affiliate along with many other state and local affiliates around the nation are forming militant social justice caucuses. The fight back has more than begun. More and more educators are demanding their unions challenge rather than acquiesce. In a blog by Tanis (2014) posted:

> I have to wonder about the relationship between Core Knowledge, American Educator and the AFT, especially in light of the fact that the former editor of American Educator now sits on the board of Core Knowledge and another, Lisa Hansel (co-author of this article) is also a past editor of American Educator and is now the communications director of Core Knowledge.... Rather than becoming part of that web, American Education and the AFT must create a safe space for dissent and resistance to policies and practices that hurt learning, promote inequality, and diminish the teaching profession.

It is now on.

September of 2014, UOO administrator Peggy Robertson and I, in a published press release, called on national, state, and local union organizations to provide legal and material support to educators who refuse to sign rights and responsibility agreements and or refuse to administer or proctor district, state, and federally mandated tests. Our intent was and is to garner safe-haven and job protection for the growing number of unionized teachers who refuse to adhere to testing mandates that range from ethically challenged and poor pedagogy to actual child abuse. Aware of the liabilities involved in the probable and problematic ethic, human and civil rights violations occurring in high stakes testing; many brave educators, such as Alachua County Education Association (ACEA) member Susan Bowles of Gainesville, FL, are refusing complicity and culpability.

Bowles, very vocal about the apparent compromised ethical considerations of the Florida Assessment for Instruction in Reading (FAIR) on early childhood education students, pointed out many factors ignored by Florida lawmakers and education administrators and in a letter submitted to administrators, refused to administer the computer based assessment to her kindergarten students. Following her refusal, the district removed FAIR from the list of tests for early childhood education for the 2014–2015 school year (Smith & Robertson, 2014).

Soon thereafter, Peggy, in her suburban Colorado school district, publicly stated her refusal to administer the Common Core State Standards PARCC assessment for reading. It prompted *Washington Post* blogger Valerie Strauss to ask American Federation of Teachers (AFT) and National Educators Association (NEA) leadership if they would support their members who refuse to partake in administering tests. AFT and NEA both stated their past support of test administration refusal by educators. NEA went on to say they would support educators "who determine that a standardized test serves no legitimate educational purpose, and stand in solidarity with their local and state association to call for an end to the administration of that test in their schools," while AFT stated that "teachers are the canaries in the coal mines, and we support their advocacy" (Strauss, 2014).

During the 2014 Florida Educators Association delegate assembly in October, a resolution and a New Business Item were passed that support the parental right to opt out of high stakes testing and "local union support to defend every local union's right to engage in collective, concerted, and constitutional activities as set forth in Florida law and the Florida constitution, including the right to voice objections to, and to mobilize and organize against, unsound educational practices" along with solidification of "community support to shield an individual teacher from punitive actions by a school board or the Florida Department of Education" (Robertson, 2014). UOO is hopeful that other state and local unions will pass similar measures.[25]

Our Declaration of Independence (Summer 2013)

Shaun Johnson

Testing "season," so to speak, ends for many teachers and students during the months of March and April. After that, educators typically keep their heads down in order to make the final push to end the school year sometime in June. Activist moments are fewer and farther between in those summer months, so our organization sought to try something different to keep momentum going. We decided to jump on the patriotic coattails of the July Fourth holiday to "declare our independence" from corporate-style education reforms.

This continued the general theme of UOO, which is to boycott or refuse prevailing education reforms. We, as professional educators, assert our professional autonomy in the face of standardization. All we seek for educators is to free them from unreasonable mandates, based on junk science, in order to be able to teach, which is what they were presumably educated to do. In our collective conversations with thousands of educators, and from our own experiences, current mandates, namely, high-stakes testing, prevent rather than stimulate innovative practice.

Co-opting the original Declaration of Independence and its language seemed like an interesting project for us. It seemed creative and something we could easily promote and share on social media. This Declaration from Corporate Education Reform consisted of two main components: the Declaration itself and a couple of online videos that we produced. For the written document, we decided to "indict" the Secretary of Education Arne Duncan in a similar fashion to revolutionary-era monarch King George III. This is not to say that Mr. Duncan is necessarily responsible for all that is contemporary education reform. It would drastically overestimate his overall impact. Targeting Mr. Duncan in this way, however, is more symbolic, since he is the current executive in charge of education policy in the United States.

Our Declaration borrowed most of the language of the original document. The various grievances were all that needed moderate adjustment. Additionally, we purposely left out any modification of the line, "We hold these truths…," because of its iconic status. To amend that line for our cause would strain credulity, and there was no way we could do it justice. The following is the full-text of our Declaration:

IN OPPOSITION, July 4, 2013

The Unanimous Declaration of the National United Opt Out,

When in the course of educating a nation, it becomes necessary for its people to restrain the political and private powers which have obfuscated the fundamental mission of a public system of education to, among other points, compensate for the proclivities of the Laws of Nature to separate and exclude swaths of humankind into those that have and those without.

That to secure this broad mission of a public education, Governments are commissioned by its people to serve unequivocally the explicit needs of those to be educated. It is not to relinquish control of the purposes of education to incorporated powers which deign the will of a free People to determine the means and ends of their cultural developments.

Whenever any Government or Agent of the State abrogates the responsibility to defend the general preparations of its future citizens from untoward profit-making, it is the Right of the Educated to alter or to refuse impositions, and to institute a new Education, laying its foundation on principles and powers to most likely effect their Autonomy, Freedom, and Happiness.

Love, indeed, will resolve that a public system of Education long established should not be upended for fickle and makeshift designs, and accordingly all experience has shown, that an aspirational People are disposed to trust, as certain evils are trustworthy, when impossible oaths are expressed as guarantees of accomplishment. That such promises are made by representatives of the Education State, to whom its People have become accustomed, is the most perverse injury of all.

But when a long record of exploitations and failures, in pursuit of objectives that evince a design to reduce the Educated to absolute Quantification, in effect leading to total economic Exploitation, it is their right, it is their obligation, to refuse such Education, and to provide new Custodians for their future achievement. Such has been the persistent sufferance of the Educated, particular to Inhabitants of the most meager of circumstances; and such is now the requisition which prohibits them from amending their rightful System of Education.

The history of the present Secretary of Education, of his maids of State, and sycophants in unelected offices, is a history of recurring ignorance and ineptitude, all having in ultimate purpose the reduction of the Educated to singularly objective values that are inherently valueless. It is with this Ignorance and Ineptitude that the current Government wields an inseparable Autocratic alliance between Incorporated and State interests against the wishes of the People.

To prove this, let United Opt Out submit these Facts to a candid world:

He has refused to reduce inequality and segregation, the most unwholesome and unnecessary for a public Education.

He has constrained the role of professional Educators and contributed to their egregious humiliation in the face of unreasonable scrutiny from the State.

He has ignored significant corrective actions necessary to diminish disparities in opportunities, resources, and human capital in Education as sanctioned by the Fiscal Fairness Act.

For refusal to recommend other Laws or Regulations for the Rightful accommodation of large groups of students, principally second language, impoverished, and students of color, unless Schools relinquish the autonomy of Educators and control of their Curriculum, needs inestimable to them and formidable to ideologues only.

He condones through inadequate and narrow investigations a professional culture of Lying, Cheating, and Exploitation within School communities.

He has endeavored to prevent School populations from selecting refusal of specific Federal impositions that hinder local needs from an erroneous Competition for funds, such that these limited monies could not possibly repair previous and egregious breaches in support, that otherwise bind Schools and Districts to compliance.

For taking away our traditional public Schools in favor of Charters, altering our most valuable laws to hasten dissolutions, and altering fundamentally the Forms of our Local Boards to enact control of Mayors as opposed to the People expressly.

For Accommodating large bodies of unprepared Educators among us.

For protecting them, by granting certain exceptions, from qualification for any Educator position which they hold in the most challenging Schools.

For imposing Subsidies on public School systems to sponsor amateurs.

For shielding open Educator positions, that should otherwise be available to qualified candidates, for provisional Recruits.

He has excited insurrections amongst us, and has endeavored to bring on the inhabitants of our cities against each other, setting as rivals the poor against the poor, to become executioners of their own friends and Brethren, to fall themselves by their Hands, to enable the affluent in escaping responsibility.

He has affected to render Corporations independent of and superior to the Civil power.

He has exacerbated the conditions dissolving elected Boards repeatedly, for opposing with effete vacillation his encroachment on the rights of the people.

He has denied sufficient protections to confidential information gathered by private entities in the process of public Education; ignored the apprehensions expressed by the caregivers of the students of our public Schools therein; and perseveres in implementation of diffuse collection methods in defiance of personal Privacy.

For conscripting the publicly Educated into labour on behalf of Private entities to refine the instruments of our own Oppression; not for the re-investment of knowledge and resources acquired, but to enrich the remunerative coffers of speculators.

He has abdicated Government in the defense of public Education by declaring Accountability greater to Preservation, and waging Wars of Attrition against us.

In every stage of these Oppressions We have Petitioned for Redress in the most humble terms: Our repeated Petitions have been answered only by repeated injury. A Secretary of Education whose character is thus marked by every act which may define a Profiteer, is unfit to be the warden of a Public lavatory let alone a free system of Public Education.

Nor have We been wanting in attentions to our Private brethren. We have warned them from time to time of attempts by their Board members to extend an unwarrantable jurisdiction over us. We have reminded them of our Allegiance to the public in Education. We have appealed to their assumed senses of innate justice and fairness, and we have summoned them by the ties of our common citizenship to disavow these usurpations, which would inevitably interrupt our cooperation and camaraderie. They too have been deaf to the voices of equality and solidarity. We must, therefore, submit to this necessity, which denounces our Disobedience, and hold them, as we hold us all, Enemies in War, in Peace Friends.

We, therefore, the Administrators of the national United Opt Out, in General Congress, Assembled, appealing to the free people of this Nation for the integrity of our intentions, do, in the Name and our Authority, defiantly publish and declare, That our public systems of Education are, and of Right ought to be, Absolved from any and all Obligations, Oppressions, and Exploitations set forth only by Private and Unelected Associations; that we assert the abilities to Choose and Refuse certain Acts and Things that violate the interminable conscientiousness of professional Educators; and that as Discerning and Intellectual personnel, charged with labors few are wont or capable to do, we have full Power to secure our own professional identities, determine to Whom and under what conditions for which we are Accountable, and succeed with significant voice to govern the Laws of our work.

And for support of this Declaration, with a firm reliance on the protection of Good Sense and a Common Destiny, we mutually pledge each other our Lives, our Fortunes and our Sacred Honor.

To complement the document, we also created two online videos,[26] one a "teaser trailer" in anticipation of the Declaration's release and a longer, full-text choral read of the text. Both of these videos are viewable on our website.

In the end, the impact of this campaign could be described as "unresolved." It is certainly possible that UOO can recycle these efforts every Independence Day, extending its potential reach. We were not seeing desirable results from this effort, or those that we could necessarily measure. On a more superficial level, the videos we created did not receive a significant number of views on YouTube or our website. We did not see a tremendous amount of traffic regarding our Declaration. Although we were pleased that some advocates (see Ravitch, 2012) were promoting our campaign, its overall sharing on social media was tepid. It did not seem to resonate with our fellow activists.

It is perhaps possible that there exist some immeasurable results of the Declaration campaign. Since imitation is the sincerest form of flattery, or so they say, then perhaps we will see some imitators this time around. In addition, we can double our efforts in sharing and promoting the Declaration since our network has expanded greatly since it was first created a year ago.

In the end, this era of quick 5-second Vine videos, bumper sticker politics, memes, and other forms of "sloganeering" might not be ideal for a roughly 1,300-word document. Maybe it's simply too much to ask of people considering how much information is changing hands daily. On an interesting political note, our Declaration may resonate more with the conservative movement, given their strong affinities with patriotism and our country's founding documents. In recent weeks and months, right-wing conservative opposition to, for example, the Common Core State Standards is growing more prevalent by the day. This would necessitate a greater effort by UOO to reach out to right-wing activists and their online communities in order to share our Declaration campaign materials. We may ultimately pique their curiosity. But if our more conservative brothers and sisters decide to delve a bit more deeply into what UOO is all about, the Declaration might be where our relationship ends. Time will tell.

ACTIVIST WORKBOOK

1. Radical activism requires risk taking. Be prepared for an effort to fail, to be hijacked, to be misunderstood, or to seem divisive.

The only way to avoid these risks is to remain neutral and avoid controversy, but then, what exactly has been accomplished? Carefully consider what risks you can afford to take and those you cannot. Consider what possible outcomes or reactions you might anticipate from others. What's the best that could happen? What's the worst that could happen? And leave room for the unexpected to occur.

2. Strategy is key. Is the action long term or short term? What does it demand of folks? What will it demand of you? Messaging and organizing the steps or sequence are key too. See Laurie Murphy's advice in Chapter 8 of this book for more advice on how to create effective strategy.

3. Play to the strengths of those helping on the action. Who is the strategist among you? Who is the publicity monger? Who is the researcher? Who is the time keeper? Who knows graphics or technology? If the action includes violations of the law, make sure you plan for what do to if you are sued or arrested, *ahead of time*.

NOTES

1. http://unitedoptout.com/essential-guides/get-tough-guide/
2. http://www.huffingtonpost.com/alan-singer/
3. http://www.schoolsmatter.info/2012/04/join-national-boycott-against-pearson.html
4. http://www.susanohanian.org/outrage_fetch.php?id=1290
5. Read more, see Carey (2011).
6. http://www.ncee.org/programs-affiliates/history/americas-choice/
7. http://www.pearson.com/news/2001/may/pearson-education-and-the-university-of-phoenix-collaborate.html?article=true
8. http://reporting.sunlightfoundation.com/lobbying/firm/bryan-cave-llp/32849A23-FB4B-4DD8-9227-8A70A0BBC058
9. http://www.pearsoned.com/stanford-university-and-pearson-collaborate-to-deliver-the-teacher-performance-assessment-tpa/#.U5OCAfldVuo
10. Sir Michael Barber published *Deliverology 101* in 2011 to serve as a comprehensive guide to education system reform and delivery. Governments and large public organizations have systematically adopted the "deliverology" approach and realized quick impact and significantly improved outcomes to their reform programs. In the summer of 2010, Sir Michael Barber teamed with leaders from the Education Trust (also funded by the holy trinity Eli Broad, Walton, and Lumina) and Achieve (funded by State Farm and Lumina) to found the U.S. Education Delivery Institute (EDI).
11. http://achieve.org/about-us
12. *Enhanced GED Testing Program Will Validate Career- and College-Readiness* http://tuckercapital.com/TC_News_ACE.html

13. http://www.ccsso.org/News_and_Events/Press_Releases/CCSSO_Welcomes_New_President_and_Board_of_Directors.html
14. GradNation Summit at http://www.americaspromise.org/Our-Work/Grad-Nation/Summit/~/media/Files/Our%20Work/Grad%20Nation/2011%20Summit/BGN%20Summit%20Agenda_3-18-11.ashx
15. The Council on Foreign Affairs report was also written by: Joel Klein, Chancellor of NYC schools, former Secretary of State Condoleeza Rice, ACT, Common Core author David Coleman, Secretary of Education Arne Duncan, Teach for America's Wendy Kopp, the American Enterprise Institute's Rick Hess, Stand for Children's Jonah Edelman, and Pearson. See http://www.huffingtonpost.com/2012/03/19/schools-report-condoleezza-rice-joel-klein_n_1365144.html?ref=education
16. http://susanohanian.org/outrage_fetch.php?id=1248
17. See http://www.care2.com/causes/bill-gates-gives-alec-big-to-reform-education.html?page=1
18. http://www.sourcewatch.org/index.php/ALEC_Education_Task_Force
19. http://www.pearsonvue.com/about/release/archive/08_03_03_nbpts.asp
20. http://jaxkidsmatter.blogspot.com/2011/12/miami-heralds-investigation-into.html
21. http://madvilletimes.com/tag/pearson-education-inc/
22. http://michaelklonsky.blogspot.com/2012/07/big-push-for-unity-at-nea-meeting.html
23. The original documentation of this rebuttal was lost when our website crashed in 2014 and is therefore no longer available.
24. http://www.nea.org/assets/docs/2014-NEA-Handbook-New-Business.pdf
25. Additionally, president of the Tulsa Classroom Teachers Association and a member of the National Education Association board of directors Patti Ferguson-Palmer is showing support for Tulsa. Oklahoma first grade teachers, Miss Karen Hendren and Mrs. Nikki Jones who declared their refusal to administer standardized tests to their students.
26. http://www.youtube.com/watch?v=oH6IDt9JHqg

REFERENCES

Carey, D. (2011, September 15). Apollo exits Connections Education via $400M sale to Pearson. *The Deal Pipeline*. Retrieved from http://www.thedeal.com/content/private-equity/apollo-exits-connections-education-via-400m-sale-to-pearson.php#ixzz1sSFSzLK0

Derstine, K. (2013, February 23). Who is Eli Broad and why does he want to destroy public education and turn teacher unions into company unions? *Substance News*. Retrieved from http://www.substancenews.net/articles.php?page=4016

Haimson, L. (2012, June 6). The lessons from Pineapplegate. *WNYC Schoolbook*. Retrieved from http://www.wnyc.org/story/301545-the-lessons-of-pineapplegate/

Klonsky, M. (2012). A big push for unity at the NEA meeting. *Mike Klonsky's Small-Talk Blog*. Retrieved from http://michaelklonsky.blogspot.com/2012/07/big-push-for-unity-at-nea-meeting.html

Johnson, S. (2012, June 21). A draft of a challenge to the #NEA to be delivered soon. Patience, my dears. *The Chalk Face*. Retrieved June 10, 2014, from http://atthechalkface.com/2012/06/28/a-draft-of-a-challenge-to-the-nea-to-be-delivered-soon-patience-my-dears/

Joseph, G. (2013, June 13). Teachers College students urge president to cut ties with Pearson. *In These Times*. Retrieved from http://inthesetimes.com/uprising/entry/15138/teachers_college_students_urge_president_to_cut_ties_with_pearson

Ravitch, D. (2012, July 8). "Declaration of Independence" by *United Opt Out*. *Diane Ravitch's blog*. Retrieved from http://dianeravitch.net/2013/07/08/declaration-of-independence-by-united-opt-out/

Ravitch, D. (2013). *Reign of error: The hoax of the privatization movement and the danger to America's public schools*. New York, NY: Knopf.

Robertson, P. (2014, October 18). Florida alert: FEA passes NBI & resolution supporting teacher refusal of test & parent/student opt out. Retrieved from http://www.unitedoptout.com/2014/10/18/florida-alert-fea-passes-nbi-resolution-supporting-teacher-refusal-of-test-parentstudent-opt-out/

Schmidt, G. (2013, July 10). Parental "Opt Out" gets national support! NEA adopting resolutions opposing "excesses" of high-stakes testing and Common Core. Retrieved from http://www.substancenews.net/articles.php?page=4389

Schneider, M. (2014). *Chronicle of echoes: Who's who in the implosion of American public education*. Charlotte, NC: Information Age.

Shanahan, T. (2011, June 2). Comparing Common Core and Reading First. *Shanahan on Literacy*. Retrieved from http://www.shanahanonliteracy.com/search/label/Reading%20First

Smith, C., & Robertson, P. (2014, September 29). UOO calls on unions to support teacher refusals to administer tests. Retrieved from http://unitedoptout.com/2014/09/28/uoo-calls-on-unions-to-support-teacher-refusals-to-administer-tests/

Strauss, V. (2014, October 6). Unions say they will back teachers who refuse to administer mandated standardized tests to students. Retrieved from http://www.washingtonpost.com/blogs/answer-sheet/wp/2014/10/06/unions-say-they-will-back-teachers-who-refuse-to-administer-mandated-standardized-tests-to-students/

Sustar, L. (2014). A fork in the road for teachers' unions? *Socialistworker.org*. Retrieved from http://http://socialistworker.org/2014/05/14/fork-in-the-road-for-teachers

Tanis, B. (2014, June 12). AFT's American Educator: Voice of the rank and file or tool of the reformers? *The Chalk Face*. Retrieved from http://atthechalkface.com/2014/06/12/afts-american-educator-voice-of-the-rank-and-file-or-tool-of-the-reformers/

Uetricht, M. (2014, February 22). Nice unions finish last. *Al Jazeera America*. Retrieved from http://america.aljazeera.com/opinions/2014/2/unions-volkswagenunitedautoworkers.html

Winerip, M. (2012, May 6). Move to outsource teacher licensing process draws protest. *New York Times*. Retrieved from http://www.nytimes.com/2012/05/07/education/new-procedure-for-teaching-license-draws-protest.html?pagewanted=all&_r=0

CHAPTER 6

EVERY NARRATIVE HAS A LENS

The Value of Social Justice

Ceresta Smith and Morna McDermott

Traversing a Shifting Terrain

Morna McDermott

Maybe I was simply naïve as a child and continue to be naive in my adulthood. I grew up firmly believing in a sense of social justice. As my education deepened I welcomed challenges to examine my own "Whiteness" and privilege. I screwed up along the way. I still do. But I am committed to living a social justice project. When I arrived at the place of being a "boots on the ground" public activist in 2011 (beyond the comforts of my own four classroom walls and my own students), I realized just how complex the world of "fighting for social justice" can be. It was easy enough to preach it in my college classes, to assign Jonathan Kozol and conduct *Theater of the Oppressed* (Boal, 1993) strategies in classrooms and at conferences. But "out here" the terrain becomes far more difficult to traverse. How does one stay true to values of ethics, equity, and justice when what those ideals "look like" are shifting beneath your feet? The number of voices, struggles for power, identities, and even egos came crashing in around me. How do I remain open to change, flexible to new realities, amenable to collaboration, and aware of how my own race and privilege intersect with my voice or perspectives in these matters, when standing upon a public platform? I say I was naïve because it was easy to assume that my perspective about what was "right and fair" was well ... what everyone else fighting for the same broad set of values wanted as well. Because I was coming at the opt out movement from the angle of justice, equity, and democracy for ALL children, I assumed that, well ... shared by everyone else. Because I was coming I had no idea what I was in for or how to negotiate this strange new world.

Opting Out for Public Education or Opting Out of Public Education?

Our first struggle on this issue arose right as we were coming out of the gate in August 2011. Within 24 hours of our Facebook site being up and available, we realized that there were many outspoken voices swarming the conversation on "opting out," and many of these voices were rather contrary to our own views and values. There was this whole world out there of organizations and individuals who supported the action of testing refusal, yet their general ideology seemed tethered to the desire to eliminate public education altogether.

We Have Just Lost Altitude

This became an issue of social justice for us because we knew how corporate reformers and profiteers were using the "anti-public school" (co-opting voucher, charter, and home school) rhetoric to advance their own agenda to privatize public education. The "founding fathers" of the American Legislative Exchange Council (ALEC) themselves (Charles Koch and Paul Weyrich) made the elimination of public education a large piece in the privatization-for-profits ALEC pie. They fund the spread of this narrative using language like "government run schools" and slogans like "home school your kids!" to manipulate public sentiment. Eric Heubek,[1] acolyte to Weyrich wrote,

> We will use *guerrilla tactics* to undermine the legitimacy of the dominant regime. We will take advantage of every available opportunity to spread the idea that there is something fundamentally wrong with the existing state of affairs. For example, we could have every member of the movement put a bumper sticker on his car that says something to the effect of "*Public Education is Rotten; Homeschool Your Kids.*" (2001, para 21; author's emphasis)

We knew that the debates warring on our fledging Facebook site were about more than simply an articulation of different personal opinions. And while we were quite sure that most folks supporting homeschooling were just that—parents advocating for their personal values—there remained a deeper ideological agenda being promulgated via trolls and agitators. And we knew we had reason to be concerned. How does this "eliminate public education" narrative affect our social justice stance? On September 10, 2011, three weeks into our existence, Ceresta stated it plainly in a comment she offered to someone on Facebook:

> There are too many children out here to think that [homeschooling] is the answer for the majority! I do not think you are being realistic about "choice." First and foremost, do you know how many children there are in the U.S. that need to be educated? Charter schools with 100–500 pupil maximums and private schools that boast of ... small class sizes and high tuitions will never be able to school all these children. Most adults work these days, so that limits the number of home schoolers. I wish one of you that are so into promoting choice can tell me where the hell all these children will go to school? I agree reform is an old tired out tag, but public school is public school. Taking taxpayers' money and channeling it into all these stupid experiments and exploitative reforms is crazy. Just fund the damn system w/o compromising teacher working conditions or local autonomy, support teacher training and quality pay, support the magnet/academy approach, get these schools integrated, stop the stupid high stakes testing, stop the racist inequities in curricula, get rid of all the damn profit making motives, put some damn recess and gym classes back in the mix, and call it a damn day!

We debated deep into each sleepless night of those early UOO days, worried that we would either alienate people we wished to support or conversely, that our own values might wind up hijacked by another narrative that was counter to the one we were just beginning to voice. Social media trolls and hijackers have a great way of forcing you to articulate where you stand. And what you *will not stand for*. After many e-mails and phone calls between us, we decided that we had to ban some of these agitators as it was clear their intention was to hijack the mission and purpose of the site. We asked repeatedly that posts remain focused on opting out of tests.

When we made our counterargument, that this group was "for" public education, and that we were opting out to support public schools and public teachers, and *politely* requested that the narrative around eliminating public education as a solution be taken elsewhere, we were soundly and routinely attacked for not being "open" to multiple opinions—opinions that were coming in the form of an avalanche into our FB site. In essence we were attacked for not allowing others to make *our* FB site *their* site. The hostile claim to one's "right" to say whatever one wished on our site was beginning to scare off others. That of course was met with more backlash; accusations that we were undemocratic and refused to allow for dissent.

We also realized that our firm commitment to public education was alienating some folks we did not wish to offend. Yet we remained transparent in our own goals. While our own shared beliefs in a social justice perspective on testing resistance has been tacitly understood between us, we erroneously assumed it was also everyone else's. And so we faced our first challenge: to *more firmly, publicly, and clearly, articulate what we were for.* This early setback forced us to establish clarity in whom we were. Sage advice came from Laurie Murphy (unpublished correspondence, 2011):

> The team: What makes a team work well?
>
> Identify clearly what you are for. Be prepared in advance for complex alliances with other groups. Determine what the guiding principles are so that when you need to, you can refer to them for deciding when you can or cannot work with other groups who may not share your end goals or values.

We realized that it was not enough to state we were for opting out of testing. We emphasized that we were opting out as a way of fighting *for* public education. Some of those who were banned for their own aggressive behaviors went to great lengths to discredit us and shut us down. One hostile response on a blog[2] wrote of UOO: "The stated purpose of the group seemed to sway from opting out of **high stakes tests** to, no, it's really about saving the public school system by getting rid of tests" (para. 1). The author would be correct on this point. The blog author adds, "It was a very enlightening experience, lending *mucho* credence to my ongoing message to parents: The system is broken, and cannot and *should not* be repaired" (para. 2)

This was our first "dividing line" with certain other opt out advocates. Yes, the system is broken, but we had to make clear, and quickly, that we did not advocate for eliminating public education as a solution. We agreed that we must remain open to varying opinions and disparate political and educational points of view but that discourse on the Facebook site must remain dedicated to advocating for public education. Home schooling is an option, but not a wholesale solution for us.

The aforementioned blog post concluded by advocating that others *not* join our site. After endless hours of trying to defend our own stance in response to hostile and defensive posts we repeatedly requested be discontinued before banning anyone, we were publicly accused of "bashing, bullying, censoring, and banning members."

Many well-meaning members might have been alienated in those early days as we were learning, and making mistakes. Did we over react? Were we too sensitive? Most likely we were—at times. But it was also clear to all of us that others were not well-meaning at all, and that our views were far too disparate to find a mutual leg of support to share. So in the end, when we refused to have our mission co-opted (or watered down) into something it was never intended to be, the angry parties left. Within a week of starting, we feared we might be completely destroyed if we did not respond.

In an effort to establish clarity and be more definitive in our cause to advocate opting out as a defensive strategy in the fight to save public education, we established "guiding principles" that reflected our individual and collective stance. We did this for others as well as ourselves because being against high-stakes testing was not enough. We sought to support those who support their children in tandem with seeking those who support public education. Three years later we are happy to report that our over 30,000 Facebook members hail from the far left, the far right, from atheists, practitioners of various organized religions, vegans, homeschoolers, communists, and anything in between. We have found ways to read between the lines and weave threads of strength from our commonalities amongst our differences. But we still occasionally run into someone bent on using the opt out movement for their own ideological agenda, or to distribute a misinformed narrative that we cannot support. Our strength lies in having what St. Francis said is "the wisdom to know the difference." And we determined that our efforts would focus on actions, not ideologies. Establishing set "guiding principles" helps us never to lose sight of our values.

Playing With Prepositions: Who Can You Stand With, and Who Can't You Stand?

Ever since Arne Duncan rolled out the inaccurate but oft-quoted phrase, "Education is the civil rights issue of our time," the education reformers and proponents of RTTT and Common Core have hijacked the messages about equity and social justice. Adding insult to injury, there are numerous statements given by conservative groups or people now opposing the Common Core (CCSS) on the grounds that it "forces progressive propaganda including multiculturalism and diversity." Or that it "brainwashes children toward a socialist ideology." While we fight for social justice because we see CCSS as a destructive force against it, ironically we witness many groups expressly opposed to CCSS because they believe that it *promotes* social justice. And social justice for some equals totalitarian-style communism (in their defense, CCSS *is* quite totalitarian, just a different breed of it).

We are constantly surprised. Everyday. The decision over with whom, as individuals or groups, we can align ourselves is a day-to-day struggle. And sometimes folks will surprise you. We are not alone in this struggle. Other groups with a social justice framework for action are equally divided within and across one another on this issue: Is the enemy of my enemy my friend? Maybe. Sometimes. It depends. Let me get back to you on this.

There seems to be a connection between the hostile cadre of advocates for the elimination of public education we encountered in 2011 and some strands or facets of the anti-testing/anti-CCSS Conservative/Libertarian/ Tea Party movements of 2015. But again, there are many conservative or libertarian folks who are fighting for public education and whom we consider strong allies. What they share in common with us is an affinity about the problem based on solid evidential facts: the abuses on children by high-stakes testing, the federal intrusion on local decision making, developmentally inappropriate curricula, concern over data mining, and costs associated with new "reforms." But then oftentimes we diverge over possible alternative solutions. Fortunately, we have had three years to practice. We learned by now that making clear our own principles and standing by them will either attract or repel others and limit alliances that may compromise too much, or open up new alliances we never expected. While some might broadly sketch the division as "progressive" vs. "conservative," this is a false bifurcation. Democrats for Education Reform are as equally willing to sell public schools to private profiteers as is Heritage Foundation. And we have found common-ground solutions with many who hold self-identified conservative views. But the devil is always in the details.

Indeed, we have come a long way baby. The mistakes and the challenges of those early weeks did not destroy us. As founding member Laurie Murphy posted April 10, 2014:

> 56 Million? What is so amazing about this number? Compared to the number 22, it is a miracle.... What am I talking about, you ask? Let me explain. Back in August of 2011, I had just finished a 15 month project of working with an amazing group to hold the first SOS March and National Call to Action in D.C. After it concluded, some equally amazing people asked if I could provide a little advice for a group that they were forming concerning Opting Out of tests. Frankly, I had never heard of such a thing, so I googled it. I typed in the terms "opt out," "tests," and "students." There were 22 responses—and most didn't contain any real information. Just 22. A tiny number. A tiny ember of life. Guess what? I googled the same terms today and got 56,900,000 responses! In 2011, my goal (not the group's—just mine) was to change the conversation. Ed reformers had taken control of the media and there was a total blackout on those who did not believe that test mania served a valid purpose. I wanted a real conversation. I knew that until that happens, no change is possible. Well, folks, the world is buzzing with conversation about testing. Exciting! Even more exciting, however, is what comes next. Conversations breed change. Change is now happening. And this change is happening because all of you spoke up. Thank you for changing the conversation.... Heck, for changing the world!

So now it's 2015. Narratives, alliances, understandings—they've all changed. And they continue to change. Especially on the individual (person-to-person) level, we have been surprised by the unlikely friendships and supports that no "match.com" process would have ever approved. No ... the difference is in agreeing on *what we want*. What we want for our own children, for other people's children and our public schools is not a narrative owned by any single ideology or political party. But the framework that guides *United Opt Out* is driven decidedly by values of social justice. In 2014 we decided to begin working more directly with interested individuals and groups according to various regions of the country to provide greater state specific assistance. We made sure to announce with transparency what we stand for: "We at UOO believe in an equitably funded, democratically based, anti-racist, desegregated public school system for all Americans that prepares students to exercise compassionate critical decision making with civic virtue" (Tim Slekar, unpublished correspondence, June 3, 2014).

So what do we mean by that?

The Challenge: What Are You For?

> *And it's one, two, three,*
> *What are we fighting for?*
>
> —I-Feel-Like-I'm-Fixin'-to-Die-Rag,
> as sung by Country Joe and the Fish (McDonald, 1967)

Any curriculum that would become successful at transforming schools and education must be grounded first and foremost in the needs of the students and the communities—not the needs of corporations. We need to have a strong and clear vision for what will happen after CCSS and other test-driven reform policies are gone. Are you opposed to public education because of what it's doing to your/our children, or are you opposed to what reformers are doing to public education? We are supporters of public education; opposed to what is happening *in* them as well as what is happening *to* them. While the former may affect only "my" children, or "my" community schools, the latter demands we focus on the bigger question:

What Do We Want For All Our Children?

We believe that whatever our solution may be, it must include the opportunity for all children to attend sustainable, equitably funded, meaningful, engaging, and accessible public schools. We are not opposed to "choice"— it is the fundamental right of every parent to choose to homeschool their child or send them to private school (or charter) if they so choose—but the availability of those options should not come at the expense of our public education system.

Is the system broken? Yes … and no. Public schools are not failing (Ravitch, 2013) in the ways which reformers would have us believe. Rather, as a society we are failing public schools. We squander the opportunity to embrace children and communities as sites of strength and (sometimes painful) beauty, by labelling them "failing." For many children, public schools are the place where they feel safest, where they can grasp at opportunities otherwise unavailable in their homes or communities because of the generations of systematized institutionalized oppression, and state and federal laws which created the profoundly impoverished and racially segregated neighborhoods which we are forced to now confront and will continue to confront until we face full responsibility for their creation. For many children around this country, schools are their place to learn how to problem-solve, to empathize, to connect, and to create. It may be the only place in their lives where such opportunities exist in what we want to be a safe and nurturing setting. And we must embrace public education as *one facet* of a set of solutions to address these concerns. Schools cannot single-handedly remediate for the effects of poverty. They cannot be expected to resolve our social ills. But *without* high quality public education as a foundation of our democracy, we are dead in the water.

What Kinds of Public Schools Can We Imagine? What Kinds of Public Education Should We Demand?

First of all, our investment in public school is supposed to be an investment in our children's future, not limited to the sole purpose of using children as investments in the future for corporations. We envision a commitment to our promise *to children* through a reimaging of *public* education that is built upon three basic and interdependent democratic values: Freedom, Equity, and Possibility.

Freedom

It's a word we love in United States. But what precisely do we mean? True freedom cannot exist without equity. How so? Freedom for me cannot come at the expense of providing for the right to those same freedoms for others. In the words of authors Tony and Slade Morrison in *The Big Box* (1999), "If freedom is handled only your way, it's not my freedom or free." Freedom is power. Schools can create spaces for free thinking, for questioning, for challenging, so that no one ideology or form of indoctrination imposes itself, because through the freedom of critical thinking, whatever the reigning ideology is, students will have the power to examine it for themselves.

Children and teachers being forced to work under constant surveillance in the name of accountability is not freedom. Race to the Top and its various iterations are a gross overstep of the federal government and must be stopped. But freedom does not mean the total absence of legislation or oversight either. Government oversight was necessary to legislate desegregation, to promote funding for Title I schools, funding for Title 9 to ensure equality in men's and women's sports programs, and laws to protect the rights of children with special needs. If all public schools are to become sites for free thinking and learning, to be places of student empowerment, as determined by our newest stake holders—the children themselves—we cannot rely on big business or the "kindness of strangers" to make it happen. We must demand that our government make good on its promise to us: to serve the people. And demand that such rights and freedoms are protected through legislation that ensures the access to these freedoms for all students.

Equity

A one-size-fits-all trudging all children toward a same nationalized curriculum of mediocrity is a piss-poor excuse for equity. We equalize opportunity not by imposing a one-size-fits-all mediocre curriculum on all children and call that fair, or tell them to master the same test material and pretend this is the equivalent of equal opportunity. We equalize education by treating all children with equal amounts of respect, voice, vision, and freedom—by empowering them with all of the resources we have at our disposal and with the myriad ways in which they can engage as the co-creators of meaning and knowledge. We create equity by alleviating implicit and explicit systems of oppression so that all children have the freedom to invest knowledge and meaning in their own lives as they so choose. "Let them eat cake" cannot sustain the future of a democratic society. Other people's children are the future citizens who will share the next generation of decision making with our own children. What kind of world we envision for our own children must include the kind of world we envision for others. Public education must remain a part of that vision.

Freedom cannot outweigh equity, nor can top-down impositions in the name of equity (but service corporate profits) outweigh our freedoms. The balance is messy, complicated, and always, as Maxine Greene (1995) says, "unfinished." But we never stop trying. In the balance between "ours" and "theirs" we can see schools as sites for possibility, not places to be stuck reciting "what is" but sites to explore what "*can be*" if we give them the chance.

Possibility

Public schools are not places to indoctrinate but places to liberate—to imagine, to empower, to transform ourselves and the world. It is astounding that while people fighting for greater democracy in other countries risk their lives to create public education for all its citizens, we have used the system to abuse children, perpetuate less democracy, and now in our worst moment, sell it off to the highest bidder. In our own history, education has been used as both a tool of oppression and liberation; both an unparalleled opportunity and a right denied to those we wished to hold down. But it doesn't have to be this way.

Public education is not a boil to be burned off the body of our social foundation. It is not a burden. It is not legislation we must endure. It is a human right to be protected. It is a fundamental need of democracy that we must claim for its powerful potential. Let's stop lending it out to those in power (whether it be governmental or corporate), whose agenda is and always has been to manage the rest of us according to their own desires. If we miss this chance, if we sell out or give up, we will lose something tremendous that we may never have the chance to reclaim. But the possibility remains—it's what we do with the framework that matters.

Complexities of Race, Racism, Language, and Resistance

Ceresta Smith

In a rather scathing and somewhat embarrassing speech I made during our 2013 Occupation of the U.S. Department of Education, I referenced those who are in that select group of "top cream," as I, in language that was filled with invective, cited how many people of color in positions of power maintain those positions by willingly undermining the various communities from which they came. During the speech, I harshly criticized President Obama, entertainer John Legend, former Newark Mayor Corey Booker, the legendary Oprah Winfrey, Senator Marco Rubio, Superintendent of Miami-Dade County Public Schools Alberto Carvalho, and former Chancellor of the District of Columbia Public Schools and current organizer and spokesperson for Students First Michelle Rhee for their culpability in embracing and promoting market-based reforms that serve to undermine as opposed to build. I addressed this in an interview with retired teacher and blogger for *Ed Week* Anthony Cody (2012):

> My greatest concern is the implementation of DoEd policies has many accepting fiction as true fact. High stakes test scores do not indicate that students have learned deeply, claimed ownership to knowledge and learning, obtained the ability to work with others, or developed the ability to think creatively. Nor do they really reflect the quality of a school or a teacher. They suggest trends in regards to cultural practices, social class, and the ability to learn test taking strategies. And to a certain extent they reveal aptitude based on assimilation and cultural bias. The Department of Education promotes

these misnomers. The student who scores high on a single math test is going to receive more respect and validation than the young man who scores poorly on a single math test but is able to create a practical and stunning fashion design using recycled materials. Consequently, we are wounding instead of empowering students, teachers, and the overall academic culture. All of us need validation, not a fictitious grade stamped on our school, a misleading number stamped into our consciousness, or a bonus check for a random number that we may or may not have had something to do with.… Another concern is the huge racial and economic divide that the standardized test culture is fostering. Many great teachers are backing away from teaching in minority and impoverished communities, and others are being tossed out of these communities. Schools are very segregated by class and color, and the divide is filled with inequity. Sadly, there seems to be a trend in that the different groups are becoming insensitive and discriminatory toward each other in very harmful and non-progressive way. (paras. 2–3)

Further into my discourse, I began to talk of the inevitable cheating that will and does occur as a consequence of such polices. As an illustration of that, as well as the inequities of America's judicial system, I compared the alleged testing cheating in District of Columbia Public Schools to that of Atlanta Public Schools. Both districts had similarities: widespread testing infractions where there were high numbers of wrong-to-right erasures, irregular math and reading score gains, accolades and merit awards issued to faculties and administrators, and investigative reports published by their local newspapers.

However, Atlanta's former superintendent Beverly Hall and 34 other educators were indicted for racketeering and corruption while all investigations into the DCPC scandal were aborted before any indictments could occur. Upon learning about the indictments in Atlanta and the initial $7.5 million bond on Hall and $1 million placed on the other educators (CNN Staff, 2013, paras. 8–9), in anger, I said that the African American educators have been indicted and are facing bonds in the millions in contrast to the "Asian bitch" who is getting off scot-free. My intent was to demonstrate the racist inequity that exists in the American judicial system, but reporter Michele McNeil (2013), in her article titled "U.S. Dept. of Ed. Protesters Turn Fierce Rhetoric on 'Corporate Reform,'" focused more on my use of language and characterized it as "racially insulting":

Standing in front of the Education Department's headquarters in downtown Washington, Miami-Dade County teacher Ceresta Smith referred to former District of Columbia Public Schools Chancellor Michelle A. Rhee—founder and CEO of the advocacy group Students First—as an "Asian bitch … Smith, the Miami-Dade teacher and an African-American, was particularly critical of Rhee and other non-white leaders, such as Booker, for embracing "corporate reform," such as high-stakes testing, that she says hurts minority children. In her speech, she suggested that while some black teachers have been indicted in a cheating scandal in Atlanta, Rhee suffered no consequences in the wake of testing irregularities when she was chancellor of the District of Columbia schools, which she headed from 2007 to 2010. (para. 2)

On her blog site, Diane Ravitch (2013) and others characterized it as an "unforgivable" racial slur, and in an effort to save the anti-reform movement from alienation, they offered condemnations of me and my use of language. Diane offered an apology to Rhee:

Yesterday I participated in the first day of Occupy the DOE, where parents and teachers spoke out against DOE policies that demand high-stakes testing and school closings. In my own presentation, I urged the DOE to stop its punitive policies and instead to follow the positive agenda of the Network for Public Education. According to an account I read later, an earlier speaker used offensive language, calling Michelle Rhee an "Asian bitch." I was not there to hear it, but I was appalled when I read about it here. I want to make clear that this kind of language is unacceptable and intolerable. No one should resort to racial, ethnic, gender, or cultural slurs to express their views. It is just plain wrong. I don't use that kind of language, and I encourage others to have a high personal standard of civility. We must be able disagree about ideas and policies without getting personal. (para. 1)

Others expressed their disgust and intolerance as well:

Steven A. Levine

April 5, 2013 at 3:56 P.M.

I find the use of this term deeply disturbing, racist and sexist. Michelle Rhee does not represent women or Asian-Americans, nor is "bitch" acceptable language to describe a woman regardless of a person's opinion of her. She is the leading representative of an educational movement and philosophy which I find destructive and abhorrent. I only hope that this speaker's words do not distract us and the media from the message of our movement.

around the pond

April 5, 2013 at 5:35 P.M.

I'm so sorry to hear that a speaker at the rally used racist and sexist language. Even if we disagree passionately with the person at whom the invective was aimed, disparaging that person with slurs will never be ok. Thank you, Diane, for taking the high road and issuing an apology, even though the offense wasn't yours.

Michele Stork (@michelestork)

April 9, 2013 at 8:16 P.M.

I wanted so badly to attend this event, but due to scheduling was not able. I was disappointed at the lack of coverage by not only the media, but also by the people who were there. I was hoping to see more in real time on social media. However, I do think the UOO has done a good job of posting post-event coverage. The racial slur made by Ceresta was inappropriate and did much more harm than good for public education. Thank you Diane for apologizing. For someone like me who is just starting the process of getting involved with this movement, the comment and coverage of it made me a little nervous about just how much can be done if the people speaking on behalf of public education resort to racial slurs and name-calling. Let's try and focus on facts—there's enough of those to sink several corporate reform "battleships."

Others displayed more understanding:

johnabramson

April 5, 2013 at 4:14 P.M.

No doubt, an apology was required. Rhee is just one of the representatives of a so-called reform movement that does damage to our kids, our school and our communities. Hand in hand with corporate sponsors, privatization, union busting, teacher degradation and devaluation and one dimensional pseudo assessments and curriculum, our kids are being made ready to take their assigned slots in our 21st century economy, under the guise of meritocracy.

We all know about the research on the relationship between income levels and academic achievement; it has been around for "ages." Yet the role of income inequality in schooling is swept under the rug by those who have coopted and misused for their own purposes the historically valid idea of educational reform.

It is no surprise that that we have learned of cheating scandals [and] conflicts of interest, when there is so much money at stake for the private sector, which could well be utilized by the public schools. No doubt there are Atlanta-like situations just waiting to be uncovered. If those who resist "educational reform" would organize and actively investigate.

Likewise, those "Educational Reform" resisters must challenge the assumptions that underlie that movement and make their challenges insistent and vocal. Active resistance involves publishing articles that counter the lies and misrepresentations that have assumed the role of commonsense "truth."

Public education is not only under fire. It is being undermined and challenged on all fronts. Those who resist will be trampled, unless there is organized resistance to the takeover and destruction of the public schools. Local resistance can only be successful when it is supported and coordinated regionally and nationally.

Yes, epithets are never polite. What is far worse is the harm that Rhee has done and will continue to engender to schools, kids and communities.

paz

April 5, 2013 at 10:57 P.M.

All this hand-wringing. Someone who was wronged lashed out and said two wrong words. The person who said it should apologize. Just like Rhee finally sort of apologized and said she probably might have been wrong for happily firing that unsuspecting principal on camera, effectively ending his career perhaps forever. Betcha he had a few choice words he's glad he didn't say out loud. It's kind of unfortunate that we need always to take the high road, let's remember the down and dirty dealing we're fending off, and give ourselves a break for a minute. Even Jesus got really mad at the garbage going down at the temple. Give the person who "mis-spoke" a bit of the same forgiveness we keep giving our dissembling, equivocating politicians, who actually do our whole country real lasting damage. At least the alleged cusser was honest about her feelings. Was it Kathy Griffin? I really like her.

shawnbeightol

April 10, 2013 at 2:52 P.M.

Last time I checked, "Asian" was not a pejorative, but an accepted adjective. To insist it is racist reveals a condescending, racial superiority. Those who are destroying public education by chopping it up and selling it to the highest bidder by enabling charters (siphoning money, parent triggering) are B****es and B****rds and history will uphold this judgment. It may have been brute to say B****, but it was accurate. Furthermore, it is necessary to identify which B**** was the focus of conversation to distinguish from other education (de)formers like Levesque (Executive Director for the Foundation for Florida's Future) and Allen (founder, Center for Educational Reform and self-proclaimed author of ALEC Parent Trigger language). By providing the qualifier "Asian," listeners had no doubt which female education (de)former was the point of the paragraph. I know and have worked with Ceresta. She is NOT racist. She is harshly critical of the individuals and corporations that are turning public education into a profitfeeding-frenzy.

In response, my UOO co-administrator Peggy, along with the other co-administrators who gallantly stood by my side amidst criticism and fear for the movement, posted my response on Ravitch's blog site:

Peggy Robertson

April 6, 2013 at 12:03 P.M.

Dear Asian American Educator,

I personally felt it important for Ceresta to speak for herself, as quite honestly, I, as a white female who grew up in suburbia cannot begin to fathom the context, the background, from which Ceresta speaks. So, I waited for her to write her response which I now repost as found on our FB group page. Please accept my sincere apologies.

Ceresta writes:

> In his discourse titled "Civil Disobedience," Henry David Thoreau cited three courses of action that can be taken when one feels laws are unjust: comply without vocalizing complaint, comply but engage in activity to encourage change, or outright break laws and engage in civil disobedience. Thoreau had a barometer to help guide when to engage in the third choice. He said if a law is unjust and harms others, it is time to break the law. I deliberately broke the laws of decency and political correctness during my opening statements for the kick-off of Occupy the DOE 2.0., as I cited the inequity and harm that is being caused by complicit non-whites that have allowed corporate reform proponents to harm all children and more particularly non-white communities in ways that have widened the gulf of racial inequity. After citing the inequity between how the African American superintendent and educators of Atlanta Public Schools and the Asian American Chancellor of D.C. Public School were dealt with after it was alleged that both school systems were wrought with standardized assessment irregularities that could possibly indicate fraud, I was cited as hurling a "racial slur" by saying "black women" in contrast to the "Asian bitch." Taken in or out of context, many would agree it was simply a descriptive adjective when I used the word Asian. Taken in or out of context, many would argue it is a racial slur. My concern is that the members of the Asian community find it offensive and a direct attack upon their race. I apologize to all those in the Asian community that see it as such and took offense. I thank all those in the Asian community that clearly understood the parallelism used to show a problematic inequity that should be addressed.

As an African American that has and continues to be battered in a society that was born and continues to be raised in racism that goes unchecked and is supported by well-paid minorities, I find it extremely difficult to be decent. Many can understand why. And if we do not find it in our hearts to acknowledged and change the fact that in these contemporary times, black people, with the aiding and abetting of other minorities, continue to suffer the worse persecution out of all ethnic and cultural groups while a guise of protecting the most vulnerable is pushed by an oligarchy that is most concerned with maintaining absolute power and control, my poor choice of wording will pale in comparison into what will be realized in the future. Honestly, other black folk and I can't take much more.

Still angry when I wrote the response, I have to say even though it was not good enough for most of my critics, it was sincere in my concern for the Asian community. I subsequently had private conversations with folks who were upset and critical of my discourse, and accordingly, meaningful dialogue changed the negative opinion that many of my critics had as a consequence of the article and or the speech. Unfortunately, the overall message was missed by many due to my poor choice of wording, which, by the way, is legally characterized as a "racial reference" and not a "racial slur." Invective, for sure, and driven by anger, it was mischaracterized as a "racial slur" and "sexist." With regard to the "sexist" tag, I grew out of adolescence during the Murphy Brown and Saturday Night Live's Roseanne Rosannadanna days where women claimed the right to use the "Bitch" archetype. It became a part of our vocabulary and was used freely to represent on one hand, the aggressive, mean female who recklessly pounces on others to attain what they want; and on the other hand, the aggressive, strong, smart, talented female that will not take any crap.

The same sentiments are expressed by Bitch Media co-founder Andi Zeisler when asked: Why title a magazine Bitch? Writer Rebecca West reported,

People call me a feminist whenever I express sentiments that differentiate me from a doormat." We'd argue that the word "bitch" is usually deployed for the same purpose. When it's being used as an insult, "bitch" is an epithet hurled at women who speak their minds, who have opinions and don't shy away from expressing them, and who don't sit by and smile uncomfortably if they're bothered or offended. If being an outspoken woman means being a bitch, we'll take that as a compliment. We know that not everyone's down with the term. Believe us, we've heard all about it. But we stand firm in our belief that if we choose to reappropriate the word, it loses its power to hurt us. (Bitch Media, 2013, About Our Name)

Many feel Ms. Rhee is one of the most damaging Teflon-coated harbingers and advocates for market-based reform policies that serve to destroy quality and equity public education. Prior to my "gaffe," she was in Florida—a state that is majority Hispanic and non-White, with significant populations of impoverished, second language, and special-needs students—helping to craft Senate Bill 736. The bill, now law, attaches 50% of teachers' pay to student test scores by using Value Added Measures (VAM) that are faulty and unreliable and are far too often attached to teachers who have never seen or taught the scored students. Moreover, it illegally overrides the collective bargaining that put in place due process clauses for teachers. Nevertheless, that does not excuse the use of the term by me, as today I have been made well aware that it represents a misogynist frontal attack that is "uncool" and in activist and other circles is an unfortunate pitfall that can get one labeled, misunderstood, and by some, "un-forgiven."

I am not the first to take a public misstep in my use of language and certainly will not be the last. Had I left that word bitch off the statement, I am sure the clarity of what I was pointing out would have resounded as two truths that many have to admit. One, on the list of non-Whites that coexist in a world controlled by a White power structure, Black people are usually dealt the worse blows in the American judicial system with regard to who is indicted, who is not; and who goes—and for how long—to prison, and who does not in a world where it would be difficult to prove we are the "worse people." Two, a major problem in our efforts to save public education and the communities of color and poverty who have suffered the worse damage from market-based reform is that many non-White people and the formerly impoverished, the "top-cream" of their ethnic, racial, or low-socioeconomic group (Michelle Rhee inclusive) hold and foster the moral values (or lack of) of a patriarchal and supremacist system and are ultimately beholden to the money-driven method of systemic exclusion and exploitation that underlies and maintains today's bipartisan attack on public education, collective bargaining, democracy, and egalitarianism overall.

ACTIVIST'S WORKBOOK

1. Know yourself, check yourself. Learn about racism, classism, and privilege, and continue to be open to criticisms when offered by people you trust and respect when your perspective or actions might need examination. *Listen* carefully to what others have to say and *continue forward on your activist trail.*
2. Know and embrace the fact that *you will fuck up*. We all do if we're in it long enough, and deep enough, and transparent enough. The only way to avoid this dilemma is to hide in the shadows and not take risks. But the issues that confront us in this fight are messy,

complicated, and constantly shifting. There must be the willingness to embrace risk and to put oneself on the line for criticism and error if you are going to take on this kind of work.

3. Create true trusting alliances and friendships. Nothing so ensures our collective success as much as having respect, transparency, and honesty in this work. Be willing to apologize, to learn, and stand firm when needed; but avoid becoming so neutralized as to cease to matter or to be effective. We cannot be quick to throw one another under the bus, but neither can we look askance when mistakes are made. Be comfortable with the murky middle terrain of the unknown and land of "uneasy answers."

4. Determine what your nonnegotiables are and stick to them. Understand that you might lose some support along the way. Get comfortable with not being liked all the time by all people.

NOTES

1. http://www.makethemaccountable.com/articles/Free_Congress_Foundation_Integration_of_Theory_and_Practice.htm
2. http://www.parentatthehelm.com/6533/high-stakes-tests-everyone-has-had-enough

REFERENCES

Bitch media. (2013). *About us.* Retrieved from http://bitchmagazine.org/about

Boal, A. (1993). *Theater of the oppressed.* New York, NY: Theater Communications Group.

Cody, A. (2012, March 22). Teachers and parents prepare to occupy the Department of Education. *Education Week Teacher.* Retrieved from http://blogs.edweek.org/teachers/living-in-dialogue/2012/03/teachers_and_parents_prepare_t.html

CNN Staff. (2013, April 3). Former Atlanta schools superintendent reports to jail in cheating scandal. *CNN Justice.* Retrieved from http://www.cnn.com/2013/04/02/justice/georgia-cheating-scandal/index.html

Greene, M. (1995). *Releasing the imagination: Essays on education, the arts, and social change.* Hoboken, NJ: Jossey-Bass.

McDonald, J. (1967). *I-feel-like-I'm-fixin'-to-die-rag* [song]. Tradition Music.

McNeil, M. (2013, April 4). U.S. Dept. of Ed. protesters turn fierce rhetoric on 'Corporate' Reform. *Education Week.* Retrieved from http://blogs.edweek.org/edweek/campaign-k-12/2013/04/education_department_protesters_turn_fierce_rhetoric_on_corporate_reform.html/

Morrison, T., & Morrison, S. (1999). *The big box.* New York, NY: Jump At the Sun.

Ravitch, D. (2013, April 9). Why I apologized for something I didn't say. *Diane Ravitch's blog.* Retrieved from http://dianeravitch.net/2013/04/06/why-i-apologized-for-something-i-did-not-say/

CHAPTER 7

A CASE STUDY IN REFORM FAILURE

The Inconvenient Truth

Ruth Rodriguez

*Young children need to spend their time actively engaging in play and
learning through direct experiences with materials, activities, peers and
teachers. Rather than measuring school success by testing, the most reliable
approach to assessing young children's learning is through ongoing observations
by skilled teachers and assessments of children's work over time.*

—Nancy Carlsson Page[1]

*An Activist Handbook for the Education Revolution:
United Opt Out's Test of Courage*, pp. 125–135
Copyright © 2015 by Information Age Publishing
All rights of reproduction in any form reserved.

Ruth Rodriguez

The Massachusetts Miracle?

Massachusetts (MA) is one of the states that is often touted as having the highest standardized test scores and consequently the largest share of the best public schools in the nation. The validity of this premise should not come into question since over the course of several decades groups and individuals encouraged policymakers to make wise investments in the schools that serve all the children of the Commonwealth. Responding to a need, policymakers implemented a campaign for equitable funding in the 1980s. One of the challenges involved in this effort included, first of all, the formula that the state uses for school funding, which is based on property taxes. This creates an unfair and unequal form of funding because affluent communities are able to provide some of the finest state of the art schools with rich curriculum, small classrooms, and all the resources needed to ensure academic success; in contrast, poor communities with limited resources are unable to accomplish the same feats as their affluent counterparts. Consequently, the premise called for a new formula that did not leave poor communities without the resources needed for quality and equity.

Prior to the state's education reform of 1993, there was visible momentum in school improvement efforts, especially important were programs for English language learners and students in need of special education. The strength of these improvements was due in part to the active role played by a highly committed community made up of families, teachers, and some respected policymakers. One would admit that there were challenges accompanying these successes, but the whole community was together in working hard to make sure that students received the quality education every child deserves.

Notwithstanding, efforts made in the 80s were canceled out by the legislation in the 90s, and today we must call into question why the promise of equity made in the 70s and the 80s was not realized as a consequence of the reforms implemented in the early 90s. The failure was documented in the report by *Citizens for Public Schools*[2] (French, Guisbond, & Jehlen, 2013): "The evidence strongly suggests that the major reforms of the 1993 law that consisted of high-stakes testing and Commonwealth charter schools two decades later have failed to deliver on their promise" (p. 5). In examining why, it seems that those who aimed to profit from public schools funding—instead of supporting educators and students—found a way to convince policymakers to adopt their business-style education reforms. They wasted little time in launching their campaign of privatizing public education. Their first step to ensure this takeover was to target teachers and the union.

MA's political and administrative leadership are often quoted, boasting that MA is proud to have the distinction of being number one in education, but it still has a long way to go to eliminate the achievement gap between White and Black/Latino students. Decision makers acknowledge that little was done to address what they term the "achievement gap" by expanding opportunity, addressing equitable funding, and promoting a broader pedagogical vision of education, one whose main goal ought to have been the strengthening of students' creative abilities and expanding the knowledge of the world around them while learning how to live in a democratic society. To the detriment of MA, the education reforms launched in 1993 were dominated by accountability measures that caused public schools in numerous MA urban school districts to be defined through the lens of a powerful corporate group that demanded schools provide a course of study that trains the student with the skills, knowledge, and credentials needed in building a workforce. There was little interest in ensuring that public schools engage students with a course of study that understands the pedagogical foundation of education as a deeply civic and political endeavor and allows the conditions for individual autonomy, taking liberation and the practice of freedom as a collective goal. Not surprisingly, the gaps persist.

The idea that MA is number one despite the "gaps" can be perceived as a double-edged sword. On one hand, MA can promote itself with a sense of arrogance and superiority, a classic hallmark of the corporate agenda, which encourages competition. On the other hand, it also leaves little time to deal with the underlying causes of "achievement gaps" that continue to fester under a system of competition. Further dismaying is that corporate moguls, legislators, and their academic administrator lackeys love to take

credit and embrace the mantra-like claim of success based on high standardized test scores even when these education measures are misnomers for
actual success, particularly for non-White and impoverished students. More
troublesome is that such claims, coupled with the continuing "achievement
gaps," simply look like promising dollar signs to carpetbagging corporate
entities who are searching for opportunities to invest in the profit-making
ventures. Many of these investors have come to see MA as "ripe" for the
corporate takeover of public schools.

It did not take long for them literally to come to MA. Soon after having
"duped" the Chicago Teachers Union, Jonah Edelman, the head of the
reform group Stand for Children, promised to take his corporate agenda to
Massachusetts. In his determination, MA was ready "for reform" (Clawson,
2012). Stand for Children came to the state as a lamb, but soon roared
like a lion. At first embracing the campaign for fair school funding, an
already established goal for a coalition of advocates for public education,
many of us welcomed Stand and believed that they shared our values of
protecting public education. I applied for a job with Stand for Children,
a job I thought consisted of organizing grassroots groups in Worcester,
especially the Spanish-speaking community. Little did I know at the time
that this job required one to organize a campaign to have teachers' job
evaluations attached to students' test scores. The candidate who was hired
soon resigned after realizing her job duties entailed executing damaging
corporate reforms.

In his first term, 2008–2009, Governor Deval Patrick launched his
Readiness Project, an initiative that brought together citizens from across
the state to advise him on issues ranging from education to health and
other important issues. I was honored to have served in this initiative
with the subcommittee, MCAS and Assessment. It is interesting because
the first meeting was held at the school where I worked, Boston Day &
Evening Academy, and it is a school that utilizes multiple forms of assessment tools, such as Exhibition, Portfolio Presentations, and Essay Projects.
These forms of assessments allow the students to showcase what they have
learned in front of a panel made up of students, teachers, parents/family
members, and community advocates. I sat through numerous sessions and
was impressed with the high professionalism shown by these presentations.
The last presentation that I attended in the 2013–2014 school year was for
a Boston Pilot School named Young Achievers. In conversation with the
panel at the end of the presentation, I offered a suggestion to the leader
to invite Governor Patrick to be a panelist for the upcoming 2014–2015
school year. The incentive was to give him firsthand experience with an
assessment tool that has merit and is an alternative to MCACs, the punitive high-stakes testing currently used in MA. Unfortunately, he was not

running for reelection, but the offer should be extended to prospective governor contenders.

Follow the Money

One of the state's biggest investors in our public schools is philanthropist Bill Gates. Personally, I consider him the Devil of public education. The story in the Bible has a similar character named Lucifer. Now it is recorded that Lucifer used his charm to entice Eve to eat the forbidden fruit. He knew it was bad for Eve to partake of this fruit, but that didn't stop him from pursuing his evil act.

See, I am sure Mr. Gates by now knows very well how harmful his pet projects have been for the public schools of MA, especially for the neediest communities. But this seems to have little or no influence in stopping him from using the communities of the poor, working class, and politically disenfranchised as guinea pigs in his laboratory world for his own gain. No, because when he fails at one project, just like he did in the early part of this century with his small-school project, well that's ok, he just goes on to his next experiment. He knows that there is not one single lawmaker with the moral fiber to say "no" to him, and those who are powerless, who have no voice at the State House, have to live with the results and be subjected to the mad scientist experiment. He has become clever in pushing his projects without having his signature name out in the public eye. No, he doesn't have to do that anymore for he has acquired enough people, who, during slavery, were known as "house negroes" and "poverty pimps" in the 1960s, to do his bidding.

Just Google the names of the state's corporate promoters, the charter school profiteers, and the testing consulting firms, and you will see the Bill and Melinda Gates Foundation as the main financial supporters. For example, the recent report from the Massachusetts Business Alliance for Education (Barber et al., 2014), co-authored by Sir Michael Barber (CEO of Pearson Publishing), reads like a *Who's Who* of corporate-education leaders. It is hard to comprehend how bad these reformers have been for public education in our state. Everybody considers Bill Gates to be such a nice guy because the first thing that comes to mind to most is that Gates gives his money to help improve people's lives. If that were the case, after decades of his investments in public schools, one would think that the United States would be number one in education, not Finland. What Mr. Gates does best is invest; he has investments in the testing industry, in the for-profit charter school, and if allowed, he plans to profit from the state's children's private information through his trademark, inBloom.

In 2002 during his run for Governor, Mitt Romney promised that if elected he would eliminate Bilingual Education-Chapter 71A. He wasted no time in bringing carpetbagger millionaire Ron Unz to carry out his promise. The millionaire contracted a marketing firm and poured thousands of dollars into launching one of the most anti-bilingual education, bigoted campaigns in the state. Lincoln Tamayo, considered a sellout, who, if it were in the 1960s would have qualified as a poverty pimp because he screwed his own community for his own financial gain, led the efforts to put an end to the Bilingual Law, and they proceeded to lead this most bigoted campaign and gathered enough signatures to put it on the ballot. Our newly elected governor had his promise of ending the 20-year-old *Education Reform Act* (see Birmingham, 2013) signed and sealed. This unfortunate legislature has been responsible for leaving many English language learners behind. The measure called for limited-English-speaking students to be immersed in English for one year, then sent back to their assigned class. One school year was all Governor Romney believed it would take for one to master the new language and be able to compete with the rest of the students. In fact, if the governor had his way, the referendum would have included a clause that would punish any teacher who used the native language of the student, even if it was for an emergency or an intervention. Under Romney's plan, any teacher in a school caught speaking a language other than English was subject to firing. The Massachusetts Teachers Union fought against this inhumane measure, and the final Unz Initiative,[3] which is still the law of the land, did not include the teacher unfair measure.

But for many, limited-English-speaking students who enter MA public schools in the ninth grade are forced to be immersed in English for one year, then take the tenth-grade MCAS. If they don't pass the test, they cannot receive a high school diploma. This led me to take a stand, and in a room full of over 300 people at Framingham State University, I challenged Governor Deval Patrick, to whom I said face-to-face:

> Governor, I thank you for giving me the opportunity to serve on your Readiness Project with the MCAS/Assessment subcommittee. I'm saddened that you did not accept our recommendation and have decided to continue the MCAS punish-style measures. But I challenge anyone in this room, including you, governor to immerse yourselves for one year in Spanish, and then take the MCAS in Spanish, for that is exactly what you are asking English language learners to do.

There was clapping by the audience, and a newspaper reporter approached me for my name. The governor directed me to one of his staff, saying he will look into this, but to this day English language learners still must pass the 10th-grade MCAS or not be able to receive a high school diploma.

The Inconvenient Truth

Massachusetts' role in the pursuit of funds under Obama's RTTT initiative created a fixation on the test-driven, privatized, and charter school reforms, as well as on the hostile takeover of public education by hedge funds and privateers offering as "choice" a test prep, "no excuses, zero tolerance" school environment; certainly an environment to which they would never expose their own children. What we have is a reform that has most urban public school districts forced to compromise on providing students with a rich curriculum, small-class-sized classrooms, full-time nurses, in some extreme cases even physical education over the pervasive testing preparation that has become the norm in the public school districts across the state. If the amount of money that has gone into the hands of the "testing-industrial-complex" (Krashen, 2013, para. 1) had instead gone to answer the needs of the resource-deprived schools in the urban districts, MA would indeed be living up to the reputation of being number one. However, as with national public education, once seen as a fundamental public good, MA schools are now reduced to what many reputable educators have come to view as a *corporate private* good, almost exclusively available to the wealthy and the politically influenced (see Ravitch, 2013; Schneider, 2014)

Acknowledging this reality has caused the corporate reforms to come under serious scrutiny; as obsessive and unreliable accountability measures have replaced excellence, any semblance of quality and equity is gone and has threatened the very essence of our democracy as we now face an apartheid system worse than before the desegregation passage of *Brown v. Board of Education*. In fact, it has been found that today, Boston schools are more segregated than before the state passed its school desegregation plan in 1974. As Horowitz (2014) reports, "Massachusetts now has seven times as many highly segregated schools as it had two decades ago" (para. 4). And poverty being the greatest factor in determining who is successful and who is not on standardized testing has many civil rights leaders in Boston acknowledging that a student's zip code is the greatest indicator of a student's academic success.

Moreover, as we have seen since the state test became a graduation requirement; it has also enjoyed the status of being number one in the achievement gap between Whites versus Black and Latino students. *When will the state realize that it is the misguided policies with a single test determining students' achievement that has created this apartheid school system and no amount of their so-called rigor is going to help reduce the achievement gap?*

Let's be real. Prior to the corporate education reform, standardized tests were administered mostly in deciding placement of students in their classes or to ascertain a student's special need. But today, in a MA education reform, test scores are used as the primary criteria for judging the success or failure of students, teachers, and schools. While few countries administer exams to children at a young age, or with such frequency as we do, the state's latest early-education initiative is set to do just that, test 4 and 5 year olds. Under this test-obsessed reform, our children are tested to an extent never seen in history. The Massachusetts Comprehensive Assessment System (MCAS), the state high-stakes test, denies a high school diploma to students who fail the 10th-grade test. There is a direct correlation between states that have high school exit exams and increased rates of adolescent/young adult incarcerations. Also, many of these same students who fail exit exams are victims of "zero tolerance" polices that likewise have direct correlations between suspensions and rates of incarceration. The "school-to-prison pipelines" are policies and practices that have been found to push out mostly students of color, those with special needs, and the at-risk out of classrooms and into the juvenile and criminal justice systems, with incarceration replacing education (see report by the ACLU[4]; Teaching Tolerance[5]; Smith, 2014).

In 2009 in Cambridge, I participated in a panel on the school-to-prison pipeline at a conference sponsored by the Harvard School-to-Prison Project.[6] I shared the panel with Suffolk Juvenile Court Judge Leslie E. Harris. Judge Harris' eloquent message rang loud and clear. He determined that since the mandate of the Massachusetts Comprehensive Assessment System (MCAS) was implemented as a high school graduation requirement, he noticed an increase in the numbers of black and Latino youth before his court. The majority of these youths had failed to pass the MCAS. Furthermore, schools may actually encourage dropouts in response to pressures from test-based accountability regimes such as the No Child Left Behind Act. In fact, some of the state charter schools have adopted a policy creating incentives to push out low-performing students in order to boost their test scores.

In its quest to implement their idea of high standards, the state went against the recommendation from the campaign for the education of the whole child. The campaign laid out the vision of how educational excellence and equity can be implemented. The vision called for educating the whole child, and that if "schools promise every child excellence in education, it had to do so by ensuring that every child had access to a rich curriculum, including social studies, world languages, science, art, music, physical education and recess, as well as reading and math." Furthermore, in order for students to succeed in school it had to stress the importance of "addressing children's basic emotional and physical needs."[7]

Testify

On July 9, 2013 I gave the following testimony on school suspension:

July 9, 2013

Boston State House

Good afternoon, my name is Ruth Rodriguez-Fay and I am a resident of Boston. I am a member of the national Save Our Schools movement and former President of Citizens for Public Schools. I am here today to voice my support to the Bills S. 631 and H. 1644, two "Acts Decriminalizing Non-Violent and Verbal Student Misconduct," S.631 sponsored by Senator Brownsberger and H.1644 sponsored by Representatives Swan and Coakley-Rivera. I thank this Joint Committee for allowing me to offer my testimony

Nationally there is a growing concern for a pervasive practice of "a systemic disregard for children's basic constitutional rights ... " following the comprehensive investigation by the Justice Department Civil Rights Division[8] in 2009 in Mississippi. The investigation found local and state authorities to be running a "school-to-prison pipeline" through the incarceration of students for minor school disciplinary infractions, in some cases as violating school dress code guidelines, and as such constituted school misconducts that were formerly addressed within the school. A recent study by the Gaston Institute at U-Mass Boston found a disproportionally high number of Latino students who are suspended and arrested annually, placing the state in line with some of the nation's worst offenders [see Reis, 2013]. We must be the leader that initiates a judicial practice that promotes an evidenced based approach for addressing students' school conduct and creates school environments that are safe for the teaching and learning process. The implementation of "zero tolerance" served to pave the way for some school districts to adopt policies that have proven discriminatory along racial lines. In a series of reports it's been found that zero tolerance has not been shown to improve school climate or school safety. In fact, a task force of the American Psychological Association in 2007 [Graves & Mersky] found these policies to be "particularly inappropriate for younger pupils, and to be applied as such it appears to run counter to the best knowledge of child development" [para 10]. "Zero tolerance" policies can exacerbate both the normative challenges of early adolescence and the potential mismatch between the adolescents' developmental state and the structure of secondary schools." This practice concentrates on punishment rather than practices such as restorative justice, and are pervasively applied in a manner that is often perceived as unjust, as in many cases is applied unevenly across race and ethnicity.

The most unfortunate result of zero tolerance is the increased referrals to the juvenile justice system for infractions that were once handled in schools, and at the same time has increased the cost of treatment dramatically. Additionally, families have seen little to no positive effects to the community and no evidence that this policy has helped parents or that the family unit has been strengthened through its use. As to improvement in academic performance, one report saw "a negative relationship between the use of school suspension and expulsion and school-wide academic achievement." A more humane and productive practice that has wide support is one that connects the home and the school in finding solutions to the student infraction, one that has long-term positive results with the establishment of healthier more positive student and adult relationship.

In conclusion, I want to appeal to this committee to vote yes on these two bills and to join those in the community that are collaborating in efforts to find solutions that are equitable and just, and that can help to create healthier and safer school environments.

Thank you for giving me this opportunity.

Ruth Rodriguez-Fay

Jamaica Plain

CONCLUSION

If the amount of money that has gone into the hands of the testing-industry complex had instead gone to answer the needs of deprived schools in the urban districts, MA would indeed be living up to the reputation of being number one. Massachusetts has the opportunity to return to the policies that helped the state established itself as the leader in education by abandoning the corporate agenda. It can be the voice that cries out in defense of all the children by denouncing the measures that are creating a dual system of schooling. It is going to take the will of honest politicians who will stand up to those who are privatizing for their own economic gain. And it is the parents, students, educators, and taxpayers who have to make sure we elect politicians who are honest with the will to do what is right by public education and those who benefit from it.

NOTES

1. http://nancycarlssonpaige.org/ECE-Brochure-8.20.13.pdf
2. http://www.citizensforpublicschools.org/
3. http://bilingualeducationmass.wordpress.com/category/information-on-the-unz-initiative-massachusetts/
4. https://www.aclu.org/school-prison-pipeline
5. http://www.tolerance.org/magazine/number-43-spring-2013/school-to-prison

6. http://prisonstudiesproject.org/
7. http://www.citizensforpublicschools.org/wp-content/uploads/2009/08/whole_
   child_summary.pdf
8. http://www.justice.gov/crt/publications/accomplishments/

REFERENCES

Barber, M., Day, S., Donnelly, K., Page-Jones, R., Rea, S., Rizvi, S., & Sandals, L.
(2014). The new opportunity to lead. *The Massachusetts Business Alliance for
Education.* Retrieved from http://www.mbae.org/wp-content/uploads/2014/03/
New-Opportunity-to-Lead.pdf
Birmigham, T. (2013, June 15). Education reform at 20. *The Boston Globe.* Retrieved
from http://www.bostonglobe.com/opinion/2013/06/14/education-reform-act-
reaches-mass-has-more/GMIIIIU8FdXLwR46qtAM7TgL/story.html
Clawson, L. (2012, May 15). Corporate education reformers take aim at Massachusetts.
Daily Kos. Retrieved from http://www.dailykos.com/story/2012/05/15/1091833/-
Corporate-education-reformers-take-aim-at-Massachusetts
French, D., Guisbond, L., & Jehlen, A. (2013). Twenty years after education
reform. A report from Citizens for Public Schools. Retrieved from http://
www.citizensforpublicschools.org/wpcontent/uploads/2013/06/CPS-20th-
Anniversary-of-ERA-Report-Executive-Summary-Online-6-10-13.pdf
Graves, D., & Mersky, L. (2007). American Psychological Association report chal-
lenges school zero tolerance policies and recommends restorative justice.
Restorative Practices. Retrieved from http://www.iirp.edu/iirpWebsites/web/
uploads/article_pdfs/apareport.pdf
Horowitz, E. (2014, May). If segregation ended 60 years ago, how come it's getting
worse? *The Boston Globe.* Retrieved from http://www.bostonglobe.com/news/
politics/2014/05/19/segregation-ended-years-ago-how-come-getting worse/
qbvuqM0yLcWrNObVlMC6zH/story.html#comments
Krashen, S. (2013, Jan.). Feeding the testing industrial complex. *Schools Matter.*
Retrieved from http://www.schoolsmatter.info/2013/01/feeding-testing-
industrial-complex.html
Ravitch, D. (2013). *Reign of error: The hoax of the privatization movement and the danger
to America's public schools.* New York, NY: Vintage Press.
Reis, J. (2013, June 26). School suspension numbers vary widely in Worcester.
telegram.com. Retrieved from http://www.telegram.com/article/20130626/
NEWS/106269962/0
Scheider, M (2014, Jan.). ALECS extensive plans for educational restructuring
in your state. *Deutsche 29.* Retrieved from http://deutsch29.wordpress.
com/2014/01/29/alecs-extensive-plans-for-education-restructuring-in-your-
state/
Smith, M. D. (2014, March 28). The school-to-prison pipeline starts in preschool.
The Nation. Retrieved from http://www.thenation.com/blog/179064/school-
prison-pipeline-starts-preschool#

CHAPTER 8

STRATEGIZING 101

What It Involves and Why It Is Important

Laurie Murphy

Laurie Murphy

An Activist Handbook for the Education Revolution:
United Opt Out's Test of Courage, pp. 137–154

There are many things that need to be considered when creating an organization. In fact, the "You Need To" list can be fairly long and overwhelming. You need to establish a basic organizational structure. You need to clarify your message and your purpose. You need to determine who should hear your message, how you will deliver it, and what actions you want them to take. You need to determine the best way to present your message and facilitate your desired change. And finally, you need to know *who* and *what* may prevent the change from occurring.

Strategic planning is key to achieving this daunting task. It allows an organization to take a string of individual actions and use them in a coordinated and purposeful manner to create something that is larger and more meaningful. No action is conducted in complete isolation. Your eyes must always remain focused on other actions, your greater purpose, and your future.

This chapter will explore some of factors that influence the success of social movements in general, as well as the strategies adopted by UOO in changing High-Stakes Testing from an invisible issue to a subject of national concern.

Taking the First Steps

The early days of the UOO could be defined as controlled, passionate chaos. Within 2 weeks of being established, the basic framework of the organization was completed. The first five administrators were recruited. Together, they developed a unified message, created a Facebook page, and shared their message with the nation. And what they said struck a nerve.

In less than 48 hours, the group's Facebook membership climbed to triple digits. It was clear that the concerns of the administrators were shared by many. A movement to address the destructive nature of high-stakes testing had been born, and it was ready for action.

The initial growth of the organization appeared to happen spontaneously. However, a great deal of credit is owed to the depth of consideration that the founder, Peggy Robertson, gave to the project prior to its official beginning. In her first e-mail to Morna McDermott on August 11, 2011, she detailed what was needed: a clear purpose, a great name, a killer marketing slogan, strong imagery, factual information, connections with others who had opted out, and parents who needed this information—all delivered in a manner with minimal cost. While she didn't have all of the answers, she had considered the important questions. That alone contributed much to the early strength and success of the organization.

Membership and postings on the Facebook page continued to grow at a rapid rate. However, it lacked control. The new administrators were busy getting their message out to others, but they had not yet taken the time to develop a formal structure for communication, policy setting, or decision making. As a result, early conversations on the group's Facebook page proved to be more problematic than expected, and no one was certain how to handle it.

A small group of posters had shifted the conversation to meet their own personal agenda, often promoting issues which conflicted with the group's intent. Administrators, lacking protocols for steering their membership in a unified direction, used different and often conflicting tactics for addressing the matter. Soon, more time and effort was being invested in addressing the problematic posts than in promoting their original message. The administrators quickly realized that a more coordinated effort was needed to effectively address evolving issues and promote a single, unified message.

Adding the Sixth Administrator

My involvement with UOO began on August 27, 2011, the day that Morna McDermott, one of the five original administrators, reached out to me (at the recommendation of SOS organizer Bess Altwerger) to ask technical advice concerning issues they were having with the group's Facebook page.

She and I had become acquainted during my days at the Save Our Schools march. I had served as the national organizer on the SOS Executive Committee and had the honor of watching the organization grow from a handful of concerned individuals to a national organization that had gained the attention of the White House and international media outlets. I also had over 15 years of experience in working with nonprofits, with my specialty being strategic and organizational development. I was familiar with the difficulty of creating unified messages and actions, and understood the additional challenges encountered when dealing with volunteer and virtual organizations.

The first day of my involvement with UOO was crazy, with over 30 e-mails exchanged among the group. My main focus at that point was to simply resolve issues related to the Facebook page and learn more about the needs of the new group. In the course of doing so, I asked questions concerning key players and offered guidance on creating a unique and memorable identity. When the dust finally settled, I was asked to formalize my involvement with the group and join them as an administrator. The other administrators had great depth of experience in the field of education, children in the school system, and actual experience opting out of high-stakes testing. The group hoped that my experience with organizational and strategic development would help them build the identity, structure, and strategy that they needed.

Establishing Communication: The First Step in Creating Organization and Structure

Based on my early questions, it was clear that a greater sense of order and direction was needed. Through a series of e-mails and phone calls, it was determined that three key factors would have the greatest influence on the final organizational structure of the group: a lack of external funding, the diverse locations of the various administrators, and the success of other social activist groups in using social media. It was also clear that the first priority was finding the means for the administrators to communicate.

After considering various options, the group decided to try to hold a Skype conference call, as it was a free service and several of the members had previously used the service.

The first Skype call that included all six initial administrators took place on August 29, 2011, just two days after I was asked to join the group. As this e-mail from administrator, Morna McDermott shows, the call quickly took on a comedic theme.

yes i am on for skype

i have no power/electricity and no internet access but across the street they do so we have a LOOONNNG ass electrical cord running over the street into our home from our neighbors-so at least our fridge and two lights are plugged in and they let me use their WIFI acct so work tonight

sheesh. (personal communication, August 29, 2011)

And the challenges continued. At first, only five of the six administrators could be on the line at once, as the addition of the sixth administrator to the group call would disconnect someone else from the call. After all six administrators finally managed to stay on the call, mysterious echoes, buzzes, and frozen screens made communication difficult at best. However, the group persisted and, by the end of its first call, they had established a sense of coordination and structure.

Throughout the years, utilization of Skype for group communications continued to be both challenging and a source of comedy relief. Many of us were utilizing outdated equipment and software and had to take a crash course in using emerging new technologies. Unexplained events, such as hearing Morse Code or voices of unknown persons on the call, created an atmosphere of dark humor that served to bond the group even closer.

Creating the Basic Organizational Framework

During the initial call, as well as the weekly calls that followed, the group discussed how the organization should work. The group decided that UOO would function best as a web-based organization, as there was no funding available to secure a physical location. While it would continue its use of Facebook as its primary source of public interaction, a website would serve as a hub for sharing more complex information with the general public. Items that would be published on the website would include documents that clarified our position on key subjects, announcements of major actions, and publication of general educational information for the community and the media. The group would utilize Skype, e-mail, and other no-cost web-based technologies for internal communication and planning.

While humor was important and ever-present, our weekly calls addressed serious issues and focused on making the group as strong and effective as possible. During the initial conference calls, the question of the appropriate size of the administrative team was explored.

We knew that too small of a leadership group could limit the diversity of representation and inadvertently prevent the group from considering important alternate points of view. However, large leadership groups posed their own problems. Based on past experience, we knew that the larger the group, the less time each person had for contributing to the discussion. Equally important was the difficulty of finding perfect agreement on complex issues within large groups. The philosophy and planned actions of UOO were considered radical by many. Increasing the size of the administrative group increased the risk that some members would attempt to alter the organization's purpose, message, or direction to better fit their own, less radical ideology or to fulfill other personal needs. After the first few phone calls, it was clear that the existing group of six administrators worked well together.

Clarifying the Message: Transitioning From Organizational Structure to Strategy

From the beginning, it was clear that the stories that each administrator had concerning the impact of high-stakes testing on their lives contained a unifying thread. High-stakes testing was diminishing the educational experience of children. It was also negatively impacting children, as well as society, in less direct ways as well. The challenge for the administrators was to create a message that was universal in scope and deliver that message in a manner which inspired individual action and change.

After much discussion, the following message was developed:

The central mission of *United Opt Out* is to eliminate the threat of high-stakes testing in public K–12 education. We believe that high-stakes testing is destructive to children, educators, communities, the quality of instruction in classrooms, equity in schooling, and the fundamental democratic principles on which this country is based.

High-stakes testing is not supported by educational research as a measure of student learning and progress. It is, however, the crucial information needed by groups who seek to privatize public education and run it for-profit.[1] (paras. 2, 4)

Implementing Strategic Actions

Nailing down organizational basics was a critical first step for UOO, but more work was required if we were to make a true difference. We still had to determine who needed to hear our message, the most appropriate methods for delivering our message, what actions we needed the recipients to take, how we should facilitate our desired change, and who (and what) may prevent this change from occurring. The questions sounded simple enough, but the answers often left us uncertain. To obtain these answers, we first decided on a basic organizational strategy, around which all other decisions would form. We knew that six people were too few to lead all of the plans of action needed to bring an end to destructive high-stakes testing. Instead, we would serve as a hub for providing information, increasing awareness, and connecting the various groups who would be responsible for conducting local actions. After some discussion, we determined that providing high-quality information would be key to establishing our credibility. We also decided that holding a single, highly visible national action, as well as attention-grabbing weekly actions, would help to increase the public's awareness of the issues. We also felt that our Facebook page would be our primary tool for building a strong network. However, we realized that even with this basic framework, our actions would lack the focus needed to achieve the depth of results we desired, unless we addressed other, more specific strategic questions.

Determining Who Should Hear Our Message

At first, we thought that the primary target of our message would be parents. After all, they were the ones making the decision whether or not to opt their children out of high-stakes testing. And, while this answer was not wrong, it was deceptively oversimplified.

Once UOO began to think strategically, we realized that the pool of people and entities we should target was actually much broader. We also realized that our specific message, the means for delivering, and the specific action that we desired would vary, depending on the specific category of our target. All of the possible scenarios threatened to overwhelm us.[2]

To keep us on track, I created a series of charts to identify the stakeholders and track the complex maze of the various players. Some charts were straightforward, designed simply to help the administrators keep track of who was aligned with whom, the name of the organization for which they worked, and basic contact information. Others were designed to be shared with others and were included in registration and press packets. Specific charts were also completed for media sources, influential bloggers, primary supporters of public education, and the primary supporters of education reform.

In the end, we realized that the list of entities that needed to hear our message was almost as complex at the issue itself. We needed to reach out to students, parents, family members, teachers, school administrators and support staff, teacher education and training programs, and school boards. We also needed to develop relationships with those working in local, state, and federal government and connect with traditional and social media sources. We also realized that each of these contacts would require different documents, methods of delivery, and requests for action.

Deciding What We Should Say: Our Broader Messages

Having a great title and tagline was wonderful, but we knew it wouldn't help us when we needed to discuss the issues in greater depth. We started to create our own internal library of issues, responses, and quotes that could be applied to specific situations. The administrators had a great deal of personal and professional experience and were already gifted communicators. Therefore, they rarely needed to actually consult the lists. However, by bringing the questions to the group for discussion, it allowed us to organize our thoughts, prioritize issues, and consider how our feelings could be best expressed.

Over the course of our meetings, many internal planning documents were created. Below is a copy of an e-mail I sent to the group on September 5, 2011. This was sent in response to Tim's announcement that he had been contacted by CBS News to discuss his involvement in the opt out movement.

My dirty-dozen. This is my list of 12 things we should be prepared to offer/answer-and these are common sense ones so you all have probably already thought of them. These answers will be part of our "library" that we can use for all sorts of purposes....

1. Be able to explain why this is all about students (Keep everything focused on students. Even if teachers get fired and a school closes, ultimately it is the students who pay the price. Be able to explain why.) Avoid making this about teachers who are trying to protect their jobs.
2. What matters most—the more varied the statistics and subject, the better. We don't know what specifically they will ask, and being able to add in a statistic or two gives us credibility and can help to counter a reform-based argument that they may toss our way.
3. Be ready to explain how today's HST is worse than the testing that "old people like me" did in my youth ... (I am calling myself old, not Tim!)
4. Be prepared with short answers as to how testing actually hurts students and examples—trauma, guilt if they don't do well (teacher loses job), and the issue of testing special needs students who will fail by definition of their condition (My hubby is asleep and he is the special education teacher, not me ... but I believe that his students are 2 grade levels below the grade level and are forced to take the test—so of course they fail. It makes them feel terrible and like losers, again...)
5. Be able to list the key corporate players who profit from testing, how much they gain financially from testing, and—if we have examples—how they contribute to politicians campaigns.... Also, how much each year is spent on testing and test preparations.
6. Explain that charters and private schools often don't use HST—and many of these expensive private schools (President's daughters, for example) have quality teachers—and that politicians are hypocritical because they are demanding things from public schools but send their own children to schools that don't follow what they consider to be essential practices.
7. Have very short answers to the two questions posed on the fb page. Create one set of answers that are sound bite length—something that can be said in 10 seconds or less; the other set of answers can be a very short paragraph that actually answers the questions:

    a. HOW DO WE KNOW THAT CHILDREN ARE LEARNING? (or *what they are learning?*) We are vexed that the curriculum has been "narrowed." They will counter that for decades children graduated from high school not being able to read or do simple math, and you're worried about art and music. Shouldn't we have a bare minimum of things students should know? Shouldn't all students be held to the same basic "standards"? Then you can deal with "the frills"...
    b. HOW WILL YOU MAKE TEACHERS/SCHOOLS *ACCOUNTABLE?* Without test scores, how do you know teachers are actually teaching anything? Don't we need some sort of external accountability measurement to ensure that teachers are teaching? They stay in their classrooms behind closed doors and what is there to prevent them from just doing what they want?

8. Have pre-arranged Quotes available:

   a. Have a quote handy from a student, teacher, parent, **and** researcher as to why HST is not appropriate, how it negatively impacts students (remember, when a teacher is fired or a school closes, it ultimately impacts students) and/or how they feel being forced to participate in competition, politics, the firing of teachers and school closures, etc.

   b. Have a quote from a student handy that specifically expresses how they feel having their knowledge and thoughts reduced to multiple choice questions.

   c. Have a personal quote ready that addresses that having a student be able to develop complex questions and to find complex answers is more critical to success than simple bubble answers.

   d. Have a quote from both Tim and Ceresta's child (if possible) about why they didn't take the test, what they hoped to accomplish, and what happened. Age appropriate—

9. Have a list of research articles that explain/support our stance on HST and a list of the key researchers that support our stance.
10. Pose the issue of teacher-fear. Something is wrong when teachers are afraid to participate in a public debate about educational policies.
11. Have a list handy of the real reasons for HST—include that this is a tool being pushed by corporations in order to create a market for their services and products.
12. Be prepared to address the legal implications: Are we asking kids not to graduate? How can you "opt out" in other ways, if opting out of the test will keep a child from being promoted or graduating?

This is a start of the kinds of things that I think that we should all be ready to answer if needed. (personal correspondence, September 5, 2011)

Building Credibility So People Will Listen

In the middle of our rush to create all the documents we needed, one of the administrators asked the following jarring question: "Why should they listen to us?" I wish I could recall who asked the question, but I can't. All I can remember was the awkward dead silence of that Skype call. For a few seconds, we were all caught in the reality of the challenge we faced. Facebook was cluttered with thousands of activist pages. The news was filled with people claiming to be educational experts. What set us apart? Why would anyone listen to us?

In our gut, we knew that this group was special. We were authentic. We had experts from all levels of education and decades of combined teaching experience. We were people who were intimately familiar with research, but who also had invaluable classroom and parenting experience. We were also free of influence from those involved in the testing and evaluation industry.

We were the real deal. But how would others know?

For social movements to inspire people to actually take action, the followers need to feel that those in charge are *true authorities*. The followers need to have confidence in the abilities of their leaders, the desire to root for their success as they go into battle, and the willingness to act when asked to do so.

UOO used their website to establish this level of credibility. A great deal of time was devoted to filling the website with information that was both useful and which showcased the experience and expertise of the administrative team. The group developed original content, created documents in partnership with other established authorities, and located valuable resources from other highly regarded authorities. They also developed a list of links to blogs and other sites in an effort to build a strong, interconnected network and expose visitors to new ideas. This information was then deposited in a central location on the UOO website.

Over time, usage of the website continued to increase and its reputation as a key resource for High Stakes Testing and the opt out movement continued to grow. The month prior to Occupy DOE 2.0, the website had over 2 million visitors.

Establishing connections not directly related to UOO was also an important element to establishing our credibility. Two of the administrators, Tim Slekar and Shaun Johnson, had a powerful and humorous radio show, *At the Chalk Face*, and often used it to promote the ideology and activities of UOO. Other members spoke frequently at local and national education-related events, participated in television and radio interviews, and presented workshops addressing many of the issues key to UOO.

UOO recognized the power of layering efforts and knew the value of strong visual images—the things that could be photographed, shared on Facebook, and attract the media's attention. Fortunately, this strategy played on the strengths and experiences of the administrators who were all known for their humor, creativity, and willingness to try new things.

Morna McDermott created an education graveyard that was often featured by the news media. She also created a huge chart showing the complex links between the various education reform groups and the American Legislative Exchange Council (ALEC) and videoed a guided tour of the chart, posting it on YouTube. Shaun Johnson created an oversized ed-reform-themed Monopoly game, which was played by students in front of the Department of Education. I created a cluster of 5-ft tall school houses that were displayed at our Occupy DOE 2.0. At all events, colorful posters were created by participants and prominently displayed.

I took on the role of writing and issuing press releases to publicize our actions, events, and successes. The releases were met with varying degrees of interest. Sometimes our press releases would be picked up by a major media outlet. At other times, it would drive additional traffic to the website or Facebook page, or generate a request from media for more information. One press release that had been dormant for over a year was picked up and recirculated in the press a year later. All of these combined activities drew the attention of the media and community members alike, and increased the number and types of people who received our message.

As a result of the depth of information and media coverage, the administrative team succeeded in establishing themselves as the go-to authority for opting out information. However, it also had unintended consequences. The increase of visits to our website resulted in a sudden surge of individuals and media staff requesting personal contact or other follow-up. The bulk of this responsibility fell on the shoulders of UOO's president, Peggy Robertson, due to her in-depth understanding of the people, information, and resources involved. The risk of advocacy-related burn out became a real concern and remains a chronic issue for most people deeply involved in social causes.

A second unexpected consequence involved the limitation of our existing server plan. In the month prior to the 2013 Occupy, the website received over 2 million visitors. The sudden increase in visits to the website exceeded the range of the plan and overwhelmed the server. UOO was forced to upgrade to a higher usage plan, placing a greater financial strain on a group that was already scrambling to find the funds needed to support their efforts.

Making Size Matter, or the Power of a Compelling Protagonist

Sometimes strategies are created only after long and exhausting discussions and research. However, sometimes the most effective strategies evolve naturally and from surprising sources. Such was the case with dealing with what could have been one of UOO's greatest weakness: the size of the administrative team.

As discussed earlier, retaining a small core leadership group was a conscious decision that was solidified only after considerable thought and discussion. As the group gained in reputation and size, an increasing number of people expressed interested in taking on a greater, official role. While the administrators truly appreciated such supportive members, there never seemed the right time to break from the mold of the original small group.

Still, we worried that a small group of six people would not have the credibility given to larger groups. We also realized that having such a small leadership group limited the amount of time and resources that could be fed into the group by the administrative team. There were many things that UOO would have liked to do, but a lack of resources dropped them from consideration.

This was not the case, however, with those leading the education reform movement. This elite group included some of the wealthiest individuals in the world, well-financed foundations, and corporations with an annual budget that exceeded many nations.[2] They wielded incredible power and had access to a virtually limitless supply of human and financial capital.

We didn't know whether to hide the fact that we were so few or wear it as a badge of honor. As it turns out, America loves an underdog.

UOO versus the Ed Reformers soon became the story of David and Goliath.

At first, people were shocked to learn only six administrators (with absolutely no external funding) and a small team of highly dedicated supporters were the force behind our many actions. They were also shocked that a team of six "regular people" had the nerve to go head-to-head with some of the most powerful individuals and corporate entities in the world.

Once the reality of it all sunk in, our supporters cheered us on, hissed at the enemy, and cringed from the thought that we could, at any moment, be squashed. Most importantly, they stuck with us, turned each new page and became engrossed in our story. And they could not accept our defeat. They contributed funds for student activists to attend Occupy the DOE, flew hundreds of miles to attend UOO events, and continued to refer others to the site and assist the group to grow.

Rather than hide the fact that only six people were driving the actions of the group, we decided to embrace it and openly referred to the group as "six pissed-off radicals" who made up for their lack of funding with the depth of their passion, knowledge, and determination.

The timing for our David and Goliath comparison was perfect, as the Occupy movement[2] had focused attention on the often abusive power of our largest corporations and richest individuals. The David and Goliath story resonated with parents, teachers, and community members, alike. Rather than ignore us, they rallied behind us. In the end, the issue of our size generated additional media attention and a new group of supporters with a penchant for cheering for the underdog.

Selecting the Methods for Delivering Our Message

Life would be much simpler if one thing worked for all situations. Unfortunately, it doesn't. With activism, you need to tailor your document, your style, and your message to fit your particular situation and audience.

UOO created dozens of different documents in its first few years, each designed for a specific use and targeted audience. We had bookmarks, flyers, brochures, lists, templates, workbooks, and countless other types of materials that we shared. However, the central messages were always the same: High-stakes testing does not reflect student growth or the value of teachers, it diminishes the opportunity to obtain a comprehensive and quality education, is harmful to the individual and society, and is used as a tool by education reformists to privatize education and secure greater profits.

We recognized the need to select the vocabulary, style, and means of delivery most appropriate to our targeted audience, and a great deal of work went into adapting messages to ensure that each was appropriate for its purpose. Sometimes the documents were short, to the point, and void of any educational jargon. Sometimes they were filled with references to the latest research and technical language. Sometimes our message was best delivered using satire on YouTube, oversized visual displays, student art projects, or on simple buttons.[3] We varied the means of delivering our message; however, the overall message remained consistent.

This was done purposefully, as we wanted to assure our audiences that our message was authentic. We delivered the same message, whether we were standing on the steps of the White House, speaking in Selma, Alabama, or meeting face-to-face with Arne Duncan.

Taking Action

UOO knew what we wanted to say. We also knew who we wanted to listen. What was less clear was what we wanted them to do. At first, it seemed simple. We wanted parents to opt their children out of high-stakes testing. Yes, this was true. But how could we motivate them to actually take this action? And what could we do to help those who were either not ready to fully opt out or who did not have children in the school system to advance our cause? Did we invest time with actions that did not include actual opting out of a test, or would this be a waste of valuable resources and a dilution of our message and intentions?

This was probably our toughest strategic question and continues to be debated.

Our Facebook page addresses the multiple layers of opting out and suggests ways for assisting our cause that are not directly related to taking a test. We know that many people want help for various reasons. They are all not just looking for something directly related to refusing a test. We also have become more aware and sensitive to the pressure experienced by teachers across the nation and the efforts underway to silence their voices. However, we also know that every time student data is obtained by corporate entities, public education in America grows a little closer to extinction.

Data is a power and a weapon that is being used against public education. However, the administrators of UOO say that the *absence of data* is also power. It is also the one weapon that we can use against our ed-reform opponents.

If we are to win this war against high-stakes testing and the privatization of public education, we need our strongest weapon. We need data to be withheld. We need people to opt out and refuse the tests.

Overcoming Barriers

As the saying goes, nothing worth doing is ever easy. This is never truer than in the case of activism and the effort to build social movements.

When we first started the UOO group, there were no charts detailing which individuals or organizations were on which side of the high-stakes testing issue. We soon learned that the names of ed-reform groups often sounded safe and supportive and were frequently very similar to other groups that supported our cause. It was hard to tell friend from foe.

To make it easier to navigate this increasingly confusing landscape, I created several documents for internal use listing the various players and their affiliations and ties and notes about each one. Another list was made for the public which detailed the various players and the strategies used by the various groups. As mentioned earlier, Morna became our expert on the intricacies of ALEC and its web of ed-reform members. Soon we developed a finely tuned *education reform radar* and were able to recognize the groups and individuals as much by what they didn't say than what they did. We once joked that if we had a nickel for every time we discovered another group tied to ALEC or the ed-reform movement, UOO would be rich.

Not knowing the players was only one of the obstacles we faced. From the beginning, we knew that a lack of money would make our job challenging. It was. We anticipated that dealing with Facebook trolls would be time consuming and frustrating. It was. We thought that if we did our jobs correctly, we would be contacted by one of the corporations that we were challenging and that such contact would be both exciting and a little nerve racking. We were contacted, and yes, it *was* both exciting and nerve racking. However, we didn't fully anticipate the level of resistance we would have from school administrators and even from the co-workers of teachers. This resulted in some of our most painful, frustrating, and soul-searching moments.

We understood that many administrators felt that their hands were tied. They were being placed in impossible situations. Many expressed regrets that they could not openly embrace our message or facilitate our cause. And while we wished that all administrators would find the strength to join those who spoke out against high-stakes testing, we understood that not all were free to do so. What we had a harder time understanding was why some within the school system—the very people we were fighting for—made it their personal mission to seek out and punish educational professions who supported the opt out movement.

We learned to adapt our strategies to match this wave of *educational cannibalism* and protect each other. Teachers began using fake names, wearing wigs to events, and guiding each other on best practices for protecting themselves. We became an informal support group for many. Unfortunately, the harsh reality was that some teachers ended up changing jobs or leaving the profession entirely. Usually this was due to the increasingly negative work environment. Occasionally, though, it would be due to their activist actions. We grieved for the loss of these professionals and for the students who would not have a chance to benefit from their expertise, experience, and passion.

I admit that, at the beginning, we may also have been a bit naïve about those in Washington. We had assumed that we would find someone willing to actively take up our cause. This proved far more difficult that we ever imagined. In turns out that profiting off of education is a bipartisan activity. Even when politicians voiced strong support for our cause, they were unable or unwilling to raise our issue to the top of their pile and lend their face and their power to help.

Again, we learned to adapt, start lower down on the rungs of power, and concentrate on reaching out to those who would truly listen in hope that someday, they would have the influence that we needed to create real change.

Searching for a Pot of Gold

To close this chapter, I will spend one moment talking about a difficult issue: money.

Money is complicated. On one hand, the thought of money, or more precisely, our worry over the lack of money, is always in our thoughts. Discussions about money, however, are often avoided. The subject lacks easy solutions and is mined with dangerous points waiting to explode. As a result, the issue is often ignored completely.

Organizations advocating for change often face additional pressures. Not only do they have the pressure of not having enough, they also face pressure when they find it. Large donations sometimes come with expectations. They may be obvious expectations or they may be subtle. Even when there are no actual expectations tied to a large donation, just the question of improper influence and expectations may stain the organization, and that stain may remain for years.

The phrase, "follow the money" has become a simple guide to determining the true position of an organization. Fair or not, organizations are identified by their sources of funding. Even when nothing improper occurs, just the possibility of impropriety is enough to destroy an organization's reputation and send existing supporters running. The more controversial the actions of the organization, the more caution must be exercised when receiving large amounts of support from others.

I am proud to say that, although the subject was often difficult, UOO incorporated financial discussion in every step of its planning. They knew the importance and implications related to the subject and were determined to remain fully independent and free of any obligations—real or perceived.

As a result, several different strategies were adopted. To begin with, UOO decided it would not accept funds from entities involved in the dismantling of public education. Period. Instead, the group kept operating expenses to a minimum and covered many costs themselves. They also registered as a nonprofit in the State of Florida. Additional funds, when needed, were raised through donations from the membership, the sale of branded promotional items, and crowdsourcing campaigns.

In truth, there is never enough money—and money does matter. UOO could accomplish much more in the fight to preserve public education if they were engaged in a Goliath vs. Goliath war, instead of having to accept the role of David. And yes, I am sure that they welcome contact from those who would like to help to support the effort.

However, at the end of the day, integrity matters. You may not find that on a high-stakes test, but it is one of the most important lessons we can teach our children. With so many short cuts and temptations surrounding our children, it is important that they understand that sometimes the right answer is not the easy one, and that sometimes you will have to sacrifice and work harder, all because of an ethical choice you made. They need to realize that, at the end of the day, your choices mattered.

I am immensely proud of the difficult decisions and actions taken by the administrators of *United Opt Out National* and the enormity of the work that they have accomplished. While I am no longer part of the administrative team, they will always remain a part of me. I cannot begin to express the value of all that they have taught me and inspired within me. I am so much richer for the times that we shared and the experience I gained. They may need to keep on searching for their pot of gold. I, however, found mine.

Laurie Murphy and others at Occupy 2012

ACTIVIST'S HANDBOOK

1. Take time to understand why you exist and what you hope to accomplish. Be prepared to answer the following questions.

   • What is your purpose and your mission?
   • How is your organization unique?
   • What do you hope to accomplish?
   • What are you doing to achieve your milestones and broader mission?
   • Who will conduct these actions, and with whom will you interact?
   • What series of milestones will mark success?
   • What impact will these changes have on the larger conversation?

2. Determine how your group will be structured, how you will communicate, who is responsible for what, and how decisions will be made. You don't need a highly structured organization to make a major difference, but you do need all of the key players to be on the same page.
3. Find something that you can do that will cause some type of change. This may be a change in policy, procedure, or awareness. It is better to build on a series of smaller successes than to try one major project, fail, and then quit.

4. Create a list of who you want to work with, who you want to hear your message, how you will share your message, and what actions you want them to take. Determine the best way for connecting with everyone on your list. Remember, one size does not fit all. Tailor your content and language to fit your intended target. Layering—using different methods, varying your emphasis, and connecting with different groups—can add depth and effectiveness.

5. Establish and protect your credibility and sense of authority. Know your facts and the issues involved. Don't just parrot what others tell you. And learn to recognize propaganda and manipulative deception.

6. Know the difference between dramatic actions and becoming involved with distracting drama. You want your actions to get attention—to stand out—but for all of the right reasons. Plan quotable sound bites and photo-friendly events to convey your key messages, then review each to ensure that they convey what you intend and not anything that could distract from your main goals. Photos and quotes can take on a life of their own. Make them count.

7. Finally, everything you do should advance you forward in some manner: building a stronger internal group, establishing new or stronger alliances, increasing awareness, or addressing some portion of your concern. If it doesn't, learn to say, "No!" Time and energy are too valuable to waste.

NOTES

1. http://unitedoptout.com/about/letter-from-us/
2. http://www.washingtonpost.com/blogs/answer-sheet/post/ravitch-billionaires-and-millionaires-for-education-reform/2011/11/15/gIQAlDAHPN_blog.html
3. http://educationalchemy.com/2014/04/03/education-hackers-theyre-heeere/

CHAPTER 9

WHERE DO WE
GO FROM HERE

Tim Slekar

Tim Slekar

An Activist Handbook for the Education Revolution:
United Opt Out's Test of Courage, pp. 155–172
Copyright © 2015 by Information Age Publishing

Chomsky's Maxim

Where should opt out go in the future? That is an interesting question. However, let me answer it quickly by saying it should continue to do what it has been doing. Opt out must remain committed to speaking harsh realities to those in power, and it must continue to advocate actions that call attention to injustices in public schools.

I have been asked about *United Opt Out's* (UOO) future plans continually. The reason people ask is because of the misleading name—*United Opt Out*. For most, the name speaks only of action that is against simple standardized testing and never offers any alternative.

In the limited conversations and debates those in power would like us to have, opt out is simply one action against testing, because in their world, opt out is simply an anti-testing movement. In their vision of opt out, there are only two competing positions. One is pro-testing and the other is no testing. But as Chomsky (2008) reminds us, boundaries of debate are usually constructed by those in power to allow "vigorous debate" within a set of parameters.

When reformers claim that *United Opt Out* is only against testing, they are trying to set the boundaries of the debate. The same is true for those who critique *United Opt Out* for not offering an "alternative." What they are trying to do is maintain ownership over the conversation. In their world, it is simply a conversation about anti-testing and pro-testing; this makes opting out a nuanced position against testing with no alternative—nothing to replace the standardized tests. This is crap! They frame the debate as only two positions and try to paint *United Opt Out* as a single dimensional, anti-testing movement.

So when critics make comments stating that *United Opt Out* would be OK if only it offered an alternative, my response is simply that we need not offer an alternative because we are not engaged in the same conversation.

We refuse to allow others to define the boundaries of the conversation. *United Opt Out* is not a simple conversation about whether to test or not to test. It is a movement that demands that America deliver on the promise of public education and fully fund all schools equitably; that all children be provided a deep, rich curriculum full of all subjects and content areas; that teachers be treated like professionals and that all assessment transition from cheap, eugenics influenced standardized tests to truly authentic forms of assessment that treat education as an open door to endless wonders. No more bullshit beliefs that the purpose of education is to measure some predetermined set of skills dictated by those in charge.

Blog Post #1: The Myth of Failing Schools and the Unforgiven Sins of Wealth and Power

AUGUST 15, 2013[1]

There are no failed or failing schools! But there are plenty of buildings that serve as museums to display the failed social policies and economic disparities inflicted by politicians and their wealthy financiers.

A kindergarten class overcrowded with 35 children who lack basic healthcare, nutrition, and access to books and safe neighborhoods is NOT an example of failing students and an ineffective teacher. This is a graphic example of societal, political, and economic neglect. None of which was caused by the school or the teacher.

There are NO failing schools, instead, these schools stand as testimony to failed politicians, failed vulture philanthropists, and know-nothing FAILED educators.

When a child shows up to school after 5 years of fighting for basic survival, the failure is not with the school or the teacher—NO, the failure belongs to those in power. The failure belongs with those that hide behind enormous wealth and political power—those that have purposely created a society that deny NEEDED (not wanted) resources to children and families fighting to survive in a world of plenty-plenty of inhumane specimens that create false scarcities and fictional narratives that absolve them of the harm they have inflicted.

Someone has to say it!

Public schools are not failing [**Krashen, 2011**]—*they are just merely living examples of political, societal, and economic failure.*

A Word About Narratives

Considering the fact that we are still debating the failed schools narrative, it seems that *United Opt Out* has a lot of work to do. The work ahead now requires an understanding that the debate around "failed schools" is not owned by any in the opt out camp. No, "failed schools" belongs to the corporate reformers and all those who support the dismantling of the American public school system.

First though, let's address some of the rhetoric and the nonsense that masquerades as opt out pushback. Let's talk about the education reform conversation. To understand where *United Opt Out* must go in the future requires that one understand that the reform conversation concerning public schools in America is a manufactured rhetorical machine.

The reform conversation was designed to only allow debate within the narrow confines of high-stakes testing and punishment, or the act of civil disobedience and opting out. Within these confines, reformers can constantly use simple rhetorical barbs and jabs to hold on to the power in owning the debate, or such as, "If you're for opt out than you must be for no assessment." "You're just afraid of accountability," or "All kids should be held to high standards." If we don't test, how will we know if students are learning? If we don't test, how will we know if teachers are teaching? If we don't test, how will we know if schools … ?

It's maddening. *United Opt Out* is not the opposite of simple test-based accountability. *United Opt Out* is a mechanism to allow a new conversation to emerge about the future of public schools in America. It demands a different dialogue, and it asks painful questions and demands—sometimes—radical action.

If we want to know where opt out has always been going we must understand this first: *United Opt Outt* is not a counternarrative to education reform. *United Opt Out* is its own kickass vehicle to reimagine the promise of American public education.

For us to reimagine the promise of public schooling in America, we must first recognize the discussions surrounding, (a) poverty, (b) purpose of public education, (c) testing, (d) standards, (e) assessment, (f) teacher education, and (g) leadership within the profession.

We own them and we dictate the debate.

Owning the Debate by Blogging

For the rest of this chapter, I am reposting some of the blogs I have written over the years. I do this as an example of how we might start to reframe the conversation and regain ownership. Obviously some of these posts do a better job than others, but each is a valid attempt to shed the corporate reform costume and reveal a deepness and honesty.

Blog #2: Can Poor Children Learn?

MAY 13, 2013[2]

By now the *poverty does or doesn't matter* dichotomy is really starting to get old. Anyone that truly cares about helping children from low socio-economic environments succeed in school knows that all children (even poor ones) can learn.[3] It's absolutely ridiculous when education reformers insist that those of us "resisting" are claiming that "poor kids can't learn."[4]

In fact, do a GOOGLE search. Type in "poor kids can't learn." Amazing what the results show isn't it?

Along with the blog posts above, it is almost impossible to find anyone "resisting" education reform having said those words. In fact the "poor kids can't learn" bullshit (Ravitz, 2010) is typically spread by faith-based reformers while decontextualizing a comment such as, "Students that live in poverty come to school with challenges to learning in traditional academic settings." It is the reformer(s) who twist the debate and declare "You just said poor kids can't learn."

No! That's not what was said. What was said was that *poverty matters*. That's it. Not a single claim of a lack of intelligence on the part of children living in poverty.

So why bring this up now? I mean, those of us resisting education reform already are quite aware of how poverty "influences" the learning situations of children. None of us said, "poor kids can't learn." So can't we move on? Maybe. Maybe not. Not too long ago, Mr. Common Core himself (David Coleman) said, "We have to get serious with each other. It is not okay to say that since poverty matters so much we should use that as a reason to evade reform. It's not responsible" (as cited in Decker, 2013, para. 12).

This utterance perplexes me. It seems as if even Mr. Coleman understands that "poverty matters." But what the hell does it mean to recognize that and then demand more "reform?" Is he saying, "Look, I get it. Poverty sucks. But we (reformers) have to keep up the pressure. We just can't let them win! That would not be 'responsible.'"

Huh? If "poverty matters," and the current reforms aren't working, why would we continue to bash poor kids over the heads with education reforms? In fact **isn't that** IRRESPONSIBLE?

This entire poverty vs. reform (as if the latter requires we deny the existence of the former) discussion needs to end, and I am going to try to do it now. In June of 2011 and June of 2012, I, along with students and colleagues, traveled to Rwanda to work with orphan children. We had a pretty simple job—use grant money to get as many orphans through a health clinic as possible, and then find schools that were willing to educate the orphans. In 2011 we were only successful at getting 200 orphans through a health clinic. Some 92% of the orphans tested positive for parasites and other infectious diseases. All were treated with the proper medical attention and given medication. However we just didn't have enough time to find school placements for any of the orphans.

In 2012 I went back to Rwanda. This time we worked exclusively with a school and tried to secure school placements for some of the orphan children. While meeting with the administration of the Rwandan school, we were shocked to find out that the school would not take any of the orphan children. Admission to the school required a guarantee that each child had a sponsor willing to pay $14 dollars a month.

Huh? But why? Don't you want to help these children? Look, we put them through a health clinic last year and that was the extent of our grant money. We don't have $14 a month for each child. Can't you just take them? Don't these orphan children deserve a chance to go to school?

That was the dialogue in my head and out loud. The school administrators looked at us with a slightly confused look on their faces. Again we asked, "Why can't you take these orphaned children?" The answer, very bluntly was, **"Sick and hungry children can't learn."**

My colleagues and I stood speechless for moment. At some point, one of us managed to ask, "What?" as if we didn't hear the answer the first time. Again, one of the administrators reminded us that, "Sick and hungry children can't learn." He then explained that since June of 2011 all of the children who went through the health clinic were probably "sick" again since there was no continued care. He explained that $14 dollars a month would be used to pay for year-round health care, proper nutrition, and adequate clothing. These three things were "essentials" if children were to have a chance to succeed in school.

After the shock and more time discussing the issue, we came to understand what the Rwandan administrators were saying. It was still hard to accept, but it was hard to argue. The Rwandan school only had limited resources. The Rwandan administrators were only willing to use those resources with children who were properly fed, free from parasites and infectious diseases, and properly clothed.

Maybe "sick and hungry kids can't learn" was a bit harsh. But were they wrong?

How is it possible for a developing third world country to understand that *poverty matters*?

Someone Has to Say It!

Poor kids *can* learn! When they're not hungry!
Poor kids *can* learn! When they're not sick!
Poor kids *can* learn! When they're properly clothed.

When education reform means that we are willing to address these three facts, then sign me up. Until then … ?

Purpose of Public Schools

Blog #3: Public Education as the *Hunger Games*.

SEPTEMBER 6, 2012[5]

Diane Ravitch [2012] reminds us:

If we keep expecting schools to close the achievement gap by testing more, by adopting higher standards, by closing schools with low test scores, by evaluating teachers by test scores, and by offering carrots and sticks to teachers, we are deluded. (para. 1)

Reform logic requires a mirage of accountability. The reality is that the corporate reform movement embraced by Secretary of Education Arne Duncan and financed by hedge fund managers with deep ties to Democrats for Educational Reform is meant to destroy public schools in America. And once complete, the schools of the 99 percent will produce "globally competitive workers."[6]

Since the Democratic National Convention began, not a single Democrat has spoken about the function of public schools in maintaining a democratic society. Public schools have now been relegated to job training and as places where kids will learn to dominate the world through economic oppression.

This is not a world view that empowers educators. We did not get into public education to train our children to take part in the "Hunger Games" [2012] of economic global warfare. We became teachers because we wanted to help all students understand their responsibilities for living in a democratic society and help them learn to change the world. Public education is not job training. It is learning for life. If reduced to worker boot camp, children will be forced to dig the "Unforgiven" [1992].

Testing

Blog #4: It is what it is. But what if it's WRONG?

OCTOBER 4, 2012[7]

Last night I attended my local school board meeting to use my three minutes of public comment time to address the board. I was there to continue my comments from last school year on teacher evaluations and discuss why the board should at least think about the consequences that will occur when our teachers and principals are forced to have 50% of their evaluation determined by the invalid high stakes test scores of the children taking these invalid measurements.

Here's what I said last year. This year I went in without a formal speech. I took my seat and once the meeting started I was immediately called on to address the board (Public comment is always first).

I reminded the board of the points I made last year concerning Value Added Measures (VAMs) and teacher evaluation and then casually transitioned into why I was addressing the board again.

Examples of real world issues that have occurred where invalid tests scores are being used in teacher evaluations. I first commented that early observations show that some of the most vulnerable children will probably be the first casualties in this idiotic war on blaming teachers. As John McKenna stated (as cited in a post by Carol Burris in *The Washington Post*):

"The 'no excuses' philosophy which seeks to blame teachers for the burden our entire society must bear is a cold and shameful response to our most disadvantaged students." [2012, para. 17]

Why? It's simple, really. Students from challenging home settings and special education students score lower on high stakes tests. Again according to Burris,

"Some principals stated that they would change their teacher's assignment next year and assign them less needy students so that they could protect these excellent teachers from the ineffective rating. The unintended consequences to students are beginning." [para. 10]

The second reason I wanted to address the board was to inform them that because of VAM's exceedingly high error rates, teachers in D.C. who had been fired based on test scores were now being hired back [Turque, 2011]. Why? They were falsely identified as ineffective teachers.

Therefore, when our school district is forced by the state to evaluate teachers using invalid test score data, some of our best teachers will be labeled ineffective and the state will sanction the school and the board will be forced to fire these teachers. Once fired, some of these teachers will sue the school district and the school will be forced to either re-hire the teacher or pay damages or both.

I used my three minutes. The board president asked if any of the board members had questions. The dead silence permitted the board president to proceed with the official board meeting.

What? You thought they would actually ask questions? I had already taken three extra minutes of their time. The real business needed to be taken care of—finishing the meeting as quickly as possible.

At this time, the public—me—was allowed to leave. Knowing that 30 minutes was considered a long meeting I decided to stay. The meeting flowed flawlessly. The board president called items 1–6. "Second." "Motion passes."

Items 7–15. "Second." "Motion passes." I think this went on for about 10 minutes and then the meeting transitioned to reports from the principals.

The first principal to report was from the high school. She also has the honor of being the assessment coordinator. She reported that although the district met adequate yearly progress (AYP) some grade levels and special populations fell short. However, according to the principal, her team would go through the assessment data (high stakes test scores) and identify where they would target instruction. This is when she uttered the words "it is what it is" for the first time.

This comment caught my attention. What the hell does that mean? "It is what it is." I tried to ask a question but for some reason I wasn't recognized (maybe they didn't see me sitting alone right in front of them). The principal continued her assessment report. She talked about the fact that NCLB cut scores were going to be elevated next year and that they would work hard to meet the unreachable expectation of having certain grades and special education students score "proficient" and that by "shooting for the stars" maybe things will turn out differently. At any rate, she repeated, "It is what it is."

Huh? Again? What-the-hell-does-that-mean?

I tried to speak again but my raised hand must not have been visible in the room occupied by the board and me. The principal continued. She went on to announce that the state DOE [Department of Education] announced that it had changed an assessment policy for this academic year. Instead of field testing NEW standardized high stakes tests for high school students the state was going to use the new tests and scores to determine AYP.

Now I wanted to scream. In my head I shouted,

"You can't use brand new standardized tests to reward and punish students. These tests must go through rigorous field testing to determine if the tests are valid and reliable. This takes at least a few years!"

No one heard me. But this time the principal finally acknowledged that the state had put the high school students and the teachers at a disadvantage and that there were sure to be problems. But in the end, "It is what it is."

Since the board president was having a problem locating me I just waited for the meeting to end. I approached the principal (assessment coordinator) and asked her a simple question.

"Have you thought about fighting the state on the grounds that the new high school standardized tests have not been normed? Issues concerning validity and reliability need to worked out before any type of consequence can be attached to the results of the new tests (something anybody with any knowledge of standardized tests knows)?"

"No Tim. It is what it is."

Feeling defeated, I simply responded, "But what if it's wrong?"

Standards

Blog #5: "It's poverty stupid!"

MAY 4, 2014[8]

What follows below is nothing original. It's simply another reminder.

I know this is an unpopular thing to say in certain education circles **but someone has to say it:** Common Core State Standards and the Smarter Balanced Assessments will do little to nothing to help eliminate the achievement gap!

Why? Because the achievement gap is really an opportunity gap [see Krashen, 2011]. Standards and tests just measure the opportunities that we fail to provide our most vulnerable students.

Since 1983's false education crisis alert (A Nation at Risk) our public schools have been subjected to a 30-year barrage of standards and tests. Some of those standards have been extremely well written and some of the testing carried out with extreme care. Some of the standards were poor in quality and the testing atmosphere was problematic. However, good and bad, both demonstrated one thing consistently—race, socioeconomics, and geography predict the test scores of test takers.

In other words, standards and tests measure the historic inequities, and racial disparities our society fails to address. Standards and tests are racially biased tools that measure systemic poverty!

This is why we should seriously reconsider spending millions of dollars implementing another set of standards and tests (Common Core and Smarter Balanced, PARCC). Standards and tests fail to address the real determinants of academic achievement. Every tax dollar spent on common core aligned curricular materials and Smarter Balanced tests is a dollar wasted.

So then what are we to do? We must stop doing the same thing over and over again expecting to get different results—test and punish. We (you and me) must insist that tax dollars are directed at reducing the trauma of living in poverty. We must demand that our public schools are equitably funded and that schools that serve our most vulnerable children become centers of care for the communities they serve.

No more funneling tax dollars to testing corporations. Instead let's invest in child health care, nutrition, and books. Why these? Because unlike standards and tests we have more than 30 years worth of research that these investments actually help children experience success in school.

Corporate driven standards and tests are political distractions that keep us from looking at the real problems facing public schools—systemic funding inequities, racial disparities and crushing poverty.

False Assessment

Blog #6: A Hill to Die On!

AUGUST 6, 2012[9]

The SOS [*Save Our Schools* 2011] convention [in Washington, D.C.] was a great opportunity to see old friends and make some new ones. A lot happened and I am not going to summarize the conference [see Strauss, 2011]. My intent is to portray what I believe is the single biggest issue facing public education that emerged and describe the only solution.

The WAR we are fighting (and it is a war) is against the mistaken belief that private interests would run public schools best. And the weapon being used—very successfully—is punitive high stakes testing. The tests and the "data" perpetuate the mythology of failing schools, failing teachers, and failing students. This mythological mass failure has convinced our neighbors that "doing anything" is acceptable and even preferable, as long as we "fix" failing schools.

However, "doing anything" only occurs because of the false narrative that is supported by data from high stakes tests. The use of high stakes tests must end.

There is nothing to compromise on this issue–nothing! We know (and we better start helping our neighbors know) that the only thing high stakes tests tell us reliably and validly is the socio-economic condition of the test takers—that's it.

Even if we cared about achievement (I don't because I care about learning) the test scores provided by high stakes tests don't tell us about achievement.

Therefore a massive "Opt Out" of high stakes testing must be used to destroy the entire reform movement! We cannot negotiate some % of acceptable use of high stakes test data in calculating student achievement, teacher effectiveness, principal effectiveness, and school achievement. There is NO acceptable use of high stakes test data—None!

Opting out and subverting any use of high stakes tests is the only solution. This is war and this is a hill we must be willing to die on!

Teacher Education

Blog #7: Teacher Education for schools as they are OR for schools as they should be? That is the question.

OCTOBER 15, 2013[10]

A mentor once told me that "our goal" in teacher education is not to prepare pre-service teachers to teach in schools as they *are* but to prepare them *"to teach in schools as they should be."*

What does that actually mean? If enacted how would teacher education look? What would we do and/or not do?

My guess is that if we (teacher educators) really took to heart the idea of *"schools as they should be"* we would experience a transformative movement in our profession. And as much as I would like to see this radical transformation tomorrow I understand that an ontological shift like this requires a lot of information and a lot of discussion in safe places. You can't mandate transformation!

Since I accepted the position I currently hold as a leader of a teacher preparation school, I have tried to engage the faculty, staff and students. Nothing in your face. I simply find powerful posts concerning edreform [education reform] and I send them to our school's e-mail list (faculty, staff, and students). Reading the posts is not required and all are free to hit the delete button. Occasionally I get some positive feedback but for the most part interested faculty and staff just stop me in the hallway and say, "Thanks for the post."

[These little communiques are] my attempt to begin a more critical conversation among colleagues. However, in the last week I received two responses— and they weren't necessarily complimentary.

Quickly, both suggested that the messages I am sending out might be confusing students or suggesting that faculty take on positions contrary to the local public schools. They were not sure if I was asking them to directly challenge reform ideas and promote a classroom atmosphere geared towards future activism. And they were concerned that taking a more critical approach to education reform might actually interfere with our students' future careers as education professionals.

These are legitimate concerns. We don't want to send half-cocked education professionals into public schools just to cause trouble or buck the system for the sake of bucking.

However, if we believe that public schools should be safe places where children and teachers and parents and community members can gather to learn about everything from sentence structure to homelessness, then moving towards a more critical discussion seems warranted. And, if this is ever to happen we must at least begin a conversation. So that is why I decided to craft the e-mail response below.

Dear Colleague,

I would be glad to come to your class to talk about these issues. I will say that my personal and informed professional position on these issues isn't why I send these posts and articles to you and all the educators and future educators on this e-mail list. These are issues relevant to the profession and we at a minimum have a professional obligation to make sure that we and our students are fully informed concerning issues that deal with our profession.

Yes, our students "need to" do a lot of things and we have to make sure they are prepared—prepared better than any other students in Wisconsin. But that does not mean that we shield them from the larger debate that is taking place in the profession. They are in a professional program and we have a responsibility to make sure that our graduates are not just prepared for things how they are but they need to be able to imagine how things might be too.

It's not an either/or.

Yes our students should know about other students that are challenging the existing structures. Yes, they should know that CCSS has limitations. Yes they should know that Pearson is making billions off the current testing ethos that has more to do with political issues than issues that deal with what's best for children, parents, teachers, principals, schools, and communities.

We are educators and we have a mission to make sure our graduates are fully prepared to make critical decisions that promote the values of Truth, Justice, Compassion, Partnership, and Community.

Please stop by my office to talk anytime.

Regards,

Tim

Someone has to ask it!

Schools as they are?

Or

Schools as they should be?

How do we have this transformative discussion at institutions that prepare education professionals?

Leadership

Blog #8: Battling Education Reform: In the End it must be a "calling."

DECEMBER 22, 2013[11]

I am the "new" Dean of a School of Education at a Catholic College in the Midwest. One of the major reasons I was attracted to this position was the prominence of the college's Dominican values (Truth, Justice, Compassion, Partnership, and Community).

Think about it. If a college was committed to these values what would it mean for a school of education to articulate these values? And what would it look like in the context of preparing education professionals during our current education reformation? A reformation that is built on the foundation of corporate greed and a disrespect for human dignity.

For me the idea of leading a school of education during this education reformation was nothing less than a *calling*.

However, lately I have been challenged for my openly critical position on the Common Core State Standards (CCSS). While I have no problem being "challenged" I do find it difficult when those that challenge me refuse to use any scholarly evidence. Instead my critics just stick to CCSS talking points—world-class internationally benchmarked standards.

Who could possibly be against anything "world class?"

Me! And a contingent of progressive scholars, teachers, and intellectuals who have never once referred to the CCSS as a curriculum "written by Bill

Ayers" that will usher in an era of "communism" and turn children into puppets for the "United Nations."

No, our critique is actually really simple.

1. There is NO EVIDENCE that CCSS will help children succeed in school.
2. There is 30 years' worth of evidence that writing standards, testing children, and holding teachers and principals "accountable" *does not help* children succeed in school [see Tienken, 2013].
3. Accountability schemes are really just "test and punish" systems that maintain the status quo.
4. The money that will be spent ushering in this new "test and punish" system should be directed towards children, teachers and communities—not common standards, testing, and data management corporations!
5. Poverty denies "opportunities" to children and is the most influential factor contributing to the "achievement gap."

Therefore, as the Dean of a School of Education in a college with core values—truth, justice, compassion, community, and partnership—I am "called" to advocate for a system of teacher education that at a *minimum* recognizes poverty's influence on teaching and learning and *ideally* helps future teachers, principals, superintendents and other education professionals advocate for the equitable resources denied children in poverty. I am "called" to nurture an atmosphere where future educators create communities of inquiry and intellectual freedom that promote the uncomfortable but needed ability to speak truth to power. I am "called" to establish partnerships with other learning communities to strengthen common bonds that resist the narrative of the status quo education reformation.

In other words, my "calling" requires me to question the dominant culture's status quo attempt to hold teachers and principals accountable for poverty and advocate for a reclaiming of the education profession that teaches truth, expresses compassion, and demands justice.

I am not really critiquing the CCSS. I'm simply leading in a direction that seeks compassion and justice for the children of poverty. I am simply modeling evidence-based advocacy that leads to the truth—the truth that the CCSS is simply just a repackaging of "test and punish" reforms that only serve to maintain the current system's appalling separation between those that "have" and those that "have not."

However, in the end does it really matter? Shouldn't I just fall in line and prepare future education professionals for the jobs of today instead of the jobs that require serious reflection and the advocacy of evidence based reforms?

How Opt Out Owns the Conversation

Hopefully we can get a sense of what it might mean to own this conversation. The narratives around the broad spectrum of social and economic beliefs that shape our collective consciousness such as "accountability" and "poverty" have been warped by myths and lies promulgated by billionaire-owned media campaigns and stories that appeal to public sentiment. The blog posts above are just examples of ways to understand how the future of *United Opt Out* can claim ownership of the conversation. We have facts, we have evidence, we have knowledge … and we have each other. Our voices matter. The shine on their glossy narrative has worn off. People are catching on. The narrative is shifting. We must own it.

United Opt Out's New Position

We demand an equitably funded, democratically based, anti-racist, desegregated public school system for all Americans, which prepares students to exercise compassionate and critical decision making with civic virtue. If you're a reformer, tell us what you disagree with and please give us an "alternative."

We own this conversation now!

THE ACTIVIST WORKBOOK

How to Reclaim the Conversation.

1. Read! The only way to reclaim the conversation is to make sure that you actually know what the hell you're talking about. Read the research on teacher effectiveness based on VAMs. Read the research on data driven instruction. Read the research on top-down school management schemes. Read! Read! Read! The information is out there. Look at the Blogs. Anthony Cody, Diane Ravitch, Schools Matter, @the chalkface, Peter Greene, EduSchyster, Mercedes Schneider, Susan Ohanian, and so many more. The reformers have absolutely nothing other than ideology supporting their anti-public-schools narrative. Learn their narrative and make sure that you can easily point out evidence—not ideology—that negates or invalidates their bullshit.
2. Start writing your own blog and sending letters to editors of local newspapers and talking to your neighbors. Presenting the truth about reformers requires practice, and it will force you to remember step one—read. But the best thing you can do is help your neighbor understand why the destruction of public schools is the goal of the

reformers. Too many of our "neighbors" are attracted to reformer propaganda because it makes them feel good because they think they're actually supporting something positive. This has been the greatest accomplishment of the reformers. Our neighbors default to the idea that if somebody is talking about "fixing" something then they should be supportive. This is what has been happening since *A Nation at Risk*. Our neighbors believe that by simply supporting reformers they are helping. Most have no idea that they are being used in a battle to dismantle public schools. So you must practice presenting the pro-public-schools position and that reformers are actually engaged in dismantling public schools.

3.   Lastly, the only way to *reclaim* is to recognize when the narrative is owned by reformers. Whenever you find yourself in a defensive position, stop, think, and then simply say, "fuck you." Then proceed to reframe the conversation making sure that the pro-public-schools narrative is the topic of debate. Remember, we want to stop reformers before they even have a chance to utter their propaganda. We want them to defend their positions—which are defenseless. This is so important. Once we expose the reformers' narrative as the real horror story that is destroying the future for millions of children, we must take the high ground back and make reformers seem like soulless creatures hell bent on destroying public schools. Reformers must be made to start defending themselves. It is our responsibility to own the truth—we do!

NOTES

1. http://atthechalkface.com/2013/08/15/the-myth-of-failing-schools-and-the-unforgiven-sins-of-wealth-and-power/
2. See original post at http://atthechalkface.com/2013/05/13/can-poor-children-learn/
3. http://www.alaskapolicyforum.org/2012/05/nea-poor-kids-cant-learn/
4. http://eagnews.org/ctus-lewis-increased-accountability-unfair-because-poor-kids-cant-learn/
5. http://atthechalkface.com/2012/09/06/public-education-as-the-hunger-games/
6. National Governors Association http://www.corestandards.org/assets/0812BENCHMARKING.pdf
7. See original blog at http://atthechalkface.com/2012/10/04/it-is-what-it-is-but-what-if-its-wrong/
8. Original blog post can be found at http://atthechalkface.com/2014/05/04/its-poverty-stupid/
9. Original post at http://atthechalkface.com/2012/08/06/a-hill-to-die-on/

10. Original post can be found at http://atthechalkface.com/2013/10/15/teacher-education-for-schools-as-they-are-or-for-schools-as-they-should-be-that-is-the-question/
11. Original blog post can be found at http://atthechalkface.com/2013/12/22/battling-education-reform-in-the-end-it-must-be-a-calling/

REFERENCES

Burris, C. (2012, September 29). New teacher evaluations start to hurt students. *The Washington Post*. http://www.washingtonpost.com/blogs/answer-sheet/post/new-teacher-evaluations-start-to-hurt-students/2012/09/29/f6d1b038-0aa6-11e2-afff-d6c7f20a83bf_blog.html

Chomsky, N. (2008, January 1). We own the world. *Znet*. Retrieved from http://chomsky.info/articles/20080101.htm

Eastwood, C. (Director). (1992). Unforgiven [film]. Warners Brothers.

Decker, G. (2013, May 10). Alone among policy heavyweights, Vallas conveys reform fears *Chalkbeat*. Retrieved from http://ny.chalkbeat.org/2013/05/10/alone-among-policy-heavyweights-vallas-conveys-reform-fears/#.U5KM4PldVuo

Krashen, S. (2011). Poverty is the problem that must be solved.... Our schools are not broken. *Substance News*. Retrieved from http://www.substancenews.net/articles.php?page=2319

Ravitch, D. (2012, Sept 6). Making sure that poverty is not destiny. *Diane Ravitch's blog*. Retrieved from http://dianeravitch.net/2012/09/06/making-sure-that-poverty-is-not-destiny/

Ravitz, N. (2010, Oct 27). Let's stop pretending poor kids can't learn! *Huff Post*. Retrieved from http://www.huffingtonpost.com/natalie-ravitz/lets-stop-pretending-poor_b_774397.html

Ross, G. (Director). (2012). *The hunger games* [film]. Lionsgate.

Strauss, V. (2011, July 30). The save our schools march. *The Washington Post*. Retrieved from http://www.washingtonpost.com/blogs/answer-sheet/post/the-save-our-schools-march/2011/07/30/gIQAhf71jI_blog.htm

Tienken, C. (2013). *The school reform landscape: Fraud, myth, and lies*. New York, NY: Rowman and Littlefield.

Turque, B. (2011, July 15). More than two hundred teachers fired. *The Washington Post*. Retrieved from http://www.washingtonpost.com/blogs/dc-schools-insider/post/more-than-200- dc-teachers-fired/2011/07/15/gIQADnTLGI_blog.html

CONCLUSION

Rosemarie Jensen

Rosemarie Jensen

An Activist Handbook for the Education Revolution:
United Opt Out's Test of Courage, pp. 173–175
Copyright © 2015 by Information Age Publishing
All rights of reproduction in any form reserved.

> *The educator has the duty of not being neutral.*
>
> —Paulo Freire (1990)

I would dare say that all of us, when we pursued our degrees in education, had no idea the path our choice would take us. I firmly believe that the decision to teach (at a subconscious level) is a choice to pursue social justice, to inspire children to find their passion, to make a small difference in the world, and to nurture children's ability to become a part of this democratic society. Did we all know that we would be fighting for resources not only for the schools in which we taught but for all schools? Absolutely. Did we all know there were glaring inequities in the system to which we were committing ourselves? Without a doubt. Did we understand that this incredibly challenging and rewarding job would be difficult? Definitely. Did we ever believe in our wildest imaginations that a few individuals would change the landscape of teaching so dramatically that we would be called to become what some would call "radical" in order to defend authentic assessment, teacher autonomy, equitably funded neighborhood public schools, and a positive and appropriate learning environment?

Unequivocally, no.

I do not believe that advocating for an equitable education for all children is radical. I do not believe that having fully funded professionally staffed neighborhood schools can be deemed radical. Schools that include wrap around services where needed—the arts, physical education, libraries, nurses, social workers, psychologists, computers, and highly degreed teachers—are not radical ideas. They are something we seem to fight for in other countries, but seem to deny our own children. That is, unless you can afford to send your children to a tony private school that boasts small class sizes; a full complement of electives; little, if any, high-stakes testing; and highly qualified teachers. I do not believe that teacher autonomy and community involvement in curricular decisions in public schools should be described as radical. In fact, I think it's downright American and democratic. What is frightening is the growing realization that there must be something horribly wrong with our collective sociopolitical climate in this country if these things for which we advocate are indeed "radical." If our demands are radical, what does that say about the current system of education reform? Freire reminds us that:

> The more radical the person is, the more fully he or she enters into reality so that, knowing it better, he or she can transform it. This individual is not afraid to confront, to listen, to see the world unveiled. This person is not afraid to meet the people or to enter into a dialogue with them. This person does not consider himself or herself the proprietor of history or of all people, or the liberator of the oppressed; but he or she does commit himself or herself, within history, to fight at their side. (1970, p. 39)

Whether we are wearing our teacher hats or wearing our parent hats, what we have seen happen to the children we teach and to our own children as the testing juggernaut has invaded our learning spaces has been catastrophic. More and more time is devoted to benchmark testing, test prep, and to the testing itself. We have watched our specials and enrichment disappear, recess reduced to a special occasion, and worse, schools completely shuttered as a result of reforms promulgated by these test scores—tests, which parents and teachers cannot see. And while the adults can shoulder much of the stress, the children, *our children*, are the ones feeling it like a rock on their backs. It's like living the myth rof Sisyphus every year. We roll that rock of test-prep up the hill, never knowing how high we have to push it past some arbitrary cut line that keeps changing, only to have it crash down on the children who are tired, burnt out, and turned off from learning. As a result, children are retained, reshuffled, removed, damning their futures. None of these reform measures have anything to do with children.

So we stand here as educators from different backgrounds, different states, and different experiences with one unifying purpose in mind. We have never been, nor can we be, neutral when it comes to the education of the children in this country. We are united in the desire to demand an equitably funded, democratically based, anti-racist, desegregated public school system for all Americans, which prepares students to exercise compassionate and critical decision making with civic virtue. Opt in to our conversation and reclaim public education. Opt out is not a counternarrative to education reform. Opt out is its own kickass vehicle to reimagine the promise of American public education.

Opt out is not the opposite of simple test based accountability. Opt out is a mechanism to allow a new conversation to emerge about the future of public schools in America. It demands a different dialogue and it asks painful questions and demands—sometimes—action perceived as radical. For us to reimagine the promise of public schooling in America, we must first recognize the discussions surrounding (a) poverty, (b) the purpose of public education, (c) testing, (d) standards, (e) assessment, (f) teacher education, and (g) leadership within the profession. We own them and we dictate the debate.

We hope that you too can no longer be neutral. We hope you too are committed to local and national action to reclaim education and to enact, embody, and empower children, educators, parents, and entire communities to actualize what public education can and should be.

REFERENCES

Freire, P. (1970). *Pedagogy of the oppressed.* New York, NY: Herder and Herder
Freire, P. (1990). *We make the road by walking: Conversations on education and social change.* Philadelphis, PA: Temple University Press

APPENDIX

Biographies of All Speakers at Occupy the U.S. Department of Education 2012 and 2013, and Denver, 2014

THE UOO TEAM

Rosemarie Jensen (joined UOO in 2014) is a former teacher and currently a parent activist. She received her MEd from the University of Florida and taught K–1 for 10 years in both Alachua and Broward Counties. In addition, she trained teachers in Alachua and surrounding counties in Math Their Way and later worked as a K–2 literacy trainer for teachers in Broward County. In the past 15 years she has been an active participant in her local schools and has worked to end high-stakes testing and corporate reforms. She has been involved in community, state, and national efforts to support public education and teachers. She has opted her son out of FCAT for the past 3 years in Florida.

Shaun Johnson, PhD, is a public school teacher, teacher educator, blogger, and online radio show host of At the Chalk Face.

Morna McDermott has been working in, with, and around public schools for over 20 years. Currently she is associate professor at Towson University in Maryland. Her scholarship and research interests focus on democracy, social justice, and arts-informed inquiry in K–postsecondary educational settings, and working with beginning and experienced educators. She recently authored a book, *The Left Handed Curriculum: Creative Experiences for Empowering Teachers* (IAP, 2012) and maintains a blog at www. educationalchemy.com. She currently lives in Baltimore with her husband and two children.

Laurie Murphy is the Director of Resource Development for a nonprofit agency serving multiple counties in central Florida. She has worked in the nonprofit sector for over 15 years. Laurie has strong ties to the educational community, as her husband, two of her children, and countless others in prior generations have all served their communities as teachers. Laurie was a charter member of Save Our Schools march and National Call to Action, Organizing Committee (left UOO in 2013).

Peggy Robertson has taught kindergarten, first, second, fourth, fifth, and sixth grade. She was hired by Richard C. Owen Publishers in 2001 to serve as a Learning Network Coordinator and spent the next 3 years training teacher leaders and administrators in educational theory and practice in the state of Colorado, as well as around the country during the summer months. In 2004 she was hired as the Literacy Coordinator in Adams 50 School District in Westminster, Colorado. She earned her master's degree in English as a Second Language at Southeast Missouri State University. She is in her 17th year of teaching as an instructional coach at an elementary school in Colorado. She is a member of the Aurora Education Association (affiliate of NEA), co-founder of the RAVE caucus, a writer, and a devoted education activist through her work at *United Opt Out National*. She is a contributor to the book, *Pencils Down* (2012, Rethinking Schools). Her blog can be found at www.pegwithpen.com.

Ruth Rodriguez holds a BA in social work and did graduate studies in Bilingual Education at Boston University. Ruth taught Kindergarten for 5 years at Chandler Magnet School, a two-way bilingual school in Worcester, Massachusetts. She was a Community Fellow in the Urban Studies Department at MIT where she researched school violence. Ruth served on Massachusetts Governor Deval Patrick's Readiness Project on MCAS and Assessment, an initiative that brought together a diverse group of educators, from superintendents, principals, parents, teachers, and community advocates, to advise the governor on the Massachusetts Comprehensive Assessment System (Massachusetts high-stakes exam for promotion and graduation requirement) (joined UOO in 2013).

Timothy D. Slekar is the Dean of the College of Education at Edgewood College in Madison, Wisconsin. Dr. Slekar began his career in education as a second-grade teacher in Williamsburg, Virginia. He also taught fifth grade in York, Pennsylvania. Dr. Slekar attended the University of Maryland at College Park where he earned his PhD in social studies education. Dr. Slekar has published research in some of the top educational research journals (*Teacher Education Quarterly, Theory and Research in Social Education*, the *Journal of Thought*). Tim and Dr. Shaun Johnson also host At The Chalk Face (BlogTalkRadio) Progressive Education Talk.

Ceresta Smith is a 25-year veteran educator and member of United Teachers of Dade. She earned her National Board Certification in Adult/Young Adult English/language arts in 2002. In September of 2008, she moved from a school deemed "high performing" to serve as a teacher leader and literacy coach in a school deemed "low performing." She currently mentors teachers and teaches language arts at John A. Ferguson High School in Miami-Dade County. Additionally, she served as a delegate to NEA, FEA, AFT, and AFL/CIO. Along with her role as an administrators for *United Opt Out*, Ms. Smith is one of the original organizers of and is an active Steering Committee member for Save Our Schools march.

SPEAKERS FROM UOO EVENTS

Bess Altwerger is Professor Emerita at Towson University. She is a founding member of Save Our Schools, a current Steering Committee member, and was a key organizer of the summer 2011 Save Our Schools rally, march, and conference in Washington, DC. She has worked with teachers on the Navajo reservation, in the barrios of New Mexico and Arizona, and in urban school districts in the northeast and mid-Atlantic states to support multicultural/multilingual, democratic, and child-centered education. Bess has published and presented widely on the negative impact of federal policies on our schools and classrooms, particularly in the area of literacy. Her books include *Literacy Policies and Practices in Conflict: Reclaiming Classrooms in Networked Times* (co-edited with N. R. Shelton, 2015). She currently serves on the Howard County (Maryland) Board of Education.

Sam Anderson is an activist-educator who has been "retired" from higher education. He is a math/popular science and Black studies professor as well as an editor of the *Black Activist Zine* (blackactivistzine.org), co-chair of the Brecht Forum (brechtforum.org) and the Malcolm X Museum (mxmuseum.org). He is a member of the NYC Coalition for Public Education (forpubliced.org), the National Black Education Agenda (blackeducationnow.org) and the Independent Commission on Public Education (icope.org).

Philip Arnold[1] is a veteran educator with 20 years of experience teaching fifth and second grade. He is also the founder of the Facebook *Educators AGAINST Tony Bennett.* He began this page in 2010 as an "angry" educator wanting to vent about Tony Bennett and his extremist tactics and overwhelming policies. In November 2013, the page took on a new role and new name (*Citizens against Tony Bennett*) with a nationwide mission to prevent Tony Bennett from becoming a National Disaster for Public Education as he made his way to Florida.

Don Bartalo (Bart) is a recognized instructional leadership developer/coach, literacy specialist, and instructional systems analyst. Bart has extensive K–12 experience as a teacher, teacher leader, assistant principal, principal, superintendent of schools, and educational consultant. Bart is the Founder/CEO of UNITY Instructional Leadership Development and Coaching with a mission to bring theory and practice together. Bart is the author of *Closing the Teaching Gap: Coaching for Instructional Leaders* (Corwin Press, 2012). He is also the developer of *Leadership for Literacy*, marketed by Rigby Education and *Standards-Aligned Instructional Leadership* (SAIL), marketed by the Ohio Association of Elementary School Administrators.

Liza Campbell is currently a teacher and education organizer in Seattle, Washington. At the time of her speech at Occupy DOE in DC, she worked in New York City, where she focused her activism energy on building a movement of parents and teachers to fight high-stakes testing, combating the school-to-prison pipeline while pushing for restorative alternatives, and occupying the New York City Department of Education. She teaches high school math.

Phillip Cantor is a science teacher at North-Grand High School—a neighborhood public school on the northwest side of Chicago. He was a strike captain during the Chicago Teachers Union strike and is an active member of Teachers for Social Justice and CODE—Communities Organized for Democracy in Education—which is fighting for an elected school board in Chicago. He began teaching in 2002 after a career in multimedia production as a cinematographer, director, and producer. He has a master's degree in education policy from the University of Illinois at Chicago.

Chris Cerrone[2] is a husband, parent of two elementary school children, veteran middle school teacher, community volunteer, and youth sports coach in western New York. As a parent, Chris is an opt out organizer in

New York State. Chris also is a member of the Hamburg Teachers' Association, which recently was one of only five districts in New York State which did not agree to a teacher evaluation system using student test scores as a factor.

Anthony Cody taught middle school science in a high poverty school in Oakland, California, for 18 years and led a mentoring program there for another 6 years. He has been writing about education reform from the perspective of a classroom teacher for the past 6 years. He was one of the organizers of the 2011 Save Our Schools march in Washington, DC. In 2012, his dialogue with the Gates Foundation took that organization to task for its misguided approach to reform. In 2013, he co-founded the Network for Public Education with Diane Ravitch.

Lauren Cohen entered teaching through the NYC Teaching Fellows in 2005 as a mid-year replacement for a K–2 self-contained special education teacher at a high-needs school in Harlem. She taught there for 2 more full school years. She spent the next 5 years at a Title 1 school in the East Village, where she gained a reputation among her colleagues for speaking out against administrative mandates that were detrimental to student learning (such as canceling extended-day enrichment programs in favor of test prep aligned to faulty and inaccurate Acuity results). She currently teaches at P.S. 321 in Park Slope, where the privileges available to her current students have only strengthened her resolve to fight for a more equitable system on behalf of all of New York's children. For the past 2 years, Lauren has worked with parents, teachers, and others in Change the Stakes, fighting against the use of standardized tests to punish schools, teachers, and students. She attended her first MORE meeting in the spring of 2012 and was thrilled to meet so many like-minded educators. She ran on the MORE slate for Elementary Executive Board in the UFT election, for a NYSUT At-Large Director position, and she now serves as co-Chapter Leader for P.S. 321.

Tracey Bowen Douglas is a classroom teacher, an "Edublogger," and is active in the union at both the local and state levels. She is a member of a California Teachers Association Think Tank and a CTA Teacher Leader Cohort.

Angela Engel is the co-founder and executive director of Uniting 4 Kids. She is the acclaimed author of *Seeds of Tomorrow: Solutions for Improving our Children's Education* (Paradigm Publishers, 2010). Angela earned a master's degree in curriculum and instruction and has spent the past 20 years in teaching and education policy. In 2008, she served as the project director for the Children's Action Agenda. She designed the "50 State Resolution" to end No Child Left Behind and authored legislation to reduce high-stakes testing, protect parental rights, and improve prevention and early intervention services for low-income children. She is in her sixth year as facilitator and Master Trainer for the Family Leadership Training Institute. She lives in Colorado with her two beautiful daughters Grace, 16 and Sophie, 14.

Matt Farmer is a Chicago public schools parent. In the lead-up to one of Matt's recent education-related TV appearances, a local host introduced him as "Matt Farmer—musician, rabble-rouser, attorney, blogger, just kind of a general in-your-face kind of guy." Matt writes frequently about education for *The Huffington Post*.

Stefanie Fuhr has been in the classroom for close to 20 years. She has a master's degree in elementary education and is a member of the National Writing Project. She is the co-founder of Voices for Public Education and a member of the Network for Public Education's grassroots discussion group. Stefanie has had a few of her writing pieces published in various journals and organizations.

Alexia Garcia was a senior at Lincoln High School in Portland, Oregon, during Occupy DOE 2.0, where she served as the Student Representative on the Portland Public School's Board of Education. She was also a member of both the Portland Public Schools Student Union and the Portland Student Union. She took a gap year in 2013–2014 before attending college to intern with the Portland Association of Teachers (PAT) and after they settled a contract she moved to Seattle to help on Jesse Hagopian and the RESPECT Slate's campaign to win over the Seattle Education Association. She is currently in Portland and will attend Vassar College this coming fall.

Nikhil Goyal is the author of *One Size Does Not Fit All: A Student's Assessment of School* (Bravura Books, 2012). An international speaker, Nikhil has spoken at NBC, Dell, Cisco, Fast Company, MIT, Florida International University, College of the North Atlantic, and other conferences around the world. He is also a guest lecturer at Baruch College. Nikhil currently serves on the board of *FairTest*.

Troy Grant received his PhD from the University of Maryland Baltimore County (UMBC) in 2013. He is a veteran social studies educator currently teaching in Maryland. He is the only person living who can recite the entire United States Constitution from memory.

Dave Greene taught social studies and coached in NYC, Woodlands High School, Scarsdale High School, and Ardsley High School since 1970. Retired from teaching in 2008, he presently is a member of WISE Services, an organization that helps high schools create and run experiential learning programs for seniors. He is also the treasurer of Save Our Schools march committee. He blogs at dcgmentor.com. He is also the author of a book, *Doing the Right Thing: A Teacher Speaks* (Freisen Press, 2013).

Michelle Strater Gunderson is in her 27th year of teaching and currently teaches first grade in the Chicago Public Schools. She is a vice president for the Chicago Teachers Union, is chair of the union's Early Childhood Committee, and is on the steering committee of the Caucus of Rank and File Educators (CORE). Michelle is grounded by her passion for social justice unionism—working equally for students' rights as well workplace justice.

Leonie Haimson is Executive Director of Class Size Matters, a nonprofit advocacy group working for smaller class sizes in New York City and the nation as a whole. She is also a co-founder of Parents Across America, a national grassroots group that supports progressive and proven education reforms. She is a graduate of Harvard University and worked at the Educational Priorities Panel. She writes for several blogs, including *NYC Public School Parents* and *Huffington Post*.

Melissa Heckler is a public school librarian and education activist from Westchester Country, New York. Melissa Heckler, a professional storyteller and the co-author of *Who Says?: Essays on Pivotal Issues in Contemporary Storytelling* (August House, 1996), founded the first in-village schools for the Ju/'hoansi in the Kalahari in Namibia, Africa. Melissa is a board member of the professional library organizations as well and has published articles about her experiences in indigenous education and storytelling.

Jeremiah James Henderson is an undergraduate student at the University of New Mexico, completing his degree in elementary education. Jeremiah became an activist for public education when he felt that something was not right with education. He started following Diane Ravitch, where in turn he met the UOO. Jeremiah is an advocate for recess, play, teacher-controlled classrooms, equitable funding for schools, and for libraries, just to name a few. Jeremiah believes that by opting out, we share a message that public schools cannot be bought and that our children are more than a test score!

Jessica Hochmann is assistant professor at Pratt Institute School of Information and Library Science (SILS) and the LMS Program Coordinator (school librarians). She teaches courses on teaching and learning in libraries, whether and how to use technology for instruction, and educational foundations. Her research interests include the nexus of youth culture and technology, informal literacy practices, discourses of teaching and teachers, and feminist theory and practice. She is from St. Louis, Missouri, and lives in Brooklyn, New York, with her partner Alex and daughter, MB.

Jim Horn has been an educator for four decades, with time pretty evenly divided between public schools and higher education. He is still, today, a proud Tennessee educator, holding licenses for English 7–12, Library Media K–12, and Administration 7–12. His PhD is from the University of Tennessee in social foundations of education. Since 1996 he has taught at four higher education institutions between Shreveport, Lousiana, and Cambridge, Massachusetts, where he teaches now in the Department of Educational Leadership. He has published widely in peer-reviewed journals and in online publications on subjects ranging from complexity theory to education reform history. He co-authored *The Mismeasure of Education*, which was published in 2013.

Sherick Hughes, PhD, is associate professor with tenure at the University of North Carolina at Chapel Hill. He is a former public school teaching assistant, G3 teacher of urban youth in foster care, and a member of the NC-ERC, the former education research wing of Governor Jim Hunt's Education Cabinet. His research, teaching, and service have earned him leadership roles in the national Save Our Schools movement and recognition from Phi Delta Kappa, the Harvard Family Involvement Network of Educators, AESA, AERA, and Border Crossers-New York City.

Brian Jones is a teacher and doctoral student in New York City and a member of the Movement of Rank and File Educators (MORE), the social justice caucus of the United Federation of Teachers. He co-narrated the film, *The Inconvenient Truth Behind Waiting for Superman* (2011), and contributed to the book, *Education and Capitalism: Struggles for Learning and Liberation*. He is running for Lieutenant Governor with Howie Hawkins for the Green Party in New York State.

Denisha Jones is assistant professor in the School of Education at Howard University. She has been active in the fight to stop the corporate takeover of public education since 2011. She has worked with Save Our Schools, *United Opt Out,* and the Badass Teachers Association to expose the dangers of privatizing public education. She blogs about education for *emPower*

Magazine, At the Chalk Face, and the Badass Teachers Association. Her research interests include the deprofessionalization of teaching, service learning, providing meaningful professional development for early childhood teachers, and promoting diversity in education.

Alex Kasch writes, "I am fortunate to go to a school that teaches me life skills and allows me to pursue my passions. But in my freshman year of high school my school was in trouble and at risk of closing. Starting my political actions in my freshman year of high school I knew something greater needed to be done. It wasn't just about me and my education or the school I attend; it is about all students of America and everyone's education." Alex is a senior and is one of the founders of Students 4 Our Schools and one of the leaders of the TCAP walkout in Denver.

Michael Klonsky is on the education faculty at DePaul University in Chicago. He currently serves as the national director of the Small Schools Workshop and is a member of the National Steering Committee of Save Our Schools (SOS). He is also the parent of three children who have been educated in Chicago's public schools. He is author of several books, including *Small Schools: Public School Reform Meets the Ownership Society* (Routledge, 2008), *Small Schools: The Numbers Tell a Story* (University of Illinois Small Schools Workshop, 1995), and co-author of *A Simple Justice: The Challenge for Teachers in Small Schools* (Teachers College Press, 2000). He has served as a member of the National Advisory Council on Youth Violence and is past president of the board of *Catalyst*, Chicago's school-reform journal.

Stephen Krashen is Emeritus Professor of Education at the University of Southern California. He was the 1977 Incline Bench Press champion of Venice Beach and holds a black belt in Tae Kwon Do. He is the author of *The Power of Reading* (Heinemann, 2004, second edition), *Explorations in Language and Use* (Heinemann, 2003), and co-author, with Jim Crawford, of *English Learners in American Classrooms* (Scholastic, 2007). His recent papers can be found at http://www.sdkrashen.com.

Kevin Kumashiro is professor of Asian American studies and education at the University of Illinois at Chicago, founding member of Chicagoland Researchers and Advocates for Transformative Education (CReATE), director of the Center for Anti-Oppressive Education, and president of the National Association for Multicultural Education (NAME). He is the award-winning author or editor of nine books on education and social justice.

Bob and Yvonne Lamothe are the creators of the documentary, *TEACH, Teachers are Talking, Is the Nation Listening?* Robert Lamothe and Yvonne Lamothe are teachers in the Boston Public Schools.

Barry Lane is an author, teacher, comedian, and singer. Barry performs a cabaret which celebrates teachers. After years of doing stand-up and parody karaoke singing as part of his academic presentations, Barry Lane has put together a genuine interactive, improvisational nightclub act for teachers. Barry's Cabaret celebrates teachers.

Larry Lawrence began as a high school math teacher in Inglewood, California. In 1966, he was brought to the University Elementary School at UCLA (UES) to work with John Goodlad and Madeline Hunter on non-grading/school organization (Goodlad) and instructional skills/classroom organization (Hunter). After several years, he left UES to serve as an elementary principal in one California district and as a Curriculum/Special Projects Director in two other districts. After retirement from UCLA, he moved to the San Diego area to work as a math education consultant for a startup educational technology company (Lightspan, bought by PLATO).

Karen Lewis is the president of the Chicago Teachers Union (CTU).

Pamela Lewis[3] is an educator, writer, and activist currently living and working in the South Bronx. A native Bronxite and product of the urban public school system, Pamela's commitment to the children for whom which she teaches runs deep. As a servant of her community, Pamela uses both teaching and writing platforms as a means to improve, empower, or educate its members, as well as others about the people, culture, and needs of her community.

Malcolm London, called the Gil-Scott Heron of this generation by Cornel West, is an internationally recognized Chicago poet, activist, and educator. He is a member of the Young Adult Council of the prestigious Steppenwolf Theater. He has appeared on PBS for the first ever televised TED Talk with John Legend and Bill Gates. He also appears on season 2 of TVOne's *Verses & Flow*. Malcolm's work has been featured on national outlets including *CBS, NPR, Huffington Post, The Root,* and the *Chicago Tribune.* London attends the University of Illinois at Chicago and is a member and co-chair of BYP100, Chicago Chapter, a national organization of Black activists and organizers.

Barbara Madeloni is currently the president of the Massachusetts Teachers Association. Prior to this, Barbara Madeloni was the director of the secondary-teacher education program at UMass. Her contract wasn't renewed after she spoke out against the Pearson teacher performance assessment. An English teacher and now a teacher educator, Barbara's activism came to national attention when she supported students in resisting Pearson's incursion into teacher education.

Jean McTavish is a 28-year veteran educator with the New York City Department of Education. She has earned degrees in anthropology and education, special education, and education administration from Columbia University Teachers College. Jean has been the principal of Edward A. Reynolds West Side High School (a Transfer Alternative High School) since 2001. In 2014, her school, and three others schools in the nation, were honored with the Alliance for a Healthier Generation's Gold Recognition. Jean is the proud mother of two children who attend the public schools. Jean believes very strongly that parents hold a tremendous amount of untapped power. Parents can withhold children's test data and demand meaningful participation in determining the future of the neighborhood schools in their communities. Jean is an organizer for SOSNJ and works with a variety of like-minded organizations, such as *United Opt Out*, Change the Stakes, Reclaiming the Conversation, and Edu4. Jean opted her children out of any potentially high-stakes testing for the third time this year.

Deborah Meier is a senior scholar at NYU's Steinhardt School and board member of the Coalition of Essential Schools, *FairTest*, Save Our Schools, *Dissent*, and *The Nation* magazines. She spent 45 years working in K–12 public schools in New York City (East Harlem) and Boston (Roxbury), including leadership of several highly successful small democratically run public urban schools—the Central Park East schools and Mission Hill. Her books include *The Power of Their Ideas* and *In Schools We Trust*. In 1987, she was the first educator to receive a McArthur "genius" Award and currently blogs for *Ed Week* with Pedro Noguera (Bridging Differences).

Rick Meyer is regents professor at the University of New Mexico and has published broadly. He was one of the organizers of the Save Our Schools march and National Call to Action in 2011 and has remained active in SOS, most recently as a member of the steering committee, working with Bess Altwerger as co-directors of national actions. Rick is also a member of the executive committee of the Latino Education Task Force and is working with various groups to ensure that New Mexico's children are fully served as demanded by the state's constitution. Rick and a small group of other SOS folks recently attended and were part of discussions at the Selma Jubilee, a civil rights celebration that occurs every year.

Helen Moore has lived in Detroit, Michigan, since she left Newport, Tennessee, in 1941. She has four children who were also educated in Detroit Public Schools. They all graduated from Cass Tech, and Helen graduated from Commerce High School. She graduated from Wayne State in 1985 after raising her children and has a law degree from Detroit College of Law at Michigan State. She is the recipient of over 200 awards and just received the Michigan State, Robert Millender Visionary Award. She has dedicated her life to fighting for our children to have a quality education and a fair chance of achieving their life goals. After over 50 years of being an activist, she is still determined to keep fighting until the goal is reached. NO JUSTICE, NO PEACE!

Mark Naison is professor of history and African American studies at Fordham University. He is the author of four books and over 100 articles on African American politics, social movements, and American culture and sports. Dr. Naison is the principal investigator of the Bronx African American History Project. When not doing historical research, Naison likes to play tennis and golf, post commentary on his blog, *With a Brooklyn Accent*, and make periodic forays into the media. During the last 5 years, he has begun presenting historical "raps" in Bronx schools under the nickname of "Notorious Phd." He is one of the founders of the Bad Ass Teachers Association.

Linda Nathan is the founding headmaster of Boston Arts Academy, Boston's only public high school for the visual and performing arts. Currently, Dr. Nathan is the Executive Director of the Center for Arts in Education at Boston Arts Academy. Dr. Nathan is a leader in education reform and has lectured and written widely on education leadership, the arts, and democratic schools, including a highly praised book, *The Hardest Questions Aren't on the Test: Lessons from an Innovative Urban School*. She teaches a course at the Harvard Graduate School of Education titled Building Democratic Schools and blogs about education and the arts at http://lindanathan.com.

Monty Neill, EdD, is Executive Director of FairTest: National Center for Fair & Open Testing, and chair of the national Forum on Educational Accountability. He has initiated national and state coalitions of education, civil rights, religious, disability, parent, and other organizations to work toward fundamental change in student assessment and school accountability. His many publications address problems with testing, benefits of high-quality assessment, and resistance to high-stakes testing. FairTest's website is http://www.fairtest.org.

Kris Nielsen has worked in education for about a decade and is a national education reform expert. He holds an MA in education, with emphasis on child development and motivational learning. He has also helped lead parent and student opt out movements in New York, Colorado, and New Mexico. Kris blogs at www.atthechalkface.com. He is author of two books: *Children of the Core* (2013) and *Uncommon: The Grassroots Movement to Save Our Children and Our Schools* (2013).

Dani O'Brien is a doctoral student at UMass, Amherst, and other students, faculty, teachers, and community members organized to support Barbara, grow a movement to fight the corporatization of education and demand education for democracy and liberation. Thus was Can't Be Neutral born.

Ann O'Halloran was the 2007 Massachusetts History Teacher of the Year and is a member of Citizens for Public Schools.

Katie Osgood is a special education teacher in Chicago. She currently teaches on a child/adolescent inpatient psychiatric unit. Before that, she taught in a Chicago public elementary school as well as spending 6 years teaching in Japan. She is a member of CORE (Caucus of Rank and File Educators) and Teachers for Social Justice in Chicago. Find out more about Katie at her blog, Ms. Katie's Ramblings.

Nancy Carlsson-Paige is Professor Emerita at Lesley University where she taught teachers for more than 30 years and was a founder of the University's Center for Peaceable Schools. She is the author of five books and many articles and op eds on a variety of education and parenting topics. Her most recent book is called *Taking Back Childhood: A Proven Roadmap for Raising Confident, Creative, Compassionate Kids* (Plume Publishing, 2009). Nancy has received numerous awards for her leadership and advocacy of early childhood and peace education.

Tom Poetter is professor of Curriculum Studies at Miami University, Oxford, Ohio. His book *The Education of Sam Sanders* (Hamilton Books, 2006), a novel set in 2029 about the future of public education, anticipates the anti-democratic, corporate takeover that is already underway! Tom is the founder of TRAAN (Teacher Resistance and Action Network). Tom was a Democratic candidate in 2014 for U.S. Representative of Ohio's 8th Congressional District.

Susan Horton Polos is an elementary school librarian at a Title I school in Westchester County, New York, a suburb of New York City. She is a National Board Certified teacher (2010) who was a member of the New York

State ELA/ESL standards review and revision panel up until New York won RTTT and had to adopt the Common Core Standards. She is a board member of the School Librarian Section of the New York Library Association and will be president elect as of November 2014. She was a member of the 2014 Newbery Committee.

Jessie B. Ramey, PhD, is a historian of working families and U.S. social policy, and an ACLS New Faculty Fellow in Women's Studies and History at the University of Pittsburgh. She writes about public education research and policy on her blog, *Yinzercation,* which also serves as the online home for a grassroots movement in Southwest Pennsylvania. Dr. Ramey is the author of the book, *Child Care in Black and White: Working Parents and the History of Orphanages*, which won the Lerner-Scott Prize in Women's History from the Organization of American Historians (OAH), the Herbert G. Gutman Prize of the Labor and Working Class History Association (LAWCHA), and the John Heinz Award of the National Academy of Social Insurance (NASI). She is regularly published in the national media and has twice been recognized by the White House with invitations to meet with President Obama's senior policy advisors.

Diane Ravitch is a historian of education at NYU. She is author of the best-selling *Death and Life of the Great American School System: How Testing and Choice Are Undermining Education* (2010) and *Reign of Error* (2013). From 1991 to 1993, she was Assistant Secretary of Education and Counselor to Secretary of Education Lamar Alexander in the administration of President George H. W. Bush. She is—A champion of teachers;—A champion of public education;—A champion for a great education for all children.

Becca Ritchie has been teaching drama and music in middle school since 1990. After getting her master's degree, she switched to teach computer skills. She is an active leader and organizer for the Badass Teachers Association in Seattle, Washington.

Stephanie Rivera is a 22-year-old senior at Rutgers University in New Brunswick, New Jersey. She is a future social studies high school teacher, current high school mentor, prison tutor, and educational justice activist. She is one of four founders of Students United for Public Education (SUPE) and runs her own blog at teacherunderconstruction.com.

Ricardo Rosa is an activist, researcher, and writer working with youth. He is assistant professor at the University of Massachusetts-Dartmouth. His research centers on neoliberalism and educational privatization and its effects on racially, culturally, and economically subordinated communities.

Dov Rosenberg is a native North Carolinian who has been teaching in North Carolina public schools since 2001. Since attending the Save Our Schools rally in Washington, DC, in 2011, he has been working with national and local groups to raise awareness about the harm done to public schools by market-based policy. He is on the executive board of his local NEA chapter and a founding member of Organize 2020 (organize2020. com), a caucus of public school teachers, parents, and other public schools advocates that is leading the charge in North Carolina against the devastating education policies of its currently extreme-right state government.

Stephen Round is a former Rhode Island elementary teacher currently tutoring dyslexic/dysgraphic primary students at New Hope Academy in Killingly, Connecticut. His recent viral YouTube resignation, entitled RI Teacher Says, "I Quit!" struck a nerve with teachers, parents, and students alike, condemning a one-size-fits-all, testing-obsessed approach to education. His website on which you can view his approach to tutoring struggling readers is www.pireading.com. He and his wife, who is also a teacher, live in Foster, Rhode Island. They have four children and six grandchildren.

Kim Runyon writes, "My social justice work started when I got involved in the start of Occupy Denver. Since then I have helped organize the Rocky Mountain Student Power Convergence. I also helped plan the TCAP Walkout and protest on Defend Education Day. I founded a Students for Social Justice Club at my high school and I am a founding member and only high school organizer of COSPA (Colorado Student Power Alliance) and am thrilled to represent in Washington DC!" Kim just completed her freshman year in college.

Pasi Sahlberg is a Finnish educator and scholar. His expertise includes international educational change, future of schooling, and innovation in teaching and learning. His best-selling book, *Finnish Lessons: What Can the World Learn From Educational Change in Finland* (Teachers College Press, 2011) won the 2013 Grawemeyer Award. He is a former Director General of CIMO (Centre for International Mobility and Cooperation) in Helsinki and currently a visiting Professor of Practice at Harvard University's Graduate School of Education in Cambridge, Massachusetts.

Carmen Scalfaro III has been a public school educator since 2002, teaching technology and support ed courses. He has taught education courses to undergraduate students at Miami University. As a doctoral student, Carmen is focused on curriculum and is interested in corporate education reform, democracy in education, and critical theory. He and his wife,

Jodie, have two children, Isabella and Blaze, and a very loyal golden re-
triever named Bailey.

Sue Schutt has worked in education for 20 years. She was a teacher for 12
years and an assistant principal for 8. She is currently assistant principal
at an urban high school. Sue spent more than half her career working in
high schools, using performance-based assessment instead of high-stakes
end-of-course exams. She was a founding teacher at a Big Picture High
School, where student interest and real-world work experiences, super-
vised by worksite volunteers, drove student learning. In addition, she
has spent the larger part of her career serving high-needs populations
in schools throughout New York City. Sue began her education activism
fighting high-stakes testing in the early days of her teaching career. Currently she works with a number of organizations fighting to protect public
education including *United Opt Out*, Save Our Schools New Jersey, and
Abbott Leadership Institute.

Ira Shor is Professor of Rhetoric/Composition at the City University of
New York's Graduate Center (PhD Program in English) and in the Department of English at the College of Staten Island/CUNY. At the College of
Staten Island/CUNY, he teaches first-year writing, nonfiction, coming-of-
age narratives, multicultural literature, and mass media. His nine published books include a 3-volume set in honor of the late Paulo Freire, the
noted Brazilian educator who was his friend and mentor. Ira also worked
with Prof. Mark Naison of Fordham University on starting "99% clubs" af-
filiated with the Occupy movement.

Ruth Powers Silverberg is Associate Professor of Education at the College
of Staten Island, CUNY, where she coordinates the Post Masters Advanced
Certificate Program for Leadership in Education. She received her doctorate from Hofstra University after serving public and private schools
for 25 years in early childhood and music classrooms and as an assistant
principal. Since connecting with anti-corporate education activist groups
in 2010, Ruth has devoted her time to opposing the privatization of public
education and to coordinating the Edu4 Parent-Scholar Collaboration for
Educational Justice Working Group.

Ankur Singh is a freshman at the University of Missouri-Columbia. He
has taken his second semester off to travel the country to make a documentary about the effects of high-stakes testing on students.

Diayu Suzuki is a former schoolteacher, a Fulbright Scholar from Japan, and
the co-founder of Edu4. Currently a doctoral student at Teachers College

at Columbia University, his research explores the trivialization of the teacher and the truncation of teaching and learning in the U.S. neoliberal educational landscape. Reflecting on his own intense relationship with a mentor teacher during the 7 years that he taught in a public junior high school in Japan, his research pursues one guiding question: "What does it mean to have a teacher?"

Henry Louis Taylor Jr., a historian/urban planner, is professor in the University at Buffalo Department of Urban and Regional Planning and is founding director of the UB Center for Urban Studies. Taylor is a nationally recognized scholar on distressed urban neighborhoods in the United States. He has written and/or edited five books and published more than 90 articles, book reviews, commentaries, and technical reports. His most recent book is *Inside El Barrio: A Bottom-Up View of Castro's Cuba* (Kumarian Press, 2009).

Faya Ora Rose Touré is a retired litigation attorney and engaged civil rights activist who is also the founder of the National Voting Rights Museum and annual Crossing the Bridge Jubilee in Selma, Alabama. A Harvard-educated attorney, she was part of the winning legal team in *Pigford v. Veneman,* the civil rights case that led to a billion dollar payout in damages to Black farmers by the U.S. Department of Education. The first African American female judge in Alabama, she is also the founder of education and cultural support centers, political and legal organizations, and community initiatives. Rose, an accomplished songwriter, playwright, and host of a daily radio show called Faya's Fire, is the winner of numerous awards: National Conference of Black Lawyer's Lawyer of the Year Award, SCLC Women Drum Major for Justice Award, and Lewis Hines Child Labor Award. Faya Ora Rose." Contemporary Black Biography. 2006. (2006, January 1). Touré, Faya Ora Rose. Encyclopedia.com. Retrieved from http://www.encyclopedia.com/doc/1G2-3482400055.html.

Jesse Turner is the Director of the Central Connecticut State University Literacy Center. He has spoken to audiences across the nation about the problems created by the No Child Left Behind Act. In 2010, Jesse created the Facebook group Children Are More Than Test Scores as a way to connect individuals and communities struggling against the NCLB law. Two years ago Jesse walked 400 miles in 40 days from Connecticut to Washington, DC, to raise awareness of the negative impact NCLB/RTTT was having on children, parents, teachers, and schools.

Jocelyn Weeda is an educator and activist who has taught in public schools for 20 years. Currently she is a doctoral candidate at Miami University in

Oxford, Ohio. Her dissertation research is focusing on teachers as resistors to current corporate policy reforms as a way to make space for social transformation through emancipatory action.

Lois Weiner teaches education at New Jersey City University. Her first book, *Preparing Teachers for Urban Schools*, was honored by the American Educational Research Association (AERA) for its contribution to research on teacher education. A book of advice based on this research, *Urban Teaching: The Essentials*, is used in urban teacher preparation programs throughout the country. She also authored *The Future of Our Schools: Teachers Unions and Social Justice* (Haymarket Press, 2012).

Pam Zich is a lifelong journalist who chose special education as a second career after braving the world of substitute teaching in 2008. While working with students in the autism spectrum, Pam discovered a passion for inclusion and for helping children learn to see beyond their differences. She returned to college after 20 years to earn her master's in special education but was driven from the local school system for reporting disparities in special education staffing. Pam currently teaches part-time while her alter ego, the Rebel Speducator, is busy reporting and conducting investigations within the educational activist community.

NOTES

1. Was a speaker for Occupy DOE 2.0 but was unable to attend.
2. Was on the schedule for Occupy DOE 2.0 but was unable to attend.
3. Was on the schedule for Occupy DOE 2.0 but was unable to attend.

ABOUT THE
AUTHORS/EDITORS

Rosemarie Jensen (joined UOO in 2014) is a former teacher and currently a parent activist. She received her MEd *emPower Magazine* from the University of Florida and taught K–1 for 10 *emPower Magazine* years in both Alachua and Broward Counties. In addition, she trained teachers in Alachua and surrounding counties in Math Their Way and later worked as a K–2 literacy trainer for teachers in Broward County. In the past 15 years she has been an active participant in her local schools and has worked to end high stakes testing and corporate reforms. She has been involved in community, state and national efforts to support public education and teachers. She has opted her son out of FCAT for the past three years in Florida.

Shaun Johnson, PhD, is a public school teacher, teacher educator, blogger and online radio show host of At the Chalk Face.

Morna McDermott has been working in, with, and around public schools for over 20 years. Currently she is an Associate Professor at Towson University, in Maryland. Her scholarship and research interests focus on democracy, social justice, and arts-informed inquiry in K–post secondary educational settings, and working with beginning and experienced educators. Recent art work and installations have emphasized the value of art as a "public pedagogy" in creating grass roots social-political-educational change. She recently authored a book *The Left Handed Curriculum: Creative Experiences for Empowering Teachers* (IAP, 2012) and maintains a blog at www.educationalchemy.com. She currently lives in Baltimore with her husband and two children.

Laurie Murphy is the Director of Resource Development for a nonprofit agency serving multiple counties in central Florida. She has worked in the nonprofit sector for over 15 years. Laurie has strong ties to the educational community, as her husband, two of her children, and countless others in prior generations have all served their communities as teachers. Laurie was a charter member of Save Our Schools March and National Call to Action, Organizing Committee (left UOO in 2013).

Peggy Robertson has taught kindergarten, first, second, fourth, fifth and sixth grade. She was hired by Richard C. Owen Publishers in 2001 to serve as a Learning Network Coordinator and spent the next three years training teacher leaders and administrators in educational theory and practice in the state of Colorado, as well as around the country during the summer months. In 2004 she was hired as the Literacy Coordinator in Adams 50 School District in Westminster, Colorado. She earned her master's degree in English as a Second Language at Southeast Missouri State University. She is in her seventeenth year of teaching as an instructional coach at an elementary school in Colorado. She is a member of the Aurora Education Association (affiliate of NEA), co-founder of the RAVE caucus, a writer, and a devoted education activist through her work at *United Opt Out National*. She is a contributor to the book, *Pencils Down*(2012), by Rethinking Schools. Her blog can be found at www.pegwithpen.com.

Ruth Rodriguez holds a BA in social work and did graduate studies in Bilingual Education at Boston University. She was a Community Fellow in the Urban Studies Department at MIT where she researched school violence. Ruth served on the MA Governor Deval Patrick's Readiness Project on MCAS and Assessment, an initiative that brought together a diverse group of educators, from superintendents, principals, parents, teachers and community advocates, to advise the governor on the Massachusetts Comprehensive Assessment System (MA high stakes exam for promotion and graduation requirement). (joined UOO in 2013)

Timothy D. Slekar is the Dean of the College of Education at Edgewood College in Madison WI. Dr. Slekar began his career in education as a 2nd grade teacher in Williamsburg, VA. He also taught 5th grade in York, PA. Dr. Slekar attended the University of Maryland at College Park where he earned his PhD in social studies education. Dr. Slekar has published research in some of the top educational research journals (*Teacher Education Quarterly, Theory and Research in Social Education, Journal of Thought*). Tim has a blog and radio show at bustedpencils.com.

Ceresta Smith is a 25 year veteran educator and member of United Teachers of Dade. She earned her National Board Certification in Adult/Young Adult English/language arts in 2002. In September of 2008, she moved from a school deemed "high performing" to serve as a teacher leader and literacy coach in a school deemed, "low performing." She currently mentors teachers and teaches language arts at John A. Ferguson High School in Miami-Dade County. Additionally, she served as a delegate to NEA, FEA, AFT, and AFL/CIO. Along with her role as an administrators for *United Opt Out,* Ms. Smith is one of the original organizers of and is an active Steering Committee member for Save Our Schools March.

Foreword by: Ricardo Rosa is Assistant Professor Specializes in Curriculum and Instruction, Language Policies, Literacy and Social Studies Education at UMass Dartmouth. Dr. Rosa's research centers on emerging articulations of educational privatization and its effects on organizational behavior in educational settings and possibilities for transformative leadership. His research also focuses on curricular theory and praxis within and beyond the boundaries of normative schooling.